# CONTENTS

| | | |
|---|---|---|
| **Preface** | | ix |
| **1** | **Modernism and modernity** | 1 |
| **2** | **Space** | 17 |
| | Henry James, Joseph Conrad, Ford Madox Ford | 18 |
| | D. H. Lawrence | 28 |
| | Dorothy Richardson and May Sinclair | 36 |
| | James Joyce | 45 |
| | Virginia Woolf | 53 |
| | Background and context | 58 |
| **3** | **Time** | 83 |
| | Striking clocks and new chronologies | 83 |
| | The time philosophy | 102 |
| | Mean time | 113 |
| | Fragment or flow | 124 |
| | Cracks and chasms: Time and the Western Front | 137 |
| **4** | **Art** | 155 |
| | Art and the novel | 155 |
| | The revolution of language | 166 |
| | Modernism and postmodernism | 195 |
| **5** | **Value** | 201 |
| | The end of modernism | 201 |
| | The evasions of modernism | 206 |
| | The value of modernism | 213 |
| **Notes** | | 225 |
| **Select bibliography** | | 235 |
| **Index** | | 243 |

For
Sarah, Andrew, Matthew and Anna

# MODERNIST FICTION
## AN INTRODUCTION

RANDALL STEVENSON

*University of Edinburgh*

**HARVESTER WHEATSHEAF**

New York  London  Toronto  Sydney  Tokyo  Singapore

First published 1992 by
Harvester Wheatsheaf
Campus 400, Maylands Avenue
Hemel Hempstead
Hertfordshire, HP2 7EZ
A division of
Simon & Schuster International Group

Typeset in 10/12pt Times
by Witwell Ltd, Southport

Printed and bound in Great Britain by
Biddles Ltd, Guildford and King's Lynn

British Library Cataloguing in Publication Data

A catalogue record for this book is available from the
British Library

ISBN 0 7450 1302 3 (hbk)
ISBN 0 7450 1303 1 (pbk)

3  4  5    96  95  94

# PREFACE

In his pioneering analysis of modernist fiction, *The Turn of the Novel*, published in 1966, Alan Friedman remarks

> The roots of the change in the novel lie tangled deep in the modern experience. Causes in fields other than literature there doubtless were – a confluence of psychological, philosophical, scientific, social, economic, and political causes, analogues, and explanations . . . I think it is probably too soon to evaluate that confluence properly. (pp. xii–xiii)

As Chapter 1 suggests, it may be more appropriate to consider the factors Friedman mentions as 'analogues and explanations' of modernist literature, rather than direct *causes* of it. Nevertheless, a quarter of a century after his work was published, it is probably no longer premature to examine modernist fiction more or less in terms of the 'confluence' he outlines. The 1990s are as distant from *Ulysses* (1922) as *Ulysses* itself was from *David Copperfield* (1849–50) and the fiction of the mid-nineteenth century. As the twentieth century nears its end, it should be increasingly possible, in looking back at modernism, to establish the kind of historical perspective Friedman considered unavailable when he wrote – to place in the context of the century's development as a whole writing which still seems both the major achievement and the continuing, central influence in its literature.

Moreover, some of the tools of literary criticism – of narrative analysis particularly – have developed considerably since Friedman wrote. The recent availability in English translation of the ideas of the Soviet theorist Mikhail Bakhtin, and the work of Gérard Genette, substantially assist analysis of how the novel changed its structure and style early in the twentieth century. *Why* it did so – the other question of principal interest to the present study – is clarified by the criticism of the United States Marxist, Fredric Jameson, as well as by the wide-ranging cultural analysis of Stephen Kern in *The Culture of Time and Space 1880–1918* (1983).

Recent critics and theorists have much to offer the analysis of modernism; so too do commentators writing from within the modernist period itself. A lengthening historical perspective offers a certain objectivity; on the other hand, such distance may simply make some things harder to see clearly. Proximity contributes to some useful and occasionally surprising perspectives in the work of contemporary critics. One of the most surprising of them, R. A. Scott-James (further discussed in Chapter 1), emphasises as follows the particular advantage of their work:

> Is it not a mockery of modesty to assert that we have less right to judge our own contemporaries, being as we are bone of their bone and flesh of their flesh, than a diffident posterity? For the writers of our time are influenced by the prevalent thoughts and feelings which move us, so that though we know nothing of their value for posterity we have the best means of knowing their value for ourselves. (*Modernism and Romance*, 1908, p. xi)

As Scott-James suggests, in some ways contemporary critics are in a much better position than later ones to recognise what is particularly valuable, new or unusual in the writing of their age, and to judge how far this is likely to have been affected by dominant thoughts and feelings which may later be forgotten, or difficult to identify with so much certainty. Throughout, the present study often relies on contemporary commentary for this sort of suggestion. Chapter 3 turns in particular to Wyndham Lewis, whose huge volumes assessing the state of culture at the time make him one of thel most substantial – and neglected – of commentators on the 1920s.

Assessed in relation to critics of the time and since, and to a range of roots and analogues in contemporary experience, modernist fiction offers a field too wide to be examined in its entirety in a single volume. Though making an exception of Marcel Proust (for reasons explained in Chapter 1), this study confines itself to fiction written in English; within this context it looks only briefly, where appropriate, at modernist developments in the novel in the United States. Though it might seem simplest to state that the focus is therefore on 'British fiction', it would be misleading, even dishonest, to do so. The authors concerned – principally Henry James, Ford Madox Ford, Joseph Conrad, Dorothy Richardson, May Sinclair, D. H. Lawrence, James Joyce, Wyndham Lewis and Virginia Woolf – could all be said to belong loosely to a British context, since they each began or spent a large part of their working lives within it. Yet by no means all of them could be said to be British by nationality. As suggested in Chapter 4, complex conditions of national or cultural identity often formed an important part of the background – even a likely source – for the modernist disposition of their work.

Wherever possible, references to their work are to currently available paperback editions, which are listed in the select bibliography. This also contains details of other volumes referred to. Where necessary, further information about the source of quotations is given in the notes, which as they rarely contain more than publishing details need not distract readers from the text. Since a feature of modernist fiction, in the work of Ford Madox Ford and Dorothy Richardson particularly, is its frequent use of a set of dots to represent pauses in characters' thoughts, a convention is required to distinguish such pauses from ellipses indicating omissions in the course of a quotation. Throughout, three narrowly spaced dots (...) reproduce authors' own usage, while three widely spaced ones (. . .) indicate that words or sections have been omitted from a quotation.

Even confined loosely within the British context, modernist fiction and the modern experience provide an exciting but wide and challenging field of study, and I am very grateful for the help I received in writing about it. Tony Seward and Jackie Jones have been patient, encouraging editors. Ideas and methods of analysis have often been borrowed from friends, or worked out in discussion with them: Brian McHale, Colin Nicholson, Susanne Greenhalgh, John Cartmell, Jane Goldman, John Orr and Roger Savage have all helped in this way. I have also learned a great deal about the material concerned when delivering lectures on it to the Scottish Universities' International Summer School, and in the course of discussion with many groups of students in Edinburgh University's Department of English Literature. My main debt is to those who read, talked over and added their ideas to various chapters in the process of their completion: to Ron Butlin, Sarah Carpenter, Vassiliki Kolocotroni and Olga Taxidou, many many thanks.

# — 1 —

# MODERNISM
## AND
# MODERNITY

> Just as authority has been undermined in religion and
> morals, so too in art. The old accepted standards cannot
> satisfy a changing age . . .
>
> The old fixed canons of taste have lost their validity . . . the
> novelist ignores the earlier conventions of plot . . . vocabu-
> lary, literary structure, and orthodoxy of opinion . . .
>
> When we come to some of the essentially modern novelists
> we feel that the psychological tendency has gone . . . as far
> indeed as it can go . . .
>
> The spirit of psychological analysis . . . this is 'modernism'
> with a vengeance.
>
> (pp. 22–3, 92, 109, 266)

Taken from various stages of his study *Modernism and Romance*,
R. A. Scott-James's views are typical of the commentary on new,
modern or 'modernist' tendencies in contemporary literature made
in the 1920s. One of several studies of fiction published at the time,
Elizabeth Drew's *The Modern English Novel: Some Aspects of
Contemporary Fiction* (1926), for example, likewise remarks that

> the great majority of the present generation of novelists . . . have
> made psychology, conscious and deliberate psychology, their
> engrossing interest, and it is natural that such an interest should
> entail their finding the older technique too clumsy for their new
> purposes. (p. 248)

Many later critics have followed the kind of thinking outlined by
Drew and Scott-James. What has come to be known as modernist

fiction – at its height in novels published in the 1920s by James Joyce, Virginia Woolf and D. H. Lawrence – is usually defined on the grounds of its rejection of techniques and conventions apparently inappropriate or 'too clumsy' for new interests at the time. A principal part of these new interests seems to have been in the kind of 'psychology' – or heightened concern with individual, subjective consciousness – which Drew and Scott-James identify. The present study traces this interest and, throughout Chapter 2, examines the stream-of-consciousness and interior monologue styles developed to reflect it.

Given how representative Scott-James's views are of critical thinking in the 1920s and since, much the most interesting thing about his comments is that they were made, not like Elizabeth Drew's in 1926 or later, but in 1908, at a time when it is unusual to find the word 'modernism' applied to literature at all. For any study of literature in the early twentieth century, there is a good deal to be learned from both Scott-James's remarks and the surprisingly early date of their publication. Firstly, his views emphasise that the disposition for change and transformation in the novel, so obvious to commentators by the 1920s, actually originated much earlier than the innovations of Joyce's *Ulysses* (1922) and the other modernist fiction of that decade. The roots of transformation in modernist writing need to be considered as reaching back at least to the fiction of Henry James – one of the novelists Scott-James refers to when he talks of 'the spirit of psychoanalysis' (p. 109) – and other authors, Joseph Conrad in particular, working around the turn of the century.

Secondly, it is worth considering a feature of Scott-James's position which actually does belong quite specifically to the earliest years of the twentieth century – the idea that transformations in art and literature were not particularly welcome or worthwhile. Scott-James may have used the term 'modernism' early, but he does not use it approvingly. In the passage quoted above, he talks darkly of ' "modernism" with a vengeance'; throughout his study, the term is most often used in relation to what are considered largely negative aspects of the age he surveys. He remarks, for example, that

> there are characteristics of modern life in general which can only be summed up, as Mr Thomas Hardy and others have summed them up, by the word *modernism*. The hybrid may not be very pleasant to

delicate ears, but perhaps what it expresses is not a very pleasant thing. (p. ix)

Scott-James's views of the indelicacy of the term modernism', and of what if signifies, are corroborated by the *Oxford English Dictionary*. This shows that at least until the early twentieth century, 'modernism' was most often used to designate fashionable, newfangled ideas, the sort of innovation that betrayed the more solid values of tradition. Even the terms 'modern' and 'modernity' were certainly not consistently ones of approval.[1] By contrast, for many of the generation of novelists coming into prominence after Scott-James wrote – and even for a few of his contemporaries – it was tradition rather than innovation that was viewed with suspicion. 'Modernism' and 'modernist' are therefore terms quite appropriately applied – however 'hybrid' they may sound – to the work of writers apparently sharing the belief that modernity and the reshaping or abandonment of tradition were necessary conditions of their art. This belief clearly distinguishes them from the many other novelists who went on writing, thoughout the early decades of the twentieth century, more or less within styles and conventions established in the latter part of the nineteenth.

Arnold Bennett, John Galworthy and H. G. Wells are examples of this sort of novelist whom Virginia Woolf chooses to discuss in essays clarifying some of the new preferences of her time, 'Modern Fiction' (1919) and 'Mr. Bennet and Mrs Brown' (1924). The 'modern' of her first essay's title is certainly not a term of dispproval, but one which helps define a kind of writing able to alter its conventions and generate new styles to accommodate the preferences of a new age. For Woolf, the work of Bennett, Wells and Galsworthy – 'the most prominent and successful novelists in the year 1910', as she calls them – remained restricted by outmoded fictional conventions. In her opinion, it was essential to recognise that 'the proper stuff of fiction is a little other than custom would have us believe it', and to follow instead the new example of 'young writers' such as James Joyce.[2] Even a few years after she wrote, it was clear that in some areas Woolf's wishes had been thoroughly fulfilled. By the mid-1920s, the example of not only Joyce but also other writers such as D. H. Lawrence, Dorothy Richardson, May Sinclair and Woolf herself had made 'the stuff of fiction' substantially different from what it had been twenty or thirty years before, in ways impossible for commentators at the time to overlook. Thomas Hardy, for example, one of the last successful Victorian novelists, remarked of contemporary fiction in 1926 – simply, if rather wearily – 'They've changed everything now . . . we used to think there was a beginning and a middle and an end.'[3] By emphasising the amendment of conventional fiction's chronological construction, Hardy incidentally indicates another area in which – along with its deepening interest in subjectivity, mentioned above – modernism concentrated its energies for change in the novel. This phase of innovation is further discussed in Chapter 3.

A third aspect of Scott-James's significance, however, is the element of reservation or qualification his views introduce into some of the distinctions just described. Woolf and other modernists acted on their belief in the need for change, and sometimes looked back rather disparagingly on authors such as Arnold Bennett who seemed to them limited by membership of a generation content with convention. Yet Scott-James suggests that such a complacent generation may never have existed. Though he hardly approves of the consequences, he indicates that even in 1908, some time before Joyce and Woolf began publishing, 'the old fixed canons of taste [had] lost their validity . . . the novelist ignore[d] the earlier conventions'. Perhaps the stylistic and structural innovation in the novel, apparently characteristic of modernism's greatest achievements in the 1920s, needs to be seen as less unique or daring than it has usually been considered. Virginia Woolf remarks at the start of 'Modern Fiction' that 'it is difficult not to take it for granted that the modern practice of the art is somehow an improvement upon the old'. However, she soon goes on to admit herself that

> In the course of the centuries . . . We do not come to write better; all that we can be said to do is to keep moving, now a little in this direction, now in that. (p. 103)

As Woolf suggests, an urge to 'keep moving' is not unique to modernism: neither its urge for novelty nor its commitment to change are new in literature. It may be that the differences between modernism and earlier writing are best considered relative rather than absolute, quantitative rather than altogether qualitative. This is a possibility to be kept in mind throughout the analysis of modernism's stylistic, structural and linguistic transformations in Chapters 2, 3 and 4. Departures from the serial, chronological construction of story-telling, for example – its usual beginning, middle and end – are by no means unique in the history of fiction. Likewise, according to one contemporary critic, Wyndham Lewis in *Time and Western Man* (1927), even the stream-of-consciousness technique – often held to be the principal innovation and distinguishing achievement of modernist fiction – had first been practised long before, by Charles Dickens in *Pickwick Papers* (1837). There is better evidence, as Chapter 2 suggests, that it was first used extensively in French fiction in the late nineteenth century.

Nevertheless, even if the stream of consciousness was not the wholly original invention of Dorothy Richardson or James Joyce, it had not been employed previously in English writing on the scale, or with the flexibility, which those authors had established for it by the mid-1920s. The evidence of Scott-James helps to avoid crediting modernism with an absolute originality it did not possess; the range and scale of changes the movement introduced, however, and the regularity and radicalism with which they were put into practice remain more than sufficient to set apart and make distinctive a period in the literary history of the twentieth century. If not totally new in kind, modernist innovation *was* spectacularly, inescapably new in extent. Thomas Hardy was by no means the only critic who recognised a contemporary urge not just for change, but to 'change everything'. Herbert Read, for example, remarks in *Art Now* (1933) that

> there have of course been revolutions in the history of art before today. There is a revolution with every new generation, and periodically, every century or so, we get a wider or a deeper change of sensibility to which we give the name of a period . . . But I do think we can already discern a difference of kind in the contemporary revolution: it is not so much a revolution, which implies a turning-over, even a turning-back, but rather a break-up, a devolution, some would say a dissolution. Its character is catastrophic . . .
>
> The aim of five centuries of European effort is openly abandoned. (pp. 58–9, 67)

As Read suggests, innovations in contemporary fiction were only one aspect of a radical change apparent in the period's artistic sensibility as a whole, and reflected in ways confined neither to the

novel genre nor to writing in Britain. Fiction by Marcel Proust or
André Gide in French, for example, or by Thomas Mann or Franz
Kafka in German, shares many of the characteristics of the new
forms appearing in the novel in English. T. S. Eliot's *The Wasteland*
(1922) marked an analogous revolution, or in F. R. Leavis's term, a
'New Bearing' in English poetry. Ezra Pound's determination to
'make it new' and his memorably simple demand 'I want a new
civilisation'[4] are likewise reflected in his own poetry; in the Imagist
movement he helped to foster around 1910; eventually, most
substantially, in the *Cantos* he began to publish in 1917.

Read's 'revolution in the history of art', and dispositions like
Pound's for a 'new civilisation', are at least as apparent in fields
beyond contemporary literature as they are within it, affecting
almost every genre of artistic enterprise throughout Europe and
eventually the United States. Equally radical changes were
introduced to the structural constitution of contemporary music,
for example. The conventional structuring of tones in Western
composition, the diatonic scale, was replaced in 1908, by Arnold
Schoenberg, with a free a-tonality – a kind of creative anarchy of
semi-tones – which he organised around 1920 into a new serial
arrangement of twelve tones, interrelated independently of traditional systems. As one later commentator expresses it, such innovations 'undertook a radical dismantling of the established syntax of
Western music':[5] what Herbert Read would have called a 'break-up
. . . a dissolution' of conventions of construction developed over
centuries of European artistic endeavour.

This kind of 'dissolution' is equally clear in contemporary
European painting. As in modernist fiction, artists made changes
not necessarily in their subject nor theme, nor in the nature of what
was represented, but in the form and structure of the representation, the style and strategy of the art itself. Pablo Picasso's early
Cubist painting *Les Demoiselles d'Avignon* (1906–7) still – more or
less – represents human forms, though the means by which it does
so are changed so radically that even this apparent depiction of
reality is not wholly convincing or clear. Picasso abandons the
unitary perspective of painting, the tradition of seeing things from a
single point in space, in favour of an apparent multiplication of
points of view which allows him to present opposite sides of a face
together in the same picture. Such fundamental changes in the
conventions of art greatly astonished the British public when they

appeared in the exhibition of Post-Impressionist painting organised by Roger Fry in London, late in 1910. This is usually thought to account for Virginia Woolf's choice, in her essay 'Mr. Bennett and Mrs. Brown', of December 1910 as an especially revolutionary time for the contemporary sensibility; a moment when, she suggests, 'human character changed' (*Collected Essays* I, p. 320).

Whether or not Woolf actually had Fry's exhibition principally in mind when she wrote 'Mr. Bennett and Mrs. Brown' is a matter further discussed in Chapter 2. At any rate, no matter how far she and other novelists were directly concerned with changes taking place in many forms of contemporary European art, these changes do often provide illuminating analogues for innovations in their writing, as well as confirming the revolutionary nature of the period as a whole. Practically, however, there are difficulties in concentrating on modernist fiction while also keeping a spectrum of European arts in view. The present study briefly refers to other art forms where appropriate, and includes the work of Marcel Proust as a major example of developments occurring elsewhere, at least in literature. Proust's fiction is in any case particularly worth examining, as in a number of ways it can be closely and usefully connected with the British context. Especially in the areas of structure, chronology and concomitant changes in views of time, some of the innovations of modernism can be more fully and easily illustrated from Proust's *Remembrance of Things Past (A la recherche du temps perdu*, 1913-27) than with reference only to fiction in English. In these and other areas, his example appealed fairly directly to several English modernists themselves. Both Dorothy Richardson and Virginia Woolf record admiration for Proust. 'Oh if I could write like that,' Woolf remarked, mentioning at certain stages an intention to try to do so – to adapt certain of Proust's styles for her own use.[6]

Such instances of admiration or possible influence among modernist writers, however, are significantly rare. Statements of antipathy, or at best indifference, are more regularly in evidence. Though Woolf admired Proust, she had much more equivocal feelings for Joyce. She praises him in 'Modern Fiction', but records in her diary finding *Ulysses* 'a mis-fire . . . diffuse . . . brackish . . . pretentious'. Joyce himself could see no particular merit in Proust's writing. D. H. Lawrence could see little merit in either Proust, Joyce, Richardson or Woolf – who for her part remarks, 'I can't help thinking that there's something wrong with Lawrence'.[7] Wyndham Lewis suggests in *Time and Western Man* and *Men Without Art* (1934) that there was a good deal wrong with almost all contemporary authors – with Woolf, Lawrence, Joyce, Proust, Gertrude Stein, Ernest Hemingway and William Faulkner – as well as with contemporary culture as a whole. His suggestions are discussed further in Chapter 3.

As Lawrence himself warned, novelists' comments on their own work are never entirely to be trusted; it is possible that in some cases the modernists may have borrowed more from each other than they were prepared to admit. Nevertheless, the statements quoted above do help to indicate that – unlike other contemporary movements such as Imagism, Futurism or Vorticism – modernism involved very little direct association of the writers involved. It was never a movement fostered through participants' contacts or collective agreement about aims, goals, ideas or styles. Modernism is a critical construct, a recognition, some years after writers completed the works involved, of substantial similarities, even a collective identity, in the initiatives they took and the styles and concerns which they made a priority. This does not make less viable the idea of modernism, or its coherence as a movement. As the present study will show, developments made by individual authors independently from each other are nevertheless clearly comparable, and often related to one another more or less logically and progressively, one change of style following incrementally from another throughout the early decades of the century. Modernist authors' independence from each other does, however, raise one obvious question about their work. If mutual association or influence cannot very much account for manifold similarities throughout this phase of contemporary writing, what can?

One answer, really as obvious as the question, has already been offered by Alan Friedman's remarks, quoted in the preface. The originality of modernist fiction for Friedman is owed to the originality of 'the modern experience' itself; to 'causes' in its philosophy, psychology, science, society, economics and politics. Along with so much contemporary art, modernist fiction changed radically in structure and style because the world it envisaged changed radically at the time, as indeed did means of envisaging it. Analogous innovations in so many contemporary art-forms may have arisen not from mutual influence – Joyce did not restructure his work because contemporary painters had done so, nor vice versa – but from common apprehension of the shifting nature of life, and methods of perceiving it, in the early twentieth century. If, as Thomas Hardy suggests, contemporary novelists 'changed everything' in their work, it would be reasonable to suppose that this was simply because they perceived everything around them as changed; even, in Woolf's view, human character itself.

Like many an obvious answer, this is one which needs to be considered further before it can be accepted as innocent of oversimplification. Nevertheless, much evidence is available that does directly support Friedman's conclusion – some of it also helps establish and clarify the present study's methods of analysing the modernist period and its writing. Many contemporary commentators confirm the extent of new challenges to the period's life and thinking, and indicate how inescapable their effects seemed at the time. As early as 1880 the German philosopher Friedrich Nietzsche was suggesting of the 'Premises of the Machine Age' that 'The press, the machine, the railway, the telegraph are premises whose thousand-year conclusion no one has yet dared to draw'.[8] Over the next thirty years very many new forms of technology and other related changes further impinged greatly on everyday life. Dedicated to the celebration of new technologies and the excitement of an accelerated pace of life and change, the Italian Futurist F. T. Marinetti was talking by 1913 of

> the complete renewal of human sensibility brought about by the great discoveries of science. Those people who today make use of the telegraph, the telephone, the phonograph, the train, the bicycle, the motorcycle, the automobile, the ocean liner, the dirigible, the aeroplane, the cinema, the great newspaper (synthesis of a day in the world's life) do not realize that the various means of communication, transportation and information have a decisive influence on the psyche.[9]

By the early twentieth century, even before the First World War, the 'thousand-year conclusions' Nietzsche saw in the machine age had been many times multiplied, with decisive effects, whether realised or not, on the contemporary psyche.

Such effects were probably further heightened, and certainly clearly expressed, by philosophy and other forms of systematic thinking at the time. Elsewhere in his Futurist Manifestos, Marinetti writes of 'The earth shrunk by speed' and suggests 'Time and Space died yesterday . . . because we have created eternal, omnipresent speed'.[10] As he indicates, technological change inevitably also became conceptual and philosophic: new speeds, a new pace of life created new conceptions of the fundamental coordinates of exper- ience, space and time. Though contemporary philosophy did not by any means entirely share Futurism's enthusiasms, it inevitably responded to the same set of conditions. Though it rarely accepted that time and space had died altogether, it did often suggest that they had ceased to exist in the form in which they were conventio- nally understood, and that a new mutual relation and place in reality had to be established for them. The work of many con- temporary philosophers considered in Chapter 3 – particularly Henri Bergson, whose popularity spread from France to Britain in the early part of the century – is concerned with new enquiries regarding the nature and relations of space and time. Spectacularly confirmed in 1919, the astonishing scientific theories of Albert Einstein made such enquiries a common concern for the age as a whole, a topic of daily interest and conversation, as well as of frequent literary reference, throughout much of the decade that followed. For example, a contemporary critic writing about the novel in 1928, John Carruthers, describes 'space-time' as 'the modern philosophical term that means so much' (p. 84). In her novel *Mary Olivier*, published in 1919, May Sinclair suggests that in general 'Time and Space were forms of thought – ways of thinking' (p. 227). Richard Aldington begins *Death of a Hero* (1929) by defining individual life itself as 'a point of light which . . . describes a luminous geometrical figure in space-time' (p. 11).

No novelist of thirty or even twenty years before would have thought of describing life in quite those terms. Destabilised by a complex of recent developments, space and time occupied a peculiar position in the imagination of the 1920s, providing – especially in the newly hyphenated form 'space-time' recorded by Carruthers – a fashionable terminology particular to the decade. Space and time therefore offer appropriate categories, areas for particular investigation, in the analysis of modernist fiction: they are used in this way in Chapters 2 and 3. After all, they were categories which also appeared particularly useful and appropriate to contemporary literary critics. One commentator remarked in 1928 that the arguments between man and world, the spiritual core of all great novels, becomes in Joyce, a great poetic-philosophical revelation about the inner and outer world, about subject and object, about matter, space, and time. They are the problems of the present philosophical and physical theories.[11]

One of the most significant of narrative theorists, Mikhail Bakhtin, likewise responded to this phase of thinking in the 1920s, referring to Einstein's ideas and coining the term '*chronotope*' (literally, "time-space") (p. 84) as a central category employed in his analysis of the novel.

Space and time provide useful categories of analysis: the new concern with them, however, is only a symptom of deeper and more general changes of outlook apparent in the early twentieth century. As the critic quoted above suggests, the interest in space and time of 'present philosophical and physical theories' belongs with something defined much more generally as 'the arguments between man and world'. There is evidence that these arguments intensified, or at any rate changed in character, in the late nineteenth and early twentieth centuries. As discussed further in Chapters 2 and 3, philosophers such as Bergson, Nietzsche and William James all suggest a change in something as fundamental as the relation of mind and world – a kind of epistemological shift, from relative confidence towards a sense of increased unreliability and uncertainty in the means by which reality is apprehended in thought. Reflecting this general shift, the work of such thinkers helps confirm the opening decades of the century as a time of change as revolutionary in philosophy – and in the outlook of the age as a whole – as in art. In life, as in art and literature, the age was one of change more serious and general than that which Herbert Read – or in his own way R. A. Scott-James – suggests occurs 'with every new generation'. The modernist period is of the sort indicated by Michel Foucault, one of the most sophisticated of recent analysts of culture and history, when he remarks that

within the space of a few years a culture sometimes ceases to think as it had been thinking up till then and begins to think in a new way. (p. 50)

Foucault confirms a culture's capacity to change radically and quickly the way it conceptualises reality and itself: he also, however, cautions against certain ways of conceiving such changes, and movements in culture generally. He raises in particular 'the problem of causality', adding that

> the traditional explanations – spirit of the time, technological or social changes, influences of various kinds – struck me for the most part as being more magical than effective. (pp. xii–xiii)

As Foucault suggests, there are some problems of logic and persuasiveness in 'traditional' attempts – such as the one suggested by Alan Friedman, which is partly followed above – to explain art or culture in terms of their supposed 'causes'. The 'spirit of the time', for example, the *Zeitgeist*, is based upon observation of an age and then used to explain what is observed, a process close to tautology: a particular shape and character is ascribed to the *Zeitgeist* on the basis of certain cultural phenomena, then these are said to owe their particular shape and character to the *Zeitgeist*.

Tracing 'influences of various kinds' – not from some general spirit of the age, but even from specific thinkers within it – can also be problematic: if not, as Foucault suggests, 'magical', at least less logical and straightforward than is sometimes supposed. The critic Lionel Trilling suggests that 'before the idea of influence we ought to be far more puzzled than we are' (p. 191), adding that, in particular, it is necessary to

> question the assumption which gives the priority in ideas to the philosopher and sees the movement of thought as always from the systematic thinker, who thinks up ideas in, presumably, a cultural vacuum, to the poet who 'uses' the ideas 'in dilution'. (p. 190)

Trilling's warning seems sufficiently self-evident to be almost unnecessary. Even if they read it at all, writers are unlikely to derive their ideas solely or originally from philosophy – they are unlikely to be converted instantly or completely, like Saint Paul on his way to Damascus, by ideas not at least partly congenial to them already. Yet in the 1920s, as in other periods, there was a surprising persistence in the assumption that ideas current in literature or elsewhere must have originated in philosophy. D. H. Lawrence illustrates something of the nature of this assumption when he remarks in 1923 that

> The metaphysic or philosophy may not be anywhere very accurately stated and may be quite unconscious, in the artist, yet it is a metaphysic that governs men at the time, and is by all men more or

less comprehended and lived. Men live and see according to some gradually developing and gradually withering vision. The vision exists also as a dynamic idea or metaphysics – exists first as such. Then it is unfolded into life and art. (*Fantasia of the Unconscious*, pp. 9–10)

Significantly, Lawrence elevates the common 'vision' of an age into an idea or 'metaphysic' which somehow controls and accounts for it. He makes shared vision into something whose 'unfolding' shapes and *causes* this vision. His views are typical of an habitual assumption that different aspects of a culture must exist hierarchically, with philosophy or metaphysics as dominant forms at the top. As Foucault suggests, this assumption may arise because philosophy – with all the respectability of its classical past – seems the most exalted authority to choose as the origin of any dominant idea or vision whose appearance elsewhere has to be explained. The creation of a *Zeitgeist* may likewise result from some ghost of theology haunting literary analysis.

Some such exalted view of philosophy seems to be held by Wyndham Lewis when he discusses the 'parallel manifestation' of certain ideas throughout the cultural field he analyses in *Time and Western Man*, but then goes on to remark:

Point for point what I had observed on the literary, social and artistic plane was reproduced upon the philosophic and theoretic . . .

There seemed no doubt, after a little examination of the facts, that the more august of these two regions had influenced the lower and more popular one. (pp. 218, 219)

Lewis suggests a possibility more promising than the one he concludes upon when he talks of 'parallel manifestation'. The philosophy, literature and social fabric of any age are more validly considered developing in parallel, rather than in 'planes' one above the other. Though it would obviously be misleading to rule out any possibility of philosophy influencing life or literature directly, relations between the various spheres need to be considered reciprocal rather than only hierarchical. As Trilling suggests, philosophers do not work in a 'cultural vacuum', but are themselves conditioned by, and express, the 'gradually developing and gradually withering vision' of their age. The views not only of philosophers, but of psychologists, scientists and other systematic thinkers are as likely to be a consequence as a cause of this vision. Considered in this way, however (as suggested further in Chapters 2 and 3), their work remains worth examining for its analogies or parallel manifestations of the concerns of contemporary literature. It can often be especially worthwhile in offering a direct, 'undiluted' formulation of these concerns; a systematic version of the general vision by which 'men live or see' at the time.

This vision, however, needs to be related to contemporary social, political and economic conditions as well as philosophic and metaphysical ones. In this area too Foucault warns about the issue of causality, and the technological or social changes he mentions need to be considered no more likely than philosophic ideas to shape literature and culture altogether directly. An exception helps confirm this general rule. The imagination of one of Marinetti's Futurist Manifestos, quoted earlier, seems overwhelmed, entirely preoccupied, by excitement about the invention of the racing car. Marinetti, at any rate, unreservedly approves of the new technologies, celebrates them throughout what he writes, and considers it right that they should shape and dictate vision in literature, art and the world in general. 'Time and Space died yesterday,' he suggests, 'because we have created eternal, omni-present speed': for the Italian Futurists, vision – or at any rate its coordinates, time and space – underwent a welcome change *because* of new technologies.

Modernist authors were confronted by much the same set of new conditions that excited the Futurists. They may even, at times, have shared in some of this excitement, which appears, for example, in Marcel's various enthralled visions of powered flight or the speed of the motor car in Proust's *A la recherche du temps perdu*. But many contemporary authors, the modernists in particular, viewed the new technologies, speeds and stresses of modern life a good deal more sceptically than enthusiastically, especially after the First World War. Rather than celebrating this modern experience, modernist authors were often chiefly concerned about its threat to the integrity of life and the individual, and more likely to react against than to accept what Nietzsche calls the conclusions of 'the machine age'. Though much readier than R. A. Scott-James to welcome change in art – indeed to emphasise its necessity – they were not always any more disposed to approve of it in reality. Modernist innovation results at least as much from an urge to resist as to reflect changes in contemporary life. As Fredric Jameson suggests, much of modernism's enthusiasm for change in art can be seen to arise, partly unconsciously, from a need to compensate for – rather than just represent – new conditions in modern experience. This need dictated the creation of new imaginative strategies able to deflect or neutralise the new pressures – industrial and economic as well as social and technological – so marked in the machine age. Unlike Futurism, modernism neither welcomed nor accepted the death of space and time. Instead – like much contemporary philosophy – it attempted a kind of surgery to keep these dimensions alive and open in human terms: reshaped in ways which could continue to allow an integral, significant existence to be construed as the natural condition of individual life, in imagination if not in reality.

This reshaping largely defines the nature of modernist fiction's structural and stylistic developments, further explored in the chapters that follow. To questions about why modernism changed the novel, the obvious answer remains – though with some qualifications – the right one. As Friedman suggests, 'the roots of change in the novel lie tangled deep in the modern experience'. As Foucault warns, unravelling these roots is rarely a matter of tracing direct causes and effects, but of untangling the various shifts of emphasis, restructurings and evasions through which modernism sought to accommodate and make tolerable contemporary reality and the modern experience in general. By looking for what aspects of this experience offer in the way of 'analogies' and 'manifestations' paralleling innovation in the novel – and by avoiding the temptation of turning correlation too easily into cause – justice can be done to the complex, fascinating processes through which modernist fiction encountered the history of its time.

# — 2 —

# SPACE

Our mistake lies in supposing that things present themselves
as they really are . . .

The kind of literature which contents itself with 'describing
things' . . . is in fact, though it calls itself realist, the furthest
removed from reality . . .

How could the literature of description possibly have any
value, when it is only beneath the surface . . . that reality
has its hidden existence . . .

It is only a clumsy and erroneous form of perception which
places everything in the object, when really everything is in
the mind. (Marcel Proust, *Remembrance of Things Past* (*A
la recherche du temps perdu*), 1913–27)

Illumine the mind within rather than the world without.
(Virginia Woolf, 'Phases of Fiction', 1929)[1]

Writing in 1932, the popular English novelist Hugh Walpole
pointed to what he considered, for contemporary authors, '*the*
question of all questions. What is reality in the novel?' (p. 25). By
the time he wrote this, many contemporary novelists had answered
his question in the terms suggested by the comments quoted above
– choosing, as Woolf suggests, to hold up the mirror of art not to
reflect nature and the world without, but to illumine the mind
within, to portray consciousness itself. Later commentators have
usually considered their attempts 'to place everything in the mind',
rather than in 'the object' or in objective, realistic description, as a
central, defining characteristic of modernist writing. As was also
suggested in Chapter 1, concentration within the mind was a feature
of contemporary writing sufficiently striking to have become a
subject of discussion even before Walpole raised his 'question of
questions' in 1932. Assessing the state of the novel in 1926, Gerald

Bullett talks of 'the subjective method' as 'so characteristic of our age' (pp. 12–13). In a study of the novel published in 1928, John Carruthers likewise remarks that the priorities Virginia Woolf expressed in her critical writing at the time were 'another indication of the trend of modern fiction from objective to subjective, from outer semblance to alleged inner reality' (p. 71).

Carruthers's study emphasises that although increased attention to inner reality was an obvious feature of writing by the mid-1920s, it appeared in the novel not altogether suddenly, but as part of a trend. Carruthers sees 'a persistent tendency away from objectivity and towards the ever more minute and analytic exposition of mental life' discernible in European fiction for many years previously (p. 64). Hugh Walpole likewise felt his 'question of questions' had preoccupied novelists for twenty years or more. New possibilities for the 'exposition of mental life' were most spectacularly exploited by Woolf and Joyce in the 1920s, but as contemporary critics suggest, a movement towards their style of fiction, a gradual development of new forms, can be traced through the work of earlier authors such as Henry James, Joseph Conrad, Ford Madox Ford, D. H. Lawrence, Dorothy Richardson and May Sinclair. Each of these authors introduced some of the transformations in the novel form, the extensions of language and style, necessary to encompass 'ever more minute' mental movements and inner realities. Following in technical detail the changes they made, this chapter traces the trend from objective to subjective in early twentieth-century fiction before going on to consider some of the contemporary factors that encouraged its occurrence.

## HENRY JAMES, JOSEPH CONRAD, FORD MADOX FORD

Another contemporary critic, C. H. Rickword, looked back in the 1920s to suggest that Henry James

> certainly was the first to realize that the interior drama might be rendered immediately by language . . . that the word was as capable of embodying mental as physical movements.[2]

Gerald Bullett also considered James as both an important source of the 'subjective method' he saw as characteristic of his age, and 'the chief channel of its ubiquitous influence' (pp. 12–13). James's influence arose not only from his novels, but from the prefaces he began to publish for them early in the twentieth century, clarifying his ideas about fiction and his priorities as a writer. A motive in producing these prefaces was his conviction that novel-writing required firm principles and a controlling aesthetic to govern what seemed to him at times rather a haphazard practice. James saw the work of many of his contemporaries as only a 'lump of life': a raw, undifferentiated transcription of reality, too full of the shapelessness, the lack of significance of actual experience, to be fully accepted as art. He considered life itself to be 'all inclusion and confusion', while art and writing should be 'all discrimination and selection', matters of 'propriety and perspective'. James sought to provide some of this selection and perspective in his own novels by the use of 'a structural centre . . . [an] organic centre' – a character through whose perceptions the material of the fiction could be carefully shaped and focused. James talks of his 'instinctive disposition' for

> placing advantageously, placing right in the middle of the light, the most polished of possible mirrors of the subject . . . these persons are, so far as their other passions permit, intense *perceivers*, all, of their respective predicaments.

This disposition can be seen in James's work at least as early as *The Portrait of a Lady* (1881): in discussing his heroine in the preface, and his tactics in the novel generally, James writes of the need to 'place the centre of the subject in the young woman's own consciousness'. His disposition also appears, in a very particular form, in *What Maisie Knew* (1897). In this case the organic centre, Maisie, is a child whose incompletely developed perception of her predicament is as fascinating for its limited, specific, suggestive nature as for its intensity. As James himself suggests, however, the most 'unmistakeable examples' of his 'instinctive disposition' appear in later mature novels such as *The Golden Bowl* (1907) and, perhaps most clearly, in the use of his hero Lambert Strether in *The Ambassadors* (1903).[3]

Even in *The Ambassadors*, however, the role of 'intense perceiver' is not as uncomplicated as James's image of the polished mirror suggests. Strether's progress in Paris embodies James's general interest in how innocence encounters experience, an issue sometimes examined – as in this case – through the encounters of Americans with the complexities of an older civilisation in Europe.

Though Strether is hardly as innocent or uninitiated as the child Maisie, he is an emotionally rather inexperienced American adrift in a Paris whose complex allures and subtleties at first elude his grasp, leaving him unable to comprehend the true situation of Chad, the young American he tries to persuade to return to his family in Massachusetts. James reports of one of Strether's puzzling conversations that

> he was in fact so often at sea that his sense of the range of reference was merely general and that he on several different occasions guessed and interpreted only to doubt. He wondered what they meant. (p. 76)

Guessing, interpreting, doubting, and constantly unsure of the true nature of what is going on, Strether is always an intense perceiver, but, initially at least, no more than a rather hazy, particular mirror of his experience, rather than a polished or neutral one. Talking to his sophisticated friend and confidante Maria Gostrey, Strether records of the complexities confronting him, 'You see more in it . . . than I'; she replies, 'Of course I see *you* in it' (p. 46). Something of the relation the remarks imply also exists between Strether and readers. Events, action and the other characters in the novel are presented almost exclusively through his view of them, yet readers' processes of deduction allow them to see more than Strether does at times, making them more intense or accurate perceivers of Chad's situation or Strether's own predicament than he is himself. *The Ambassadors* is in a way a detective story, in which Strether's understanding gradually catches up with truths sometimes known or guessed before he has discovered them. Resulting ironies and the sense of Strether's inadequacy help to withdraw attention from what he reflects as a 'mirror' of life in Paris, redirecting it on to the nature of the mirror itself – on to Strether's mind, its reactions, its developing capacity to grasp what is happening. Consciousness and its devices for assimilating complex experience, even its ability to do so at all, thus become 'the centre of the subject'. This satisfies the preference James expresses for 'the reflected field of life' rather than 'the spreading field, the human scene'.[4] It is also a twofold anticipation of later developments of modernism: not only, as contemporary commentators saw, in moving the attention of the narrative away from the external world and on to subjective consciousness, but also, consequently, in raising questions about how the areas of mind and world can be related; about how, and how accurately or completely, individual perception can reflect the world it encounters.

James, however, represents an early stage in the growth of these interests. *The Ambassadors* concentrates with a new exclusiveness on the vision of a single character: readers encounter little more of Parisian life and society than Strether does, and except for deduction and implication, know no more than he does of the novel's 'human scene'. Yet the manner in which this vision is communicated remains relatively conventional. James employs few of the tactics later developed by modernist writers to communicate the inner mental experience of their characters or their immediate thoughts as they occur. Strether's perception is recorded throughout, but not in the form in which it immediately impinges on his mind, nor for the most part quite as he might express it in his own voice, but instead in the more objective, reporting terms of James as the author. *The Ambassadors* in this way provides an excellent illustration of the sort of distinction the narrative theorist Gérard Genette draws, within the general category of 'point of view', between 'who sees' and 'who speaks'. The point of view in *The Ambassadors* is almost always Strether's, in the sense that he envisages and provides a focus for the action of the novel, functioning in fact as what Genette calls a focaliser, a character whose 'point of view orients the narrative perspective' (p. 186). Yet although Strether 'sees' the action of the novel, it is James who speaks, reporting Strether's thoughts and vision. Thus the best metaphor for the novel's practice is provided not by James's reference to the 'polished mirror', but by the critic Hugh Kenner's view that James 'employ[s] a foreground character over whose shoulder auctorial infallibility permits us to look' (p. 79). Individual consciousness in James's fiction determines the field of the novel's vision, rather than the processes through which this vision is communicated.

Such tactics create for James a transitional role, poised between nineteenth-century and modernist fiction. *The Ambassadors* shares modernism's fascination with inner consciousness, intense perception and the nature of individual vision, and goes further than earlier fiction in making such matters an exclusive centre of attention for the novel. James also, however, retains a nineteenth-century disposition for an authorial voice which speaks from a position aloof from the events it reports; for an objective authorial infallibility even in reporting the subjective experience of a thoroughly fallible individual perceiver. Critics for some time after James wrote suggested that he had taken the novel and its capacities to present subjective experience as far as it was possible to go. Aware of the range of techniques subsequently developed which undermine authorial infallibility and confine the novel further within the consciousness of characters, later critics have usually placed James as an early figure in the 'trend from objective to subjective' – as much a forerunner of modernist initiatives as a central figure in the movement itself.

Joseph Conrad is often considered a similarly transitional figure. Fredric Jameson, for example, suggests that

> Conrad marks . . . a strategic fault line in the emergence of contemporary narrative . . . in Conrad we can sense the emergence . . . of what will be contemporary modernism. (p. 206)

This new form of narrative Jameson sees emerging as a consequence of what he calls, in discussing *Lord Jim* (1900) 'a structural breakdown of the older realisms' (p. 207). Older realism, what Proust calls the supposition that 'things present themselves as they really are', is undermined by several aspects of Conrad's writing in *Lord Jim*. A scepticism about how things present themselves is directly stated, for example, when Jim faces the Court of Enquiry set up to investigate his desertion of his ship, the *Patna*. The novel records Jim finding that the court

> wanted facts. Facts! They demanded facts from him, as if facts could explain anything . . .

> The facts those men were so eager to know had been visible, tangible, open to the senses, occupying their place in space and time, requiring for their existence a fourteen-hundred-ton steamer and twenty-seven minutes by the watch . . . and something else besides, something invisible, a directing spirit of perdition that dwelt within. (pp. 27, 29)

For Conrad, as for Proust, the tangible, visible object world is of less significance, almost of less reality, than what is invisible and dwells within. It is remarked of the range of spectators at Jim's trial that 'the interest that drew them there was purely psychological', and that the inquiry's preoccupation with asking Jim purely factual questions is

as instructive as the tapping with a hammer on an iron box, were the
object to find out what's inside . . . the questions put to him
necessarily led him away from what . . . would have been the only
truth worth knowing. (p. 48)

Taciturn, evasive and unable to string together more than a
couple of broken sentences at a time to describe himself, Jim
resembles an iron box in the hermetic surface he presents to outside
scrutiny, no matter how many varying points of view are directed
upon him. Conrad's narrator Marlow communicates most of the
story of *Lord Jim*, but much of what he tells is pieced together from
other views of Jim and the testimony of other characters who have
encountered him. Marlow includes, among others, the stories of the
French naval Lieutenant who eventually rescues the *Patna*, and of
Gentleman Brown, the pirate who eventually destroys Jim's sanctu-
ary in Patusan, together with briefer views of Jim from his
employer Egström, from the German merchant Stein, even from
the mad guano-picker Chester, as well as from the Court of Enquiry
itself. Diverse views of Jim, however, provide only further tapping
on the box: the psychological interest, what dwells within Jim,
never seems fully exposed, at least for the characters within the
novel.

The inclusion of so many narrators and points of view, however,
fully exposes the impossibility of facts given the uncertainties of
subjective, individual views of the world, and the discrepancies
which appear between them. Conclusions about Jim constantly
vary depending upon the viewpoint recorded at the time. His
nature, even his stature, remain persistently difficult to define,
literally from the novel's first sentence to its last. *Lord Jim* opens
with the statement, 'He was an inch, perhaps two, under six feet'. A
sense of slight shortcoming in Jim himself is immediately implied
by his falling just short of the imperial measure of six feet. A
shortcoming in the factual accuracy of perception, however, is
suggested equally immediately by 'perhaps', indicating the
viewpoint of a narrator not provided with firm facts and therefore
forced to conjecture about appearances. Even Marlow, the
principal observer of Jim, admits that it was 'impossible to see him
clearly' (p. 255), adding:

I don't pretend I understood him. The views he let me have of himself
were like those glimpses through the shifting rents in a thick fog –

bits of vivid and vanishing detail, giving no connected idea of the general aspect of a country. (pp. 62-3)

Jim presents for Marlow an enigma more unresolvable than Chad's is for Strether in *The Ambassadors*. As in James's novel, however, the opacity of the character envisaged does not diminish the primary psychological interest of the novel itself, but redirects it upon the character who does the envisaging. Since Jim – and external reality generally – is not straightforwardly 'open to the senses', but conflictingly envisaged and ultimately impalpable, perception itself, and the nature, motives and mental processes of the perceiver, become central subjects of the fiction. In this way, particularly in *Lord Jim* and the other novels in which the narrator Marlow appears (*Heart of Darkness* (1902) and *Chance* (1913), for example), Conrad, like James, shifts the interest of his fiction from 'the human scene' to 'the reflected field'. This breaks down, as Jameson suggests, an old realism that assumes relatively unproblematic contact between the mind and 'things as they really are'. For Conrad and James any attempt to perceive 'things as they really are' is inevitably coloured by the perceptual apparatus of the individual perceiver. Both authors accepted a label borrowed from recent developments in visual art, 'Impressionist', as a description of their style: it aptly suggests techniques in which objective certainties dissolve and the human scene of the novel is markedly suffused with the consciousness of the figure observing or narrating it. This modification in the attention of fiction at the turn of the century (one which, as the term 'Impressionist' helps to suggest, can be more widely considered in relation to the art and thought of the time) is as Jameson indicates a significant departure, a 'fault line' representing a break from earlier interests and conventions. The critic J. Hillis Miller follows Jameson in seeing *Lord Jim* as sharply differentiated from earlier fiction, suggesting that

> Victorian novels were often relatively stabilized by the presence of an omniscient narrator . . . a trustworthy point of view and also a safe vantage point . . . in *Lord Jim* no point of view is entirely trustworthy.[5]

In this way Conrad departs further from convention than James. James stabilises Strether's problematic perceptions with his own authorial voice; in *Lord Jim*, no narrator is omniscient – every voice is idiosyncratic and often highly particularised in style and language. As Jameson suggests, the breakdown of older realism achieved by Conrad is specifically structural, depending on a construction which juxtaposes disparate views of the world in order to make inescapable the conflicts between them and the consequent uncertainties of perception itself. Conflicting visions leave no single view of the world secure, and the fiction necessarily focused on the subjective processes through which reality may be known by each individual.

Henry James saw Conrad's use of the narrator Marlow as creating 'a prolonged hovering flight of the subjective over the outstretched ground of the case exposed'.[6] A comparable 'flight of the subjective' appears in the work of another early twentieth-century novelist, closely connected with James and Conrad, Ford Madox Ford. His critical study *Henry James* appeared in 1915, the same year as one of his best novels, *The Good Soldier*. Like some of James's fiction, *The Good Soldier* traces the perplexities of a naïve, inexperienced American encountering the complexity and deceptiveness of European society. The narrator of *The Good Soldier*, John Dowell, often admits to a puzzled, limited knowledge of English society, at one stage concluding that in certain areas 'Englishmen seem to me to be a little mad' (p. 137).

Ford collaborated with Conrad in jointly writing novels such as *The Inheritors* (1901) and *Romance* (1903) and also, as he records in his dedicatory letter to *The Good Soldier*, in exhaustive studies of 'how words should be handled and novels constructed'. In some aspects, construction included, *The Good Soldier* resembles *Lord Jim*. Dowell is perplexed yet fascinated by the silent, inscrutable, rather unreliable Englishman Edward Ashburnham, much as Marlow is by Jim, and Dowell's notion that he is telling his story 'in a very rambling way', as if to 'a silent listener', makes *The Good Soldier* into the sort of 'free and wandering tale' which Marlow's after-dinner monologue, in Conrad's view, made *Lord Jim*.[7]

There are also, however, significant differences between *The Good Soldier* and *Lord Jim*. One of Marlow's difficulties, and a reason for including in his narrative so many testimonies other than his own, is his distance, emotionally and often geographically, from Jim himself. Dowell, on the other hand, is consistently involved, personally and emotionally, in the events he recounts – principally his wife's protracted infidelity with Ashburnham – and always much concerned with his own responses to them. However much he reveals his own nature in the process, Marlow talks mostly about Jim rather than himself. Dowell is a more obvious, explicit centre of his own attention than is Marlow. In one way this places *The Good Soldier* close in strategy to the sort of half-confessional, first-person narratives found in Victorian fiction, for example in Charles Dickens's *Great Expectations* (1860-1) or *David Copperfield* (1849-50). By comparison such Victorian novels nevertheless remain, in Hillis Miller's terms, at least relatively stabilised by 'a trustworthy point of view and a safe vantage point'. Neither Pip's childhood perspective in *Great Expectations*, nor David's in *David Copperfield* is entirely trustworthy either morally or perceptually: this unreliability, however, is carefully indicated by their later, narrating selves. One of the structuring principles of the sort of fiction in which they appear is that the narrator progresses, in the course of the story, from earlier existence as a child towards the sort of maturity possessed throughout by the older, narrating self who looks back on past limitations or mistakes. John Dowell does not achieve stability in this way, and his narrative never offers a safe vantage point. The eventual revelation of his wife's epic infidelity does show him the extent to which he has been an 'ignorant fool', but he remains thereafter only less ignorant – not always a trustworthy observer of his world or himself, nor even a consistent one. Denial that 'analysis of [his] own psychology matters at all to this story', for example, is quickly followed by mention of a 'mysterious and unconscious self' and of 'unconscious desires' (pp. 88, 99, 100, 213).

Far from being irrelevant to the story, as he suggests, Dowell's psychology and the particularity of his outlook are central, unavoidable issues in *The Good Soldier*. Self-contradictory, frequently biased and jealous, and often ruled by unconscious desires he seeks to ignore, Dowell is an excellent example of an unreliable narrator. Some critics consider such figures character-istic of modern fiction, a decisive step in the breaking down of older realism, secure omniscience and the relative stability of Victorian fiction. Figures such as Dowell enforce a sceptical scrutiny of the means through which a story is told, as much as of what is told within it. Such scepticism installs in the fiction an epistemological doubt, an uncertainty about how completely or truthfully the world can be known or communicated through any individual's idiosyncratic vision of it. Though Ford's fiction may be less completely comparable to the work of Conrad and James than he suggests, he clearly shares in these authors' shifting of some of the novel's interest away from the perceived world in order to examine in more depth the nature of perception and the psychology of the perceiver. This shift further marks the 'fault line' between Victorian and modernist fiction. As Gérard Genette suggests, the interest of narrative at the turn of the century was 'caught between what it tells (the story) and what tells it (the narrating)' and was moving increasingly towards 'domination by the latter (modern narrative)' (p. 156).

Shifts of interest of this kind, from perceived to perceiver, from the world without to the mind within, had become such an obvious feature of contemporary fiction by the mid-1920s that Gerald Bullett could suggest in *Modern English Fiction* (1926) that

> the young intellectual who sits down to write his first novel instinctively interposes between us and the events of his story the consciousness of its chief character. (p. 12)

The fiction of Conrad, Ford and James shows the origins and early forms of this instinct. The use of what James calls 'a definite intervening first person singular' [8] – figures such as Strether, Dowell or Marlow, who provide mirrors polished, cloudy or warped through which the world of the novel is mediated – marks one stage in the development of the subjective method, the instinct for interposing consciousness whose dominance in the 1920s Bullett records. A comparison of Ford's *The Good Soldier* with some of his later fiction – particularly the *Parade's End* tetralogy (1924–8) – suggests ways in which novelists, by the end of the 1920s, had learned to enter more deeply and intimately into the consciousness of their chief characters or intervening first persons singular.

In *Parade's End*, Ford records as follows, for example, the thoughts of his hero Christopher Tietjens, disturbed by his experience as a combatant in the First World War, and by the monstrous infidelities of his wife:

> Panic came over Tietjens. He knew it would be his last panic of that interview. No brain could stand more. Fragments of scenes of fighting, voices, names, went before his eyes and ears . . . Years before . . . How many months? . . . Nineteen, to be exact, he had sat on some tobacco plants on the Mont de Kats . . . No, the Montagne

Noire. In Belgium ... What had he been doing? ... Trying to get the
lie of the land. ... No. ... Waiting. (pp. 492–3)

Frequent self-questioning and self-contradiction, together with
abbreviated, fragmentary sentences, repeatedly interrupted with
ellipses, imitate the rhythm, hesitation and something of the nature
of thoughts as they occur to Tietjens. Such passages appear
frequently in *Parade's End*, and are often extensive: the reflections
beginning above, for example, continue for more than two pages.
They obviously represent a development from the tactics employed
in *The Good Soldier*: this is no longer the manner of a narrator
telling a story to a silent listener, but a style which follows the inner
voice – if not always the actual words – of a character silently
addressing himself. Ford's employment of this voice helps to
indicate (and may itself have directly benefited from) some of the
developments in fictional style made between around 1915 and
1928. To the subjective methods Ford might have learned from
Conrad and James there were added, in this period, further
techniques for entering the mind within, variously introduced by
D. H. Lawrence, Dorothy Richardson, May Sinclair, Virginia
Woolf and eventually, most famously, by James Joyce.


## D. H. LAWRENCE

Critics sometimes seem unsure whether D. H. Lawrence should be
considered a modernist or not. David Daiches, for example,
suggests that

> in his mature novels Lawrence was at least as revolutionary as Joyce
> ... a great innovator, one who puts the novel form to genuinely new
> uses. (pp. 139–40)

Peter Faulkner, in his general study *Modernism*, sees Lawrence as
'a deliberate innovator in his method as a novelist', but adds that he
had 'scant respect' for the modernists (p. 60), several of whom he
criticised precisely because they were so firmly – Lawrence thought
fussily – attentive to the minutest movements of inner consciousness. W. W. Robson's conclusion that Lawrence was 'profoundly
traditional as well as profoundly modern' (p. 88) is the easiest to
justify, especially in the light of Daiches's suggestion that

innovative qualities may be chiefly apparent in Lawrence's mature novels, *The Rainbow* (1915) and *Women in Love* (1921), each strongly concerned with 'the mind within'. Earlier work such as *Sons and Lovers* (1913) is closer to traditional phases of writing. A partly autobiographical novel about growing up towards maturity, *Sons and Lovers* shares some characteristics with other examples of the sort of *Bildungsromans* (novels of personal education and growth towards adulthood, such as *David Copperfield*, especially popular in Victorian times) that continued to appear in the early twentieth century.

*Sons and Lovers*, however, does show an early form of the interests that extend throughout Lawrence's fiction, particularly his concern with close sexual relations and their consequences within the individual psyche. *Sons and Lovers* deals with the difficulties created for Paul Morel in his affairs by his inability to separate himself and his affections sufficiently from his mother, a problem he remains long unaware of himself. Paul remains equally unconscious of his true feelings for Miriam, described as follows:

> He did not know himself what was the matter. He was naturally so young, and their intimacy was so abstract, he did not know he wanted to crush her on to his breast to ease the ache there. He was afraid of her. The fact that he might want her as a man wants a woman had in him been suppressed into a shame. (pp. 220–1)

In Paul's relations with both Miriam and his mother, *Sons and Lovers* introduces a regular problem for characters in later novels. Like Paul, they often do not know themselves what is the matter, encountering strong forces and desires which nevertheless cannot be fully grasped or contained within their conscious minds. In *The Rainbow*, for example, Lawrence explains of Tom Brangwen that 'a daze had come over his mind, he had another centre of consciousness . . . unable to know anything' (p. 39). Lawrence likewise suggests of one of his heroines in *Women in Love*, Gudrun, that she 'knew in her subconsciousness, not in her mind' (p. 508), and remarks of the other, Ursula, that 'she could not imagine what it was. It merely took hold of her . . . beyond thought . . . she was translated beyond herself' (p. 221).

Such movements into 'another centre of consciousness . . . beyond thought' suggest that, even in his mature fiction, Lawrence remained in part a traditional writer not so much despite as *because of* what seemed profoundly modern – sometimes, in his own day, even profoundly shocking – interests in sex and the psyche. Profoundly modern techniques, such as stream of consciousness, cannot be altogether adequately applied to characters whose most crucial experiences are often not conscious at all. Transcribing the inner voice of such characters obviously does not help to gain access to aspects of their experience which cannot be reached or spoken within it. Instead, Lawrence has to remain aloof from his characters, reporting or dramatising authorially what they cannot wholly know themselves; relying on the sort of authorial omniscience described in *Lady Chatterley's Lover* (1928) as the novelist's conventional licence 'to reveal the most secret places of life . . . the *passional* secret places' (p. 104). If Lawrence's tactics are 'profoundly modern', it is not so much for the style through which he reports or describes consciousness and what lies beyond it as for the extraordinary frequency with which such passages appear, at times almost overwhelming action and dialogue. Quantitatively, Lawrence entirely shares in the modernist trend from objective to subjective, at least in *Women in Love* and *The Rainbow*, in which even single lines of conversation are often separated by whole paragraphs describing the exfoliating inner feelings of the conversants.

Such passages, however, sometimes strain the patience of Lawrence's readers. Critics of Lawrence often suggest that his urgency in seeking out the deepest core of his characters' being leads him to employ a language overfraught with portentous vocabulary – repeatedly, ineffectually gesturing at 'dark', 'mystic', '*passional*' but ultimately vague or ungraspable emotions. Part of Ursula's experience of Birkin in *Women in Love*, for example, is floridly described in terms of 'rivers of strange dark fluid richness . . . full mystic knowledge of his suave loins of darkness . . . magical, mystical, a force in darkness, like electricity' (pp. 354, 358). Some explanation of this uneasy style is offered by another description of Ursula's relations with Birkin which suggests they are characterised by 'unspeakable communication . . . that can never be transmuted into mind content' (p. 361). Some of her communication with Birkin may be unspeakable not only for Ursula herself, but also for the author, able to go only so far in communicating experience beyond thought, and to do no more than gesture awkwardly at what lies beyond. Certain impulses – physical passions especially – lead not only beyond thought, but beyond what can be conventionally rendered in language: an inevitable problem for modernist writing, with its deepening fascination for the mind within, which is further considered in Chapter 4.

One of Lawrence's better solutions to this problem is not to attempt a report of characters' feelings but to dramatise them in symbolic episodes, such as the following account of cruel mistreatment of his mare by Gudrun's eventual lover Gerald:

> He held on her unrelaxed, with an almost mechanical relentlessness, keen as a sword pressing into her . . .
>
> Gudrun looked and saw the trickles of blood on the sides of the mare, and she turned white. And then on the very wound the bright spurs came down, pressing relentlessly. The world reeled and passed into nothingness for Gudrun, she could not know any more. (p. 124)

Though Gudrun 'could not know' consciously what the scene means for her, this is made clear enough by her physical reaction to it. Blood drains from her face as it does from the sides of the mare: in 'another centre of consciousness', a level of physical cognition or even 'blood consciousness' as Lawrence sometimes called it, she identifies herself with the horse, anticipating the destructive flaunting of cruelty and power which will characterise Gerald's relations with her. Especially in *The Rainbow* and *Women in Love*, Lawrence shows a particular talent for creating such symbolic scenes, at once relatively natural – simply a picture of a man controlling a horse at a level crossing, for example – yet simultaneously highly endowed with wider significance and suggestion about the deepest emotions of his characters and about the unconscious forces that structure their relationships.

These mature novels also benefit from Lawrence's development of a tactic rarely employed in *Sons and Lovers*, one able in certain instances to adapt language to represent inner thought and the movements of the psyche. Lawrence's use of this device is evident in the following account in *The Rainbow* of Ursula's passionate feelings for religion and for the early spring:

> The passion rose in her for Christ . . . But how did it apply to the weekday world? What could it mean, but that Christ should clasp her to his breast, as a mother clasps her child? And oh, for Christ, for him who could hold her to his breast and lose her there! Oh, for the breast of man, where she should have refuge and bliss for ever . . .

Again she felt Jesus in the countryside. Ah, he would lift up the lambs in his arms! Ah, and she was the lamb. Again, in the morning, going down the lane, she heard the ewe call, and the lambs came running . . . to the udder . . . sucking, vibrating with bliss . . . Oh, and the bliss, the bliss! She could scarcely tear herself away. (pp. 286–7)

No matter how passionate an author Lawrence may be considered in general, the passion of this passage, as it begins by indicating, is Ursula's and not his. The voice in the passage which says 'Oh' and 'Ah' and 'Oh, and the bliss, the bliss!' cannot therefore be plausibly ascribed to Lawrence as the narrator of the novel, nor can all the questions and exclamations that predominate throughout. Not, or at any rate not purely, representing the author's voice, the passage must in some way be transcribing Ursula's. But this is not conventionally marked for the reader, either in the form of direct speech – which would read ' "Ah," she thought, "and I am the lamb" ', with pronouns in the first person and verbs in the present tense – or indirect speech, which would give 'She thought that she was the lamb', with verbs in the past tense, pronouns in the third person, and the character's questions and exclamations deleted. Instead, much of the passage has characteristics of both direct and indirect recording of speech or, in this case, of inner thought. 'Free Indirect Discourse' is the name usually given to this technique of presenting a character's voice partly mediated by the voice of the author; instances where, as Gérard Genette puts it,

> the narrator takes on the speech of the character, or, if one prefers, the character speaks through the voice of the narrator, and the two instances are then *merged*. (p. 174)

The term Free Indirect Discourse is perhaps best reserved for instances where words have actually been spoken aloud, while instances such as the above, where a character's voice is probably the silent, inward one of thought, can be described as 'Free Indirect Style'.

Free Indirect Style of this kind, transcribing unspoken or even incompletely verbalised thoughts, appears very frequently throughout *The Rainbow* and *Women in Love*. It is especially predominant in chapters (such as VI, 'Anna Victrix', or XI, 'First Love', in *The Rainbow*; or 30, 'Snowed Up' in *Women in Love*) where characters experience crises or strong desires, or engage in extended inward reflection about their lives and relations. One such passage, again presenting Ursula's feelings, appears at the beginning of Chapter 15 of *Women in Love*, at an early stage of her 'deep and passionate' love for Birkin:

> She sat crushed and obliterated in a darkness that was the border of death . . . Darkly, without thinking at all, she knew that she was near to death. She had travelled all her life along the line of fulfilment, and it was nearly concluded. She knew all she had to know, she had experienced all she had to experience, she was fulfilled in a kind of bitter ripeness, there remained only to fall from the tree into death. And one must fulfil one's development to the end, must carry the adventure to its conclusion. And the next step was over the border into death. So it was then! There was a certain peace in the knowledge . . .
>
> Of the next step we are certain. It is the step into death . . .
>
> It was a decision. It was not a question of taking one's life – she would *never* kill herself, that was repulsive and violent. It was a question of *knowing* the next step. And the next step led into the space of death. Did it? – or was there – ?
>
> Her thoughts drifted into unconsciousness, she sat as if asleep beside the fire. (pp. 214–15)

In a letter of 1914, Lawrence suggested to his publisher, 'You mustn't look in my novel for the old stable ego . . . of the character', adding that it required 'a deeper sense than any we've been used to exercise' to create and sustain a recognisable individuality for characters.[9] The last lines in particular of the passage above demonstrate the deepening effect of Lawrence's Free Indirect Style, equipping his narrative with the potential to record what Ursula knows 'without thinking', following her thoughts in their drift towards the very edge of unconsciousness.

The passage as a whole also illustrates one of the ways in which Lawrence's writing destabilises the ego, dissolving any easy, secure sense of identity in the voice of author or character, increasingly fused together in various shades and tones of intermingling. The opening lines can be read as relatively stabilised, almost in the manner of a Victorian omniscient narrator, seeming to view Ursula from outside and simply reporting her condition as 'crushed and obliterated'. But the apparently objective 'she' in these lines quickly slides into the less definite 'one' and 'we': in 'she would *never* kill herself', even 'she' has become, in Free Indirect Style, a kind of equivalent for 'I', and the passage seems directed largely by Ursula's unspoken thoughts, as the last line confirms. Exclamations, questions and italicised emphases – more plausibly features of character rather than author discourse – help to trace this progression into Free Indirect recording of Ursula's own thoughts, but there remain intermediary stages in which author and character voice are almost impossible to identify or separate – for example, in the sentence 'And the next step was over the border into death'. Such intermediary sentences allow the novel a certain freedom of suggestion, a possibility of statement precisely located with neither character nor author, but as if drawn from the whole atmosphere or situation the narrative develops. Much of Lawrence's moral and religious vision depends on this sort of freely located statement, a frequent condition of what is often called his 'prophetic' style. At the end of Chapter X of *The Rainbow*, for example, the voice that asks, 'Can I not, then, walk this earth in gladness, being risen from sorrow . . . after my resurrection?' is one which can be ascribed neither to Ursula, even in the 'visionary world' she inhabits at the time, nor to Lawrence himself, nor even to the risen Christ, belonging instead to a sort of 'visionary world' the whole novel creates for itself from the freewheeling interfusion of all its many voices.

Free Indirect Style is an extensive, distinctive feature of *The Rainbow, Women in Love* and some of Lawrence's later fiction, but it is by no means his invention. Following Mikhail Bakhtin's suggestion that the novel form fundamentally depends upon interminglings of languages, recent narrative criticism and theory have increasingly concerned themselves with forms of what Bakhtin calls the 'hybridisation' of speech.[10] Narrative theory now sometimes envisages the merging of character and author discourse in Free Indirect Style as a distinctive, even definitive, feature of fiction in general. Some such merging, at any rate, is evident long before Lawrence's appearance in the history of the novel: as Bakhtin himself points out, it is often clearly present in the fiction of Charles Dickens, for example. It is also at times a feature of Jane Austen's style. As the last chapter suggested, many aspects of modernist style need to be seen not altogether as innovations, but as changes of emphasis – even as quantitative rather than wholly qualitative differences from earlier writing. In this way, though it is not at all new to the twentieth century, Free Indirect Style does help distinguish the work of the modernists from the 'relatively

stabilised' fiction of their predecessors, if only on the grounds of the
new frequency and extent of its employment – though perhaps also
the particularity of its use as a register for unspoken thoughts,
rather than as just another way of recording dialogue. Free Indirect
Style is used as a means of illumining the mind within not only in
the mature fiction of D. H. Lawrence, but in much of the writing so
far discussed. In *The Ambassadors*, for example, it is regularly used
by James as a means of keeping the narrative close to the point of
view of Strether, of allowing 'auctorial infallibility' to remain at the
shoulder of the protagonist. Ford's use of the style in *Parade's End*
is more extensive, forming a principal means of transcribing
Tietjens's thoughts, as for example in the passage recording
Tietjens's 'panic', quoted earlier. Such passages seem to appear
more frequently as Ford's novel-sequence progresses in the 1920s.
By the last volume of the tetralogy, *The Last Post* (1928), his Free
Indirect Style is not just a regular feature of his writing, but at times
a very striking and even extravagant one. It extends, for example,
into transcription of the inner thoughts of Tietjens's brother Mark,
and of the highly idiosyncratic English of his French mistress.
Ford's narrative also at one stage enters into, for a whole chapter (I,
iii), the heavily dialectal voice of Tietjens's servants, one of whom
reflects, for example, that

> if you 'as to 'ave Quality all about you in the 'ouse tis better not to
> 'ave real Quality . . . 'E coudn' say as 'ow 'e liked the job the
> Governor give 'im. He had to patch up and polish with beeswax – not
> varnish – rough stuff such 's 'is granf'er 'ad 'ad. An 'ad got rid of.
> Rough ol' truck. Moren n 'undred yeers old. N'more! (pp. 704–5)

Even when, at the end of the First World War, Mark is so enraged
at the peace made with Germany that he vows never to speak aloud
again, his resolution passes almost unnoticed, so richly is his inner
voice sustained by Ford's style.

Used with increasing diversity and extravagance throughout
*Parade's End*, Free Indirect Style is a mark of Ford Madox Ford's
increasing modernity in the 1920s. In its earlier uses by James and
Lawrence, it indicates an intermediary stage in the 'trend from
objective to subjective'; from Victorian to modern. It shows
Lawrence in particular poised, as some of his critics suggest,
between nineteenth-century and modernist fiction. Free Indirect
Style moves towards deep and full entry into a character's con-

sciousness, yet cannot abandon altogether the authority of the author's own voice. Its use shows Lawrence still partly traditional in retaining an element of authorial infallibility, a stabilising omniscience; yet also partly modern in using so extensively a language and a style which offer a flexible means of transcribing inner thoughts and mental experience. A further, crucial step towards abandonment of the voice of authorial omniscience, towards complete containment of narrative within the minds of characters, remained to be taken by Dorothy Richardson in some of the early volumes of her 13-novel sequence, *Pilgrimage* (1915–67).

## DOROTHY RICHARDSON AND MAY SINCLAIR

This step is not immediately apparent in the first volume of *Pilgrimage*, *Pointed Roofs* (1915). Dorothy Richardson records her admiration both for Marcel Proust's 'reconstruction of experience focused from within the mind of a single individual', and for Henry James 'keeping the reader incessantly watching . . . through the eye of a single observer'.[11] From the beginning, *Pilgrimage* is similarly focused through the mind and observation of Miriam Henderson, Richardson's chief, completely central, character. But J. D. Beresford makes a useful observation when he remarks in his introduction to the first edition of *Pointed Roofs* that he finds it 'the most subjective thing I have ever read', while also describing it as 'realism . . . objective'.[12] As Beresford suggests, though Miriam Henderson is an entirely subjective centre for the novel's attention, she is nevertheless treated objectively enough at times. Initially, and at many stages throughout, Richardson relies like Henry James on authorial report to record the movements and contents of her protagonist's mind. She also moves beyond such methods, as in the following passage, showing Miriam pondering her place in society:

> Never daring to tell anybody. . . . Did she want to tell anybody? To come out into the open and be helped and have things arranged for her and do things like other people? No. . . . No . . .
> Her thoughts hesitated . . . Sivvle . . . Something grand – all the grand girls were horrid . . . somehow mean and sly. . . . Sivvle . . . *Sivvle* . . . *Civil*! Of course! Civil *what*?
> Miriam groaned. She was a governess now. Someone would ask

her that question. She would ask pater before he went. ... No, she
would not. ... (I, p. 31)

Exclamations, rhetorical questions and italicised emphases
resemble D. H. Lawrence's Free Indirect Style, while the frequent
use of ellipses to indicate how 'her thoughts hesitated' are close to
Ford's tactics in the passage quoted earlier from *Parade's End.*
Elizabeth Drew might have had Ford or Richardson specifically in
mind when she commented in 1926 that

> the twentieth-century novel, indeed, might almost be identified with
> that device of punctuation so liberally employed by its creators, and
> called the Novel of the Three Dots. (p. 37)

Richardson's principal contribution to the twentieth-century
novel, however, was neither a device of punctuation nor her
extended use of Free Indirect Style to communicate her heroine's
thoughts, but the development of a new 'subjective method' different from any of those employed by James, Conrad, Ford or
Lawrence. Her progress towards the use of this method can be
traced through the various registrations of Miriam's impressions
which take place in the following passage:

> She was surprised now at her familiarity with the detail of the room
> ... that idea of visiting places in dreams. It was something more than
> that ... all the real part of your life has a real dream in it; some of the
> real dream part of you coming true. You know in advance when you
> are really following your life. These things are familiar because
> reality is here. Coming events cast *light.* It is like dropping everything
> and walking backwards to something you know is there. However
> far you go out, you come back. ... I am back now where I was before
> I began trying to do things like other people. I left home to get here.
> None of these things can touch me here. (II, p. 13)

The passage begins objectively enough with the pronoun 'she',
though the three-dot device and the movement into the second-
person 'you' form soon begin to indicate a Free Indirect transcription of Miriam's thoughts. 'You' is used much in the sense of 'one'
or even 'I', part of a subtle progression, a gradual slippage, from
third person to first. This makes the final appearance of 'I' in the
last lines seem quite natural, though it actually marks a decisive
change from an indirect register of Miriam's inner vision, mediated

by the author, to a direct recording of her thoughts themselves, supposedly in the form in which they occur to her.

Such sections of direct recording of thought – of Miriam's 'mind . . . rushing on by itself' (I, p. 268) – appear more frequently as the sequence of novels goes on: perhaps as Richardson's confidence with 'the subjective method' grew, or as a general 'trend from objective to subjective' began to be more clearly shared by other contemporary authors. At any rate, by *The Tunnel* (1919) the method of the passage above turns up not just in occasional phrases, but is sustained more or less throughout whole chapters, or in long passages such as the following:

> I *must* have been through there; it's the park. I don't remember. It isn't. It's waiting. One day I will go through. Les yeux gris, vont au paradis. Going along, along, the twilight hides your shabby clothes. They are not shabby. They are clothes you go along in, funny; jolly. Everything's here, any bit of anything, clear in your brain; you can look at it. What a terrific thing a person is, bigger than anything. How *funny* it is to be a person. You can never not have been a person. Bouleversement. It's a fait bouleversant. *Christ*-how-rummy. It's enough. Du, Heilige, rufe dein Kind zurück, ich habe genossen das irdische Glück; ich habe geliebt und gelebet . . . Oh let the solid ground not fail beneath my feet, until I am quite quite sure. ... Hallo, old Euston Road, beloved of my soul, my own country, my native heath. (II, p. 256)

Richardson alternates between use of the pronouns 'you' and 'I' to represent the first person, while the more external, objective 'she' is entirely missing from this long passage, indicating the suppression of the voice of aloof authorial report. Stabilising authorial omniscience disappears, replaced by Miriam's 'registration of impressions' (I, p. 431) – the wandering, associative, '*Christ*-how-rummy' polyglot inner mutter through which her thoughts address themselves and swirl around the core of 'what it is to be a person'.

Marked by present-tense verbs and by use of the 'I' form to indicate an unmediated directness of thoughts as they occur, such writing in *Pilgrimage* is the earliest example in English of what has come to be known as the stream-of-consciousness form. The phrase was probably first used critically by May Sinclair in a review of early volumes of *Pilgrimage* in 1918, in which she suggests:

> In this series there is no drama, no situation, no set scene.

Nothing happens. It is just life going on and on. It is Miriam Henderson's stream of consciousness going on and on. And in neither is there any grossly discernible beginning or middle or end.[13]

Sinclair may have borrowed the concept of consciousness as a stream from the philosophy of Henry James's brother William. William James remarks in his *Principles of Psychology* (1890) that

consciousness, then, does not appear to itself chopped up in bits . . . it is nothing jointed; it flows. A 'river' or a 'stream' are the metaphors by which it is most naturally described. *In talking of it hereafter, let us call it the stream of thought, of consciousness, or of subjective life* . . .
The wonderful stream of our consciousness. (I, pp. 239–43)

Later critics have come to consider the invention and use of a literary form of 'the wonderful stream of consciousness' one of the central achievements of modernism: commentators even in the 1920s were quick to praise its improvement on earlier means of representing subjective life. For example, while claiming the stream of consciousness as the invention of a Frenchman, Edouard Dujardin, and discussing its later borrowing by James Joyce, Valery Larbaud pointed out in 1925 the form's

audacity; the possibilities it offers for forceful and rapid expression of the most intimate and spontaneous thoughts, ones which seem to be formed beyond consciousness and seem outwith organised discourse . . . a form which makes it possible to reveal and seize upon the welling up of thoughts so deep within the self.[14]

Larbaud also points out the form's 'novelty'. As he suggests, the stream of consciousness is in one way a technical breakthrough; a radical new step in the forceful expression of thought; a more direct, intimate entry to consciousness than anything hitherto available to the novel. Dorothy Richardson's writing suggests, however, that this new technique can also be seen to have evolved steadily, even inevitably, rather than altogether suddenly and unexpectedly. The paragraphs which appear throughout *Pilgrimage*, moving freely between 'she', 'you' and 'I', and sometimes remaining within the final 'I' form of stream of consciousness, suggest the form develops as a kind of natural, logical continuation of earlier techniques for registering thoughts deep within the self.

Once Henry James had focused his fiction around the mind and experience of a single individual; once Lawrence, Ford and Richardson herself had expanded the use of Free Indirect Style to allow narrative such extensive contact with the inner voice of characters, the fuller entry to the mind offered by stream of consciousness required only a couple of further transformations of the language of the novel – changing of verbs into the present tense, and of the 'she' and 'you' pronouns into the 'I' which they had in any case always strained towards representing. Sooner or later, such transformations were bound to be made. The appearance of stream of consciousness in English writing may thus be seen not only as a breakthrough, but as an extension of the evolving literary history, and the evolution in fictional language, of the first decades of the twentieth century; as a natural consummation of general trends from objective to subjective.

There is a good deal of truth in this conclusion, but important details remain to be added to it. As always, the evolution of literary history needs to be seen in the context of the wider historical forces which condition the shapes imagination creates for experience. *Pilgrimage* in particular, the work of a woman writer representing a female character, needs to be placed in the context of the changing status, consciousness and social role of women at the time, developments which affect modernist fiction – and literature throughout the early part of the twentieth century – very widely and variously. In 1899 Henry James suggests both that 'nothing is more salient in English life today . . . than the revolution taking place in the position and outlook of women' and that new possibilities for fiction would result.[15] Some of his expectations seem to Elizabeth Drew to have been fulfilled by 1926, when she remarks in *The Modern English Novel* that 'the full development of the intellect and imagination of women is possible now in a way it has never been before' (p. 105). As she suggests, by the 1920s characters even in novels by male authors had moved decisively beyond what she calls the 'definite design in conduct which all Victorian heroines follow' (p. 107) – though not necessarily always in favourable directions. The fiction of Aldous Huxley, Ford Madox Ford, Wyndham Lewis and others at the time is fraught with the menace of many *femmes fatales*, figurations of male anxiety about women's rejection of conventional 'designs of conduct' and their generally less passive attitudes during the suffragette period.

D. H. Lawrence appears more sympathetically interested in what he calls 'woman becoming individual, self-responsible, taking her own initiative', showing in the figure of Ursula in *The Rainbow* a woman at least determined and free enough to reject many Victorian designs of conduct, including the institution of marriage. Yet Lawrence remains suspicious of what he describes as 'the cold white light of feminine independence',[16] and is often criticised for his portrayals of women – after her self-determination in *The Rainbow*, Ursula's final alliance with Birkin in *Women in Love*, for example, seems a compromise, a tame conclusion. 'The full development of the intellect and imagination of women' is a much more sustained, central aspect of *Pilgrimage*. Much of Richardson's narrative is concerned with Miriam's struggle to maintain an independent financial existence, and with her experience of new social possibilities for women at the time, even at the banal level of smoking in public or cycling alone. Miriam's convictions make her what she calls 'something new – a kind of different world' (I, p. 260), a 'new woman' (I, p. 436) whose struggle to develop intellect and imagination for herself disposes her firmly against the restraining attitudes of men, whom she sometimes finds 'simply paltry and silly – all of them' (II, p. 206). In her view, 'all the men in the world, and their God, ought to apologise to women' (I, p. 459).

Such resentments, central to the theme of *Pilgrimage*, also have significant consequences for its form. Rejection of restraining social conventions extends into rejection of the conventions of fiction. Miriam feels there are 'whole heaps of books, millions of books I can't read' (I, p. 284), largely because they are written with

> some mannish cleverness that was only half right. To write books, knowing all about style, would be to become like a man. Women who wrote books and learned these things would be absurd . . . a clever trick, not worth doing. (II, p. 131)

Like her heroine, Richardson was sceptical of male-dominated conventions in fiction, seeking instead, as she explains in her foreword to *Pilgrimage*, 'a feminine equivalent of the current masculine realism . . . [a] feminine prose . . . moving from point to point without formal obstructions' (I, pp.9, 12). Such priorities encouraged Richardson's development of the stream-of-consciousness form, its fluid nature – not 'chopped up in bits' but shaped by an unconstrained, wandering, freely associative presentation of Miriam's thoughts – obviously contributing to the unobstructed 'feminine prose' she demands. More generally, Richardson's increased interest in consciousness, whether stream-like or not, follows from her wish to avoid conventions of 'current masculine realism': like Proust, Richardson sees a truer realism created by placing everything in the mind rather than in the object.

Her views of this matter, however, are most appropriately seen in relation not only to Proust's, but to those of another woman author of the period committed to writing specifically as a woman, Virginia Woolf. Woolf remarks in *A Room of One's Own* (1929)

> If one is a woman one is often surprised by a sudden splitting off of consciousness, say in walking down Whitehall, when from being the natural inheritor of that civilisation, she becomes, on the contrary, outside of it, alien and critical. (p. 96)

Woolf's views suggest that male structuring of society, Whitehall, civilisation generally, encourage women in particular to split off in consciousness from the external world. If women seek a room of their own, it is in the private domain of the mind that it may most easily be established. Women writers, such as Richardson or Woolf, may thus have been especially disposed to develop new narrative forms in which the workings of consciousness, split away from external reality and the object world, could be fruitfully sustained and explored. The particular nature of such narrative forms, in Richardson's writing at least, may further reflect particular conditions imposed by a male-dominated world. One of the pressures this world exerts is in seeing women not just objectively, but quite often actually *as* objects, evaluated principally for external appearance, however inwardly or subjectively they may wish to see themselves. Much as Miriam resentfully retreats from this external evaluation towards subjective enclosure within her mind and self, some vestigial consciousness of it inevitably remains: her consciousness is not only 'split off' from an external, male-dominated world, but partly split *by* it. Such a mixture of objective and subjective awareness of the self is probably present in any mind: regardless of gender, any sense of identity is partly split between external, public visions of the self and inward, private ones. *Pilgrimage* suggests, however, that the contemporary, rapidly changing situation of women made this split more acutely felt in female consciousness.

Most attracted by the subjective privacy of the mind within, women were also most pressured by a sense of the world without. Even when Miriam is most engrossed in her private thoughts, an awareness of herself from a more objective point of view can still intrude; an awareness of her as 'she' as well as 'I'. This uneasy doubleness in identity keeps the 'she', 'you' and 'I' pronouns in tense yet fluid equilibrium in Richardson's writing, facilitating the transitions between them required for the final emergence of the stream-of-consciousness form. The form may have emerged logically and naturally from the evolving literary history of the early twentieth century, but it is particularly natural and logical that it should have first appeared in *Pilgrimage*, a new woman's vision of a new woman's mind. The most comprehensive analysts of women's relations to modernism, Sandra M. Gilbert and Susan Gubar, can justifiably point to a complex of literary and historical evidence for their argument that

> in their problematic relationship to the tradition of authority, as well as to the authority of tradition, women writers are the major precursors of all 20th-century modernists, the *avant-garde* of the *avant-garde*, so to speak. (*The Female Imagination and the Modernist Aesthetic*, p. 1)

Further evidence of a particular disposition towards innovation can be found in several other contemporary women writers, appearing in an early and influential form in the work of the Paris-based United States author Gertrude Stein. Stein was a former student of William James, and the unpunctuated, flowing quality of some of her prose can be seen as an early, idiosyncratic form of stream of consciousness. In the British context, May Sinclair, for example, followed Richardson fairly directly in style and interests. She worked for the Women's Suffrage League, as well as in the first stages of the psychoanalytic movement, and her early, intelligent appreciation of Richardson is illustrated by the review of *Pilgrimage* quoted above.

In her best novel, *Mary Olivier* (1919), Sinclair is much concerned with the constraining conventions imposed on contemporary women. As in several of her other novels, her heroine endures a life of enforced renunciation and self-denial which leaves her 'mind battering at the walls of her body, the walls of the room, the walls of the world' (p. 260). This 'battering' and the movements of Mary

Olivier's mind generally are recorded in a variety of sensitive inner registers, principally an extended Free Indirect Style, most often expressing in the second-person form how 'your thoughts go on inside you' (p. 99). Like Richardson, however, Sinclair can quickly move from 'she' to 'you' to an 'I' form, as in the following passage recalling Mary's renunciation of a lover:

> She knew only one thing about perfect happiness: it didn't hide; it didn't wait for you behind unknown doors . . .
>
> If you looked back on any perfect happiness you saw that it had not come from the people or the things you thought it had come from, but from somewhere inside yourself . . .
>
> Not Richard. He had become part of the kingdom of God without ceasing to be himself . . .
>
> I used to think there was nothing I couldn't give up for Richard.
>
> Could I give up this? If I had to choose between losing Richard and losing this? (pp. 378-9)

Constraints on Mary's life and experience are generated not only by the general situation of women at the time, but by her particular position within a family dominated by a strong religious faith, especially influential on Mary's childhood. Much of her later sense of release and genuine selfhood comes through discovering in writing and in art an escape from, or a means of reshaping, the constraints of reality and personal circumstance. Many of her problems, however, continue to arise from conflicts between the exigencies of religious faith, of art and, sometimes, of sex. These interests, along with the closeness with which Sinclair's writing follows the thought, language and point of view of a partly autobiographical central figure, have often led to comparisons between *Mary Olivier* and another novel much concerned with evolution from a constraining childhood towards the free flight of art and creation – James Joyce's *A Portrait of the Artist as a Young Man* (1916). Such comparisons have not always been favourable and indicate a problem in the evaluation of the work of both Dorothy Richardson and May Sinclair. Each was considered a very important writer in her day, but their reputations had begun to be partially eclipsed by Joyce, even as early as 1925, as the following review of one of the volumes in Richardson's *Pilgrimage* series suggests:

> Probably no one has done more than Miss Richardson to transform

modern fiction. She popularised, if she did not invent, the subjective novel, and genius, beside which her own meagre talents
insignificantly fade, has been expended on it. Once, and not very
long ago, Miss Richardson's novels, or rather the instalments of Miss
Richardson's novel, were reckoned as quite important. She was
parodied, discussed, esteemed. But now . . . Miss Richardson has
failed to fulfil her earlier promise. The bleak truth is that Miss
Richardson perfected a way of saying things without having
anything to say . . . Is there anything there but an excellent manner
execrably applied.[17]

To suggest that she uses her excellent method 'execrably' is much
too bleak a view to take of Richardson, whose literary standing has
recently been rightly restored by critics interested in both her
pivotal position within the evolution of modernist style, and the
issues addressed in *Pilgrimage*. Joyce is nevertheless still judged the
principal 'genius' of modernism, the writer in whose work the trend
from objective to subjective received its most comprehensive and
sophisticated embodiment. Even Valery Larbaud, insisting on a
Frenchman as the original inventor of stream of consciousness,
acknowledged that it received its fullest and finest employment in
*Ulysses*.

## James Joyce

Joyce's writing did not immediately display the modernist techniques so spectacularly and flexibly deployed in *Ulysses*, but passed
through several stages of the development, discussed above, which
appeared in the work of his contemporaries. The short stories
eventually collected as *Dubliners* (1914) are fairly conventionally
realistic, sometimes satiric, in their portrayal of drab, deadening life
in a city Joyce shows suffering from paralysis of will, energy and
imagination. Joyce, however, also keeps most of his narratives
quite closely focused around the minds and inward experiences of
his protagonists – obviously in the opening three stories, written in
the first person; in later stories more subtly, in frequent, extensive
uses of Free Indirect Style, as well as authorial report of thought.

An increasing reliance on this inward focus can also be traced
through the changes Joyce made in the draft novel *Stephen Hero*,
begun around 1904 and eventually transformed into *A Portrait of
the Artist as a Young Man*, published in 1916. For the most part

*Stephen Hero* is a straightforwardly realistic narrative, presenting characters through report, dialogue and observation by a narrator who remains at an objective distance from the action. As Theodore Spencer explains in his introduction to *Stephen Hero*, which was eventually published in 1944, Joyce revised much of his draft material, 'aiming at economy, and . . . trying to place his centre of action as much as possible inside the consciousness of his hero' (p. 15). Some of the manuscript revisions to *Stephen Hero* indicate Joyce experimenting with Free Indirect Style: in *A Portrait of the Artist as a Young Man* itself, Joyce omits some of the realistic detail of the earlier draft, and practises a Jamesian exclusiveness of focus on – sometimes within – a single mind. Complete concentration on Stephen Dedalus makes him, in James's terms, the 'definite intervening first person singular' around whom the material of the novel is entirely shaped.

A particular form of this concentration is immediately evident in Joyce's opening paragraph, as unusual as anything in the novel which follows:

> Once upon a time and a very good time it was there was a moocow coming down along the road and the moocow that was coming down along the road met a nicens little boy named baby tuckoo. . . .
> His father told him that story: his father looked at him through a glass: he had a hairy face.
> He was baby tuckoo . . .
> The Vances lived in number seven. They had a different father and mother. They were Eileen's father and mother. When they were grown up he was going to marry Eileen. He hid under the table. (pp. 7–8)

Without always or obviously recording his actual thoughts, this opening passage nevertheless dramatises Stephen's consciousness through an infantile language whose simple vocabulary and observation, and abrupt, arbitrary juxtapositions mimic the mental and linguistic habits of the child. This is a kind of mimicry Joyce scarcely returns to – or at least not so ostentatiously – in *A Portrait of the Artist as a Young Man*, but it is variously, extensively, employed in *Ulysses*. Gerty McDowell, for example, the girl Leopold Bloom meets on the beach in Chapter 13, 'Nausikaa', is introduced as follows:

> Gerty was dressed simply but with the instinctive taste of a votary of

Dame Fashion . . . A neat blouse of electric blue selftinted by dolly dyes (because it was expected in the *Lady's Pictorial* that electric blue would be worn) . . .

A sterling good daughter was Gerty just like a second mother in the house, a ministering angel too with a little heart worth its weight in gold. (pp. 287, 291)

Joyce himself remarked that ' "Nausikaa" is written in a namby-pamby, jammy marmalady-drawersy style'[18] – a clichéd language designed to mimic the pretty, precious, cheaply romantic idiom of women's magazines such as *Lady's Pictorial*. A later section of *Ulysses*, Chapter 16, 'Eumaeus', set in the Cabman's Shelter, is equally occupied with endless, weary clichés. Bloom, exhausted himself at the time, suggests an explanation for this when

To improve the shining hour he wondered whether he might . . . pen something out of the common groove (as he fully intended doing) at the rate of one guinea per column. *My Experiences*, let us say, *in a Cabman's Shelter*. (p. 528)

Bloom does not realise these ambitions in the course of the novel, but the chapter in which they are mentioned is written almost as if he had, and as if the chapter itself were the result. The passages introducing Gerty, or Stephen in *A Portrait of the Artist as a Young Man*, similarly appear as if written by the characters who feature in them; as if the characters were somehow helping to tell their own story, shaping its style around their distinctive linguistic habits and expressive idioms. Such mimicry is very close to Free Indirect Style, which Gérard Genette sees as distinguished by the narrative 'taking on the speech of the character'. Yet it cannot be exactly labelled as Free Indirect Discourse or Style, since the narrative takes on Gerty's manner, or Bloom's or Stephen's, without necessarily or consistently transcribing their actual speech or thought. Critical commentators on this aspect of Joyce's tactics have coined various other terms for it. Richard Ellmann describes it as a 'magnetization of style and vocabulary by the context of person, place, and time' (p. 146). Dorrit Cohn talks of 'stylistic contagion' (p. 33), suggesting that the speech habits of characters temporarily infect the narrative in which they appear. Hugh Kenner sees this sort of writing as a distinctive feature of Joyce's style, pointing to its 'characterising vocabulary'; the repeated inclusion of 'a little cluster of idioms which a character might use if he were managing the narrative'. Summing up such tactics, Kenner suggests that in Joyce's work, 'words are in such delicate equilibrium that they detect the gravitational field of the nearest person'(pp. 16, 17).

Such 'gravitational fields' are neither altogether new, however, nor an invention of Joyce's. His stylistic imitation of characters' idioms extends what Mikhail Bakhtin sees as a perennial feature of the intermingling systems of language fundamental to fiction. Bakhtin suggests that

> A character in a novel always has . . . a zone of his own, his own sphere of influence on the authorial context surrounding him, a sphere that extends – and often quite far – beyond the boundaries of the direct discourse allotted to him . . . this zone surrounding the important characters of the novel is stylistically profoundly idiosyncratic. (p. 320)

Many authors – Charles Dickens is again one of Bakhtin's own examples – exploit this 'idiosyncratic zone' surrounding character. Once again, modernism may be best distinguished quantitatively rather than qualitatively from earlier writing: the 'gravitational fields' or spheres of influence exerted by characters within Joyce's writing may be neither unique nor new, but they are employed unusually frequently and adroitly and extend unusually far. Joyce's idiosyncratic zones of language are not used exclusively to reflect the sphere of influence of characters, but even (as suggested by Ellmann, and discussed further in Chapter 4) to indicate certain linguistic idiosyncrasies associated with particular places. The setting of Chapter 7 ('Aeolus') in a newspaper office, for example, helps to account for the intrusion into the text of newspaper headlines and other fragments of journalese, sometimes even between single lines of dialogue. Nevertheless, it is most often the linguistic resources and habits of speech not of places but of individuals that shape the idiosyncrasies of Joyce's language. In this way, sometimes obliquely and subtly, the whole medium of Joyce's fiction is constructed to reflect the consciousness, inner discourse or cast of mind of its characters.

In much of *Ulysses*, of course, representation of consciousness is not oblique but clear and direct. Valery Larbaud and other critics in the 1920s praised Joyce not for his creation of a language of delicate equilibrium, but for the brilliant advances he made in the use of a stream-of-consciousness style able to 'seize upon' every thought or movement of characters' minds. Its potential is most apparent in the eighteenth and last chapter of *Ulysses*, 'Penelope'. Dorothy Richardson admired Joyce as one of the authors of the 'feminine prose' she advocated, and it may be appropriate that by far the longest sustained section of stream of consciousness in *Ulysses* communicates the thoughts of neither of Joyce's male protagonists, Leopold Bloom or Stephen Dedalus, but of Bloom's wife Molly, somnolently, inwardly soliloquising as her mind hovers on the edge of unconsciousness. As Richardson recommended, the prose of this section moves 'without formal obstructions': punctuation is almost entirely missing from the concluding thirty-five pages of *Ulysses*. Its absence suggests a mind flowing freely, associatively, sometimes arbitrarily between subjects, between thoughts, in flickering, almost seamless succession – as in the following passage, for example, in which Molly seeks sleep:

> a quarter after what an unearthly hour I suppose theyre just getting up in China combing out their pigtails for the day well soon have the nuns ringing the angelus theyve nobody coming in to spoil their sleep except an odd priest or two for his night office or the alarmclock next door at cockshout clattering the brains out of itself let me see if I can doze off 1 2 3 4 5 what kind of flowers are those they invented like the stars the wallpaper in Lombard street was much nicer the apron he gave me was like that something only I only wore it twice better lower this lamp and try again so as I can get up early (p. 642)

As the above passage shows, 'Penelope' not only drops the formal obstruction of punctuation, it discards other formal constraints of grammar and coherence. Joyce's concluding stream of consciousness moves, as Larbaud suggests, 'outwith organised discourse' in its pursuit of the quivering of 'thoughts deep within the self', even leading towards what is 'formed beyond consciousness'. Joyce goes on to investigate this area beyond the conscious mind in *Finnegans Wake* (1939; further discussed in Chapter 4), though there are several points in *Ulysses* which anticipate this direction in his later writing – in Chapter 15, 'Nighttown', for example, and at moments in some of the chapters which follow. *Ulysses* itself, however, ends at the point where unconsciousness, the sleep that has hovered around Molly throughout 'Penelope', finally overtakes her. Molly's soliloquy remains – just – within consciousness, a final consummation of the trends in early twentieth-century narrative to place 'everything in the mind' of characters and to suppress from view the stabilising, controlling presence of an omniscient author.

Though *Ulysses* provides this consummate example of the stream-of-consciousness form, this should not obscure – as it sometimes seems to for critics – the real variety of Joyce's writing throughout the novel. *Ulysses* is not only, nor purely except in its last chapter, a stream-of-consciousness novel. On the contrary, one of the strengths of Joyce's writing is its exploitation and integration within a single novel of the widest possible range of the styles discussed so far. Their variety is in evidence, if not immediately from the novel's opening, certainly from its first introduction of its central figure:

> Mr Leopold Bloom ate with relish the inner organs of beasts and fowls. He liked thick giblet soup, nutty gizzards, a stuffed roast heart, liverslices fried with crustcrumbs, fried hencods' roes. Most of all he liked grilled mutton kidneys which gave to his palate a fine
> 5 tang of faintly scented urine.
> Kidneys were in his mind as he moved about the kitchen softly, righting her breakfast things on the humpy tray. Gelid light and air were in the kitchen but out of doors gentle summer morning everywhere. Made him feel a bit peckish.
> 10 The coals were reddening.
> Another slice of bread and butter: three, four: right. She didn't like her plate full. Right. He turned from the tray, lifted the kettle off the hob and set it sideways on the fire. It sat there, dull and squat, its spout stuck out. Cup of tea soon. Good. Mouth dry.
> 15 The cat walked stiffly round a leg of the table with tail on high.
> – Mkgnao!
> – O, there you are, Mr Bloom said, turning from the fire.
> The cat mewed in answer and stalked again stiffly round a leg of the table, mewing. Just how she stalks over my writingtable. Prr.
> 20 Scratch my head. Prr.
> Mr Bloom watched curiously, kindly the lithe black form. Clean to see: the gloss of her sleek hide, the white button under the butt of her tail, the green flashing eyes. He bent down to her, his hands on his knees.
> 25 – Milk for the pussens, he said.
> – Mrkgnao! the cat cried.
> They call them stupid. They understand what we say better than we understand them. She understands all she wants to. Vindictive too. Cruel. Her nature. Curious mice never squeal. Seem

30  to like it. Wonder what I look like to her. Height of a tower? No, she
    can jump me. (p. 45)

Bloom's first presentation to the reader is a parody of formal
introduction, the excessively polite 'Mr Leopold Bloom' followed
by the kind of authorial report of distinguishing characteristics,
likes and dislikes, which often appears in Victorian fiction. Bloom's
tastes, however, are comically insalubrious, undermining the
formal tone of the passage's opening, though they curiously suggest
a direction much of the rest of it will take: kidneys are followed into
Bloom's mind by the narrative itself. By the end of the second
paragraph, oddities and colloquialisms – 'Made him feel a bit
peckish' – suggest it is moving towards a Free Indirect transcription
of Bloom's thoughts. Though line 10 returns to what may be
authorial objectivity, the movement into Bloom's mind continues in
the next lines: 'she' is a pronoun without antecedent in the novel so
far, one which, like the counting phrase 'three, four: right', makes
complete sense only to Bloom. After returning to an objective,
reporting voice in lines 12 and 13, the paragraph ends with the kind
of abbreviated, telegrammatic sentences – 'Cup of tea soon. Good.
Mouth dry.' – which also appear at the conclusion of the whole
passage. Some way from organised discourse, they are the principal
device throughout the early part of the novel for representing
Bloom's stream of consciousness and its barely verbalised movements.

The next section sees an intrusion into Bloom's inner world by
domestic reality, the cat determinedly forcing itself upon his
thoughts. Joyce's fascination for sound, for phonetic music,
creates in *Ulysses* a novel in which 'everything speaks in its own
way' (p. 100), and it is typical that the cat moves beyond the    No!
conventional 'miaow' to 'mkgnao', 'mrkgnao' and even, just after   Irish
the passage quoted, 'mrkrgnao' – probably in a feline attempt to
demand 'milk now'. It is also typical that Joyce's communication
of consciousness spreads beyond the strict confines of a single
mind. Bloom's thoughts flow out not only to speculate about the
cat's nature and perspective in lines 27–31 ('Wonder what I look
like to her'), but even to encompass her possible thoughts and
impulses; almost her language at 'Prr. Scratch my head. Prr'. Such
extensions of consciousness over other creatures or objects in the
characters' world frequently brings to life unlikely situations

and points of view in *Ulysses*. Stephen, for example, imagines in Chapter 1 the words which might be spoken by a drowned corpse dredged back to the surface. Bloom's curious, kindly mind repeatedly extends to encompass the likely thinking of other creatures or people – such as the 'blind stripling' whose thoughts and feelings he constructs at some length after a chance meeting (pp. 148–9).

Such interfusions of consciousness into context spread a bright cast of thought over the whole novel: they are not only part of the novel's communication of the mind within individual characters, but an enlivening of descriptions of the 'world without' in which they live. Recording Bloom's reflections on the cat, for example, not only adds to the warmth and intimacy of the passage's communication of Bloom's mind and inner world. Use of the cat's lowly point of view adds to the variety of perspectives used to delineate Bloom in his kitchen, and to the completeness with which he is seen from outside as well as in. Joyce explained that he sought to create in *Ulysses* a 'complete all-round character' and, of Bloom, that 'I see him from all sides, and therefore he is all-round'.[19] Typical of his writing, the above passage practises a kind of literary Cubism, an almost simultaneous use of alternative perspectives, points of view which repeatedly switch between cat, character and author, inner consciousness and objective distance. In its 'Cyclops' chapter (12), *Ulysses* warns against any narrow, single-minded or, literally, one-eyed view of reality. The novel's own practice works against any such narrowing of vision. No wonder Bloom, always fascinated by science, at one stage speculates about 'parallax' (p. 126) – changes in what is seen caused by alteration of the point of observation. *Ulysses* itself employs a kind of parallax to resist the paralysis of Dublin. However drab or static Dublin life may be in reality, its presentation is made lively and colourful by Joyce's parallactic tactics, constantly shifting the narrative through a spectrum of techniques and points of view.

Hugh Kenner provides an image which helps to define the range of these techniques, perspectives and registers when he describes *Ulysses* as a sort of 'duet for two narrators' (p. 67). For the most part, each sentence in the passage quoted – or in the early part of *Ulysses* generally – can be assigned either to the author/narrator who initially establishes an objective view of Bloom and his curious tastes, or to the subjective inner discourse of Bloom himself, a second voice constantly present in the novel. But there are also many areas – in lines 7 to 9, for example – which cannot be exclusively assigned to either voice, but are a mixture of both. Throughout *Ulysses*, the two voices of Joyce's duet often interfuse, harmonise and split apart again as they do in this passage, creating a range of modulations, a flickering movement into and out of characters' minds, sometimes even within a single line of text. The passage begins clearly enough with a parodic form of nineteenth-century narrative and ends with a decisive movement into a thoroughly subjective, modernist style: the forms employed between, however, demonstrate a full range of the possibilities – Free Indirect Style, authorial report of thought, stream of con-sciousness – developed or extended by modernist narrative in the early years of the century to deepen the novel's grasp of the minds of its characters. If, as Hugh Kenner suggests, *Ulysses* is 'the decisive English-language book of the century' (p. xii), this is not only for its outstanding achievement with the stream-of-conscious-ness form, but for its fluent movement among *all* the devices developed in the course of progress towards that most effective of inward styles. In this way, the passage not only introduces readers to Bloom. It also offers a kind of encyclopaedia of the new strengths and possibilities developed by fiction in English in the first decades of the twentieth century; an illustrated introduction to the new techniques created for narrative's steady movement from objective to subjective.

## Virginia Woolf

Virginia Woolf's fiction may have benefited from the example of *Ulysses*: Woolf admired Joyce for what she called his attempts to come 'close to the quick of the mind' and 'to reveal the flickerings of that innermost flame which flashes its messages through the brain'.[20] But she also had reservations about *Ulysses*, as pointed out in Chapter 1, and the subjective method of her own novels differs significantly from Joyce's. Her particular style can be illustrated from the opening pages of *Mrs Dalloway* (1925):

Mrs Dalloway said she would buy the flowers herself. For Lucy had her work cut out for her. The doors would be taken off their hinges;

Rumplemayer's men were coming. And then, thought Clarissa
Dalloway, what a morning – fresh as if issued to children on a beach.
    What a lark! What a plunge! For so it had always seemed to
her . . .
    For having lived in Westminster – how many years now? Over
twenty, – one feels even in the midst of the traffic, or waking at night,
Clarissa was positive, a particular hush, or solemnity . . . Such fools
we are, she thought, crossing Victoria Street. For Heaven only
knows why one loves it so, how one sees it so. (pp. 5–6)

The passage begins to move away, as early as its second line, from
an objective position of authorial report, unexplained mentions of
'Lucy' and 'Rumplemayer's men' suggesting the frame of reference
of Mrs Dalloway herself. The exclamations 'What a lark!' and
'What a plunge!' and the rhetorical question 'How many years
now?' belong still more clearly to the inner voice of the character.
This voice, however, never replaces the author's completely, or for
very long: on the contrary, the frequent cues such as 'thought
Clarissa Dalloway', 'so it seemed to her', or 'Clarissa was positive'
are a constant reminder of an authorial organisation and presentation of thoughts. Though in moving freely between 'she', 'we'
and 'one' *Mrs Dalloway* seems close to the styles of Dorothy
Richardson and May Sinclair, Woolf does not follow these authors
in making further moves towards unmediated transcription of
characters' minds in the first-person, present-tense form of stream
of consciousness.
    The six characters' monologues presented by Woolf in *The
Waves* (1931) might seem closer to the subjective methods of Joyce
or Richardson, since thoughts and feelings are presented in the first
person, in great detail, and largely uninterrupted by an authorial
voice. Yet the inner life of each of Woolf's six characters is
presented almost as if written in a letter. Their thoughts are
carefully organised, clearly expressed, and show a sophisticated
capacity to find metaphors for states of mind and the various pangs
of contact between consciousness and the intractable world around
it. As in *Mrs Dalloway*, Woolf's representation of thought in *The
Waves* has none of the anarchic fluency of Molly Bloom's mind in
*Ulysses*, nor the syntactic fragmentation which often marks entry to
Leopold Bloom's. Far from a stream of consciousness that moves,
as Larbaud suggests, 'outwith organised discourse', *The Waves* is so
elegantly reflective and carefully structured that it comes as close as

any novel to the condition of poetry. As in much of Woolf's work, subjective experience forms the whole substance of the novel, but interior monologue, rather than stream of consciousness, is the appropriate term for the style in which it is recorded, both in *The Waves* and in Woolf's writing generally.

By comparison with stream of consciousness, interior monologue appears a relatively conventional form. As the repeated speech or thought cues in the above passage from *Mrs Dalloway* suggest, most of Woolf's representation of the 'innermost flame' of the mind is in the 'she thought to herself that' form of indirect discourse. The same tactics appear in *To the Lighthouse* (1927), at any rate in the novel's first and third sections. Woolf herself remarks that 'it is all in oratio obliqua' (indirect speech). Hillis Miller particularly admires Woolf's use of this form as a sensitive register for communicating inner experience, praising her

> indirect discourse, the consciousness of the narrator married to the consciousness of the character and speaking for it ... *To the Lighthouse* is a masterwork of the exploration of the consciousness of others with the tool of indirect discourse.[21]

The capacity of these tools to reach 'the quick of the mind' in *To the Lighthouse* can be illustrated by the following passage from the first section of the novel, describing Mrs Ramsay at her triumphal dinner party:

> Everything seemed possible. Everything seemed right. Just now (but this cannot last, she thought, dissociating herself from the moment while they were all talking about boots) just now she had reached security; she hovered like a hawk suspended; like a flag floated in an element of joy which filled every nerve of her body fully and sweetly, not noisily, solemnly rather, for it arose, she thought, looking at them all eating there, from husband and children and friends; all of which rising in this profound stillness (she was helping William Bankes to one very small piece more and peered into the depths of the earthenware pot) seemed now for no special reason to stay there like a smoke, like a fume rising upward, holding them safe together. Nothing need be said; nothing could be said. (pp. 120–1)

'The world without' – second helpings and banal conversations about boots – is relegated in this passage to parentheses, showing Mrs Ramsay mentally 'dissociated from the moment', free to float like a hawk, flag or fume. Such similes describe the character's mind rather than recording thoughts plausibly arising within it, but there is also much in the passage that represents more directly the particular influence or 'gravitational field' of the character herself. In particular, the complicated syntax in the extended third sentence ('Just now . . .'), and the rhythm that results, strongly suggest the gradually unfolding associations and qualifications emerging within Mrs Ramsay's pattern of thought. This is also present at least occasionally in forms other than simple 'oratio obliqua': as Hillis Miller's metaphor of a 'marriage' between the voice of narrator and character actually suggests, Woolf's style moves at times beyond indirect discourse and towards Free Indirect Style.

Sometimes employing this form, sometimes the more ordinary oratio obliqua, writing such as the above is sustained throughout much of the first and third parts of *To the Lighthouse*. It achieves, in its own way, as comprehensive an enclosure of narrative within individual consciousness as appears in *Ulysses* or *Pilgrimage*, for example. The inner life exists so richly that 'nothing could be said' to equal it, in direct speech, in the everyday, external world. Woolf's style represents the mind of Mrs Ramsay so thoroughly in the first part of the novel, also moving so fluently into and between the consciousnesses of several other characters, that the external, object world of boots and earthenware almost disappears, as it does at times in the third section. The harsher physical realities which Mrs Ramsay fears and which her husband sometimes too insistently represents to her fade from the novel. The insistent physical presence of the lighthouse across the bay, observed by all the characters, comes to provide an almost unique point of stable external reference, a clear, 'stark and straight' (p. 211) object to counterpoint the shifting tides of thought which flow around the novel in its first and third sections.

At the beginning of its second part, however, roles and priorities are reversed. In the Ramsays' holiday home, 'one by one the lamps were all extinguished' (p. 143) as the family falls asleep, leaving the lighthouse beam the only illumination in the darkness of the night – later many nights – shown passing through the house. With the characters asleep or, later, departed or dead, Woolf's style changes radically from the subjective methods of the first part. The second goes on to dramatise the workings of the world beyond the mind, making some of this world and its constituents not inert but subtly, sinisterly active. Woolf employs a style of sustained personification that endows mere objects with the usual attributes – will, reason and emotion – of a now-unconscious humanity. For example, it is observed that

> certain airs . . . entered the drawing room, questioning and wondering . . . the wind sent its spies about the house. (pp. 144, 151)

> Weeds . . . tapped methodically on the window pane. (p. 151)

> the Lighthouse . . . with its pale footfall upon stair and mat . . . the stroke of the lighthouse . . . laid itself with such authority on the carpet in the darkness . . . laid its caress and lingered stealthily and looked and came lovingly again . . . [and] leant upon the bed . . . sent its sudden stare over bed and wall. (pp. 144, 151, 157)

Values, family life, human life itself, crumble under the constant questioning of the wind and the sky: 'Will you fade? Will you perish?' (p. 148). In a reversal of earlier tactics, brief parenthetical asides separate and diminish the human domain, rather than, as in the first section, setting apart an external world irrelevant to the flow of characters' thoughts. Casual mention, in brief parentheses, of the deaths of Mrs Ramsay and several members of her family emphasises the transient irrelevance of humanity in an indifferent universe of stones, stars and things. The first and third sections of *To the Lighthouse* concentrate comprehensively on the subjective life of the mind: the second creates a style not so much objective as adept in bringing objects themselves to life, dramatising, equally comprehensively, the domain beyond consciousness which inexorably resists its order and light.

So sharply divided in style between its three parts, *To the Lighthouse* enacts formally the theme of Mr Ramsay's philosophy: 'Subject and object and the nature of reality' (p. 28). Even the novel's setting on an island, washed around by the endless chaos of the sea, figuratively extends a sense of the mind and its subjective orders threatened by the randomness that surrounds it. Much the same sense preoccupies Mrs Ramsay, even at the moment of her greatest security, domestic order and social success, her triumphal dinner party, when she feels that

> inside the room seemed to be order and dry land; there, outside, a reflection in which things wavered and vanished, waterily . . . they

were all conscious of making a party together in a hollow, on an island. (p. 112)

Juxtaposing order and chaos, subjectivity and objectivity, at the level of both form and theme, *To the Lighthouse* provides a kind of paradigm for the new priorities of modernist fiction, its growing inclination to turn from the world to the mind.

## BACKGROUND AND CONTEXT

So concerned in her own fiction with disparities between the mind within and the world without, Woolf is naturally enough one of the clearest of critical commentators on the division between subjective and objective methods in the writing of her period. In her essay 'Modern Fiction' (1919), she defines as 'spiritual' the attempt by Joyce and others to come 'close to the quick of the mind', distinguishing their work from the 'material', realist style she sees characterising the work of H. G. Wells, Arnold Bennett and John Galsworthy. In 'Mr. Bennett and Mrs. Brown' (1924), Woolf goes on to discuss in more detail the inability of realist method truly to represent a hypothetical character, Mrs Brown. Methods that concentrate on observable aspects of this character – the facts about Mrs Brown's dress, appearance, background and material circumstances – allow the spirit or inner nature to escape. Woolf, like Proust, saw it as a mistake to place 'everything in the object' rather than in the mind. Too close attention to what is perceived precludes Woolf's favoured interest in perceivers, human subjects with all their complex thought processes and emotions. What Woolf calls in 'Modern Fiction' the 'enormous labour of proving the solidity, the likeness to life, of the story' is therefore 'not merely labour thrown away, but labour misplaced'. 'Is life like this?' she asks. 'Must novels be like this?' In reply, Woolf provides a summary of her own priorities for modern fiction:

> Look within and life, it seems, is very far from being 'like this'. Examine for a moment an ordinary mind on an ordinary day. The mind receives a myriad impressions – trivial, fantastic, evanescent, or engraved with the sharpness of steel. From all sides they come, an incessant shower of innumerable atoms; and as they fall, as they shape themselves into the life of Monday or Tuesday, the accent falls differently from of old ... Life is not a series of gig-lamps

symmetrically arranged; life is a luminous halo, a semi-transparent envelope surrounding us from the beginning of consciousness to the end. Is it not the task of the novelist to convey this varying, this unknown and uncircumscribed spirit, whatever aberration or complexity it may display, with as little mixture of the alien and external as possible? We are not pleading merely for courage and sincerity; we are suggesting that the proper stuff of fiction is a little other than custom would have us believe it.

It is, at any rate, in some such fashion as this that we seek to define the quality which distinguishes the work of several young writers, among whom Mr. James Joyce is the most notable, from that of their predecessors. (*Collected Essays*, vol. II, pp. 106–7)

Woolf's views in 'Modern Fiction' provide one of the most comprehensive and celebrated statements of the priorities of modernism. Several other modernist writers discussed or sought to redefine 'the proper stuff of fiction' – or dismissed some of Joyce's predecessors – in similar terms. Ford Madox Ford, for example, also considered John Galsworthy as too little inclined to 'look within', describing him as 'a scientific observer' offering 'the Literature of organised materialism . . . simply the results of his observations in life'. D. H. Lawrence attacked a lifelessness in Galsworthy's characters, which he attributed to 'the collapse from the psychology of the free human individual into the psychology of the social being'. Such beings, in Lawrence's view, further suffer from being 'too much aware of objective reality' and too involved in the 'materialist' disposition of their age. Much of Henry James's criticism of his contemporaries also arises from his view that their work reflected 'simply the results of . . . observation of life'. James's essay 'The Younger Generation' (1914) extends to Arnold Bennett and other contemporary novelists the sort of criticism he had made earlier of Wells – that their realist style of fiction provided only a shapeless 'lump of life', encumbered with 'innumerable small facts and aspects'. This sort of meticulous attention to the external, perceived world omitted James's preferred interest in the 'intense perceiver' around whom experience could be 'wrought and shaped' into art.[22]

Comments by some of the novelists the modernists attacked often confirm such differences in their outlook. Hugh Walpole, for example, himself a prominent novelist in 1910, briskly dismisses the modernist answer to the 'question of questions. What is reality in the novel?' which he asks in his open *Letter to a Modern Novelist*. He tells the determinedly modern author he addresses:

> All that *your* school of novelists has to say about the novel seems to us nonsense . . .

> I find your novel unreal just as you find mine to be so. (pp. 6, 25)

John Galsworthy and H. G. Wells defend some of the preferences modernism rejected: Galsworthy admits that it is not the individual psychology of characters that interests him so much as their existence as types, through whom he can satirise a whole society. H. G. Wells similarly sees his subject as 'contemporary social development and its problems', suggesting that he would 'rather be called a journalist than an artist'. Though ready to admire Conrad for his 'depth' and 'subjective reality', Wells suggests in *Kipps* (1905) that 'the business of the novelist is . . . facts' – obviously not a business of much interest to Conrad, or at any rate to his hero in *Lord Jim*, sceptically questioning whether 'facts could explain anything'.[23]

Such radical differences between the modernists and some of their contemporaries established the terms for a debate about 'the proper stuff of fiction', the true locus of reality in the novel, which has continued throughout the twentieth century. Philip Henderson and Wyndham Lewis in the 1930s, and Angus Wilson and J. B. Priestley in the 1950s, for example, all return to re-examine the views Woolf expresses in 'Modern Fiction' and 'Mr. Bennett and Mrs. Brown'.[24] Most of these reassessments see injustice at least in Woolf's treatment of Arnold Bennett. Bennett may have been less interested than Woolf in the details of his characters' inner natures, but he was nevertheless able to investigate this area with some of the subtlety, and even using some of the methods, Woolf subsequently employed herself. As later commentators suggest, Woolf's views have sometimes been used too sweepingly to glorify modernist writing at the expense of the fiction – which continued to be written throughout the first decades of the twentieth century – whose more traditional storytelling aims were adequately realised within conventional patterns established in the Victorian period. The modernist writers considered in this chapter did much more, in some of the ways suggested, to discover and develop new styles, languages and priorities for the novel, but this did not necessarily grant them exclusive access to 'the proper stuff of fiction'. Woolf's views are best used not necessarily to evaluate, but, as she suggests, to 'distinguish the quality', the characteristics, which set Joyce and the modernists apart from their predecessors and many of their contemporaries. 'Modern Fiction' and 'Mr. Bennett and Mrs. Brown' provide clear statements not only of Woolf's own position, but also of the priorities that distinguished, in general, a modernist writing no longer satisfied with 'observation of life' but determined to 'look within' instead.

Novelists, of course, have always looked within and examined the mind: as Woolf indicates, certain writers in the early twentieth century did so with new concentration, exclusiveness and intensity. Her essays also suggest some of the factors at work in the early twentieth century which may have encouraged this new concentration. Woolf's demand for new fictional styles and structures, in 'Mr. Bennett and Mrs. Brown', is made on the grounds that the life the novel sought to reflect was itself, in her view, 'a little other than custom would have us believe it'. 'In or about December, 1910', Woolf suggests, 'human character changed' (*Collected Essays*, vol. I, p. 320). The exactness of the date Woolf chooses for such a radical change has often provoked attempted critical explanations. As was observed in Chapter 1, these explanations usually suggest that Woolf must have had in mind the exhibition of Post-Impressionist paintings, on show in London at the time and organised by her friend Roger Fry, as the source of a new sort of vision strange and revolutionary enough to change humanity's apprehension of itself. A fuller explanation should probably take account of December 1910 as the time when – following the General Election in that month – it became clear that the Liberal Government could, if necessary, abolish the powers of the House of Lords if forced to do so in order to carry out its programme of radical reform. Some of the hierarchies and stratifications of English life, deeply inscribed in its novelists' views of character and relationship, seemed as a result more shifting and precarious after December 1910 than they ever had before. For some authors this may have been an incentive to examine the depths of inner nature rather than look out upon society and the increasing uncertainties of the individual's place within it.

Woolf's own view of the matter, however, may have been neither aesthetic nor political but principally psychological. In a draft,

unpublished form of 'Mr. Bennett and Mrs. Brown', she explains
that the rapidly changing views of 'human character' which she felt
novelists had to take account of resulted from what she calls
'scientific reasons' such as the influence of Sigmund Freud. Her
essay 'Modern Fiction' likewise concludes that a distinguishing
feature of the new writing she admires and recommends is that 'for
the moderns . . . the point of interest lies very likely in the dark
places of psychology' (*Collected Essays*, vol. II, p. 108). Other
contemporary commentators shared Woolf's view. Elizabeth Drew,
for example, suggests that modern novelists found 'the older
technique too clumsy for their purposes' because of an 'engrossing
interest' in 'conscious and deliberate psychology' (p. 248).

As Woolf and Drew suggest, modernism's urge to examine the
mind more completely and constantly than earlier fiction seems
likely to have resulted from the new extent to which psychology had
recently, startlingly, become an area both of 'conscious and deliberate' study and of widespread public interest. The investigations of
dream and the unconscious which Freud began to publish in 1896
were quickly influential outwith the English-speaking world, and
fairly quickly within it. English translations of Freud's work – some
of it already familiar from the studies of Havelock Ellis – began to
appear in English in 1909.[25] By 1913 May Sinclair was helping
establish the first psychoanalytic clinic in London. Dorothy
Richardson reviewed books on psychoanalysis for *Dental Review*,
later commenting on a whole atmosphere of 'Freudianity' (*Pilgrimage*, vol. I, p. 12) that had grown up by the end of the First World
War. Looking back in 1928, John Carruthers similarly (though
more sceptically) suggests that when the work of Freud and his
followers 'reached England and America in translation . . . psychoanalysis became for a time an appalling craze' (p. 56). Much the
same view of Freud's ubiquitous influence in the years around the
First World War can be found in Richard Aldington's war novel
*Death of a Hero* (1929): its early pages show Freud's theories
achieving in certain areas of society the status of a fashionable if
rather shallow cult. Ford Madox Ford indicates something similar
in *Parade's End* when he shows Christopher Tietjens's fashionable
wife Sylvia deciding to 'pin [her] faith to . . . Freud' (p. 37). Freud's
continuing hold on the popular mind in the 1920s is confirmed by
D. H. Lawrence, who suggests of certain of his ideas that

the Œdipus complex was a household word, the incest motive a commonplace of tea-table chat . . .

Does it need a prophet to discern that Freud is on the brink of a *Weltanschauung* . . .

The old world is yielding under us. (*Fantasia of the Unconscious*, pp. 197-8)

The appearance of this *Weltanschauung* (world-view) in contemporary fiction can be traced in several ways, both general and specific. In general terms, several authors show a new readiness to discuss and examine what Ford Madox Ford calls in *The Good Soldier* 'that mysterious and unconscious self that underlies most people' (p. 100). Interest in this aspect of the self also leads modernist authors to emphasise areas of experience previously of much more limited interest in the novel. E. M. Forster, still assessing fiction largely in terms of its older conventions, remarks in *Aspects of the Novel* (1927) that sleep is an area generally ignored by novelists, who make 'no attempt to indicate oblivion or the actual dream world' (p. 61). Yet what Proust calls 'the world in which we live when we are asleep' (II, p. 84) is quite often an interest of *A la recherche du temps perdu*: Proust sometimes analyses the nature of sleep and dreams for several pages at a time (e.g. II, pp. 1012-18). The subject is immediately introduced in the novel's opening paragraph, showing how his narrator and hero Marcel falls asleep when a child. Throughout, sleep and dream continue to provide Marcel with a favoured, fascinating means of 'escape from the perception of the real' (II, p. 84), one which at times colours the novel's own perceptions of consciousness and reality. Of one dream Marcel records, for example, that it 'had the clarity of consciousness. By the same token, might consciousness have the unreality of a dream?' (II, p. 1018).

Unreality and dream, if not quite oblivion, are also occasional interests of *Ulysses*, especially in the phantasmagoric, dream-like 'Nighttown' chapter (15). Warped by the hallucinations and suppressed obsessions of its characters, 'Nighttown' anticipates the more extended entry into 'night language' made by Joyce, after the publication of *Ulysses*, in his 'Work in Progress' which continued in the 1920s, eventually published as *Finnegans Wake*. Outwith 'Nighttown', however, *Ulysses* does not entirely confirm Elizabeth Drew's contemporary judgement that 'Joyce apparently accepts the Freudian dogma that the activities of the subconscious mind are the true personality' (p. 88). The stream of thoughts Joyce records is subvocal, but not by any means always subconscious. As discussed earlier, *Ulysses* remains for the most part a stream of consciousness – not, like *Finnegans Wake*, of unconsciousness – abandoning its protagonists at the moment oblivion or unconsciousness overtakes them.

More thoroughgoing acceptances of 'Freudian dogma', and more specific connections with the ideas of the new psychoanalysis do appear in modernist fiction. In Woolf's *Mrs Dalloway*, for example, Septimus Warren Smith's treatment for shell-shock and general mental debility by Sir William Bradshaw, 'the ghostly helper, the priest of science' (p. 104), reflects the expanded influence of psychoanalysis brought about by the need to treat traumatised victims of the First World War. Freud himself remarked how greatly the war had helped to further his work, and interest in the psychoanalytic movement generally. May Sinclair's direct, personal interest in the new movement is emphasised by Jean Radford in her introduction to Sinclair's *Life and Death of Harriett Frean* (1922), when she points out that

> the new science of psychoanalysis offered her a theory of mental functioning, and she drew in particular on the Freudian notions of repression and sublimation.

Each of these 'notions' can be seen to be particularly examined in a single novel. *Mary Olivier* is an extended study in sublimation, the heroine diverting into learning, literary activity and the life of the mind the energies which family life, religious belief and the behaviour expected of women otherwise allow little outlet in personal development or sexual fulfilment. *Life and Death of Harriett Frean* offers a grimmer view of a heroine for whom – as the title begins to suggest – life scarcely exists independently of a deathly, repressive proclivity that gradually extinguishes vital instincts altogether.

Contemporary commentators, such as Drew and Carruthers, often saw D. H. Lawrence's work shaped at least as much as Sinclair's by the new theories of mental functioning. In particular, Paul Morel's lingering possession by his mother makes *Sons and Lovers* seem almost a casebook illustration of Freud's idea of the Oedipus complex, while the general emphasis on sexuality throughout Lawrence's fiction seems to ally it more widely with some of

Freud's views of the roots of personality and behaviour. Lawrence's interest in 'another centre of consciousness . . . beyond thought' also shows his fiction moving into darker areas of mental life towards which Freud's work had encouraged attention. Some of this sense of previously hidden depths in human experience is figured in Gerald's disquieting discoveries in the 'Water Party' chapter of *Women in Love* – typical of Lawrence's talent for creating complex implications around plausibly natural action; for creating highly symbolic scenes. Out on the lake, Gudrun waits in a boat uncertainly balanced upon 'the surface of the insidious reality', while Gerald seeks his drowning sister in the depths beneath, returning appalled by

> a whole universe under there . . . so endless, so different really from what is on top . . . you're as helpless as if your head was cut off. (pp. 203, 206)

The scene has particular implications, first of all, for Gerald himself. Like the earlier episode discussed above in which he viciously struggles with his horse – a creature often used in Lawrence's writing to represent 'something else besides mind and cleverness' [26] – 'Water Party' indicates a kind of self-division in Gerald. His frightened response to the unfamiliar, subaqueous universe, 'so different from what is on top', indicates the extent to which his own severe rationality, his life in the head, cuts him off from elemental depths in his own nature. In another way, however, Gerald's encounter with this new universe – dark, fluid, of surprising scale, yet hidden beneath an apparently safe, smooth surface – can be seen as more widely emblematic of the deeper, less rationally controlled mind and self which interested Lawrence throughout his fiction, and whose existence Freud's work helped establish as part of the general outlook of the twentieth century. The episode can also be seen as typical of a more general employment of symbol in modernist writing. More than earlier fiction, modernist novels rely on ordinary enough episodes or things – the lighthouse or rainbow immediately highlighted by Woolf and Lawrence in their titles, for example – which are endowed with a symbolic significance leading far beyond the 'surface of the reality' which contains them. Such tactics may have been encouraged by Freud's work in the interpretation of dreams and the patterns of symbolic significance they can be shown to contain.

Other phases of Lawrence's writing, however, challenge any view of Freud as a decisive or unique influence on modernism's tactics, or on its general trend from objective to subjective, certainly where Lawrence himself is concerned. Through his German wife Frieda, Lawrence was aware of Freud's ideas earlier than most British writers, but rather than wholly welcoming them, he complained about the 'vicious half-statements of the Freudians', and acknowledged only that 'what Freud says is always partly true'. Rightly, in Lawrence's view, Freud's work suggested the existence of areas of mind and self beyond complete rational, intellectual control, but it was exactly these areas which Freud sought to *submit* to rational, intellectual analysis. For Lawrence, this was a threat to the deepest sources of spontaneity, life and vitality, since it returned to consciousness and intellect the very areas of experience most essentially liberated from them. Lawrence considered 'the first bubbling life in us, which is innocent of any mental alteration, this is unconscious': the systematic, rational aspect of Freud's thought made it for Lawrence the kind of process that threatened to subject 'everything spontaneous to certain machine principles called ideals or ideas'.[27] As far as Lawrence relied on ideas of mind in his own highly idiosyncratic studies, *Fantasia of the Unconscious* and *Psychoanalysis and the Unconscious* (1923), these are taken very much less from Freud, criticised throughout, than from the German biologist Ernst Haeckel. His suggestion that unconscious forces originate not only within the mind but also in the ganglionic cells easily adjusts with Lawrence's own belief in 'blood consciousness' and the opinion that

> real knowledge comes out of the whole corpus of the consciousness; out of your belly and your penis as much as out of your brain and mind. The mind can only analyse and rationalize.[28]

Virginia Woolf's views of psychoanalysis in *Mrs Dalloway* are hardly more favourable than Lawrence's, partly on account of a similar mistrust of its rationalisation of areas where more natural feelings – even simple sympathy – might be more appropriate. The analytic approach of Sir William Bradshaw, the 'priest of science', makes him an unsympathetic figure in the novel, and an unsuccessful one: none of the various counsellings of the medical profession can reach Septimus Warren Smith's disturbed mind, or save him from suicide. In 'Mr. Bennett and Mrs. Brown' Woolf also shows in the end more doubt than conviction about the likely value of Freud for her contemporaries. References to Freud were deleted from the final version of the essay: even in its draft form, Woolf questioned, in relation to Freud, 'how much we can learn from science . . . and make use of . . . and make our own'.[29]

The question is a crucial one, relating not only to the likely influence of Freud but to the discussion, in the last chapter, of how literature can be validly assessed in terms of the wider context of an age and its possible influences. That discussion suggested – contrary to the views of Wyndham Lewis, and many critics before and since – that figures such as Freud can confirm the ideas of novelists, but are rarely a sole source or cause of them. No doubt Freud's work did contribute to or confirm, in some of the ways suggested above, an inclination to move from objective to subjective in the fiction of the early years of the twentieth century. But as Lionel Trilling remarks, neither Freud nor any other thinker creates ideas in a vacuum, nor single-handedly builds the consciousness of an age. On the contrary, all thinkers are themselves conditioned in outlook and imagination by the nature and dominant concerns of the historical period in which they write. This shapes their work, as well as being shaped by it. Freud was at most a partial rather than an ultimate *cause* of the new literary apprehension of human character Woolf saw originating in December 1910: he remains a good witness to the nature, direction and effects of the particular forces and habits of mind that existed at the time. Seeing Freud in this way, as Lawrence suggests, as a significant part of the *Weltanschauung* of the time, allows the new delvings into consciousness in modernist fiction to be understood not as isolated phenomena, but as part of the wider movement of contemporary thought; of the more general conditions to which 'the old world yielded'. One or two other thinkers are worth considering in this way – as witnesses to, as well as architects of, the *Weltanschauung* of the early twentieth century – before going on to examine the historical, political and social conditions which also informed their individual views and the modernist movement generally.

The ideas of the German philosopher Friedrich Nietzsche were fairly widely disseminated in Britain after the translation of *Beyond Good and Evil* in 1907 and the popularisation of his work in the journal *The New Age* around the same time. Wyndham Lewis remarked in his editorial in the second volume of *Blast* (1915) that 'Nietzsche has had an English sale such as he could hardly have anticipated in his most ecstatic or morose moments' (p. 5). Admired by D. H. Lawrence, who variously examines the Nietzschean 'Wille zur Macht' ('will to power') in *Women in Love* (e.g. p. 167), Nietzsche's ideas are often given as much credit as Freud's for establishing the conditions under which 'the old world yielded'. Two aspects of Nietzsche's relation to such conditions can usefully be considered in connection with modernist fiction. The first is his much-publicised pronouncement that 'God is dead'. This statement sums up with maximum concision the conclusion of a trend of decline in religious faith which orginated well before the twentieth century began. It particularly gathered pace in the 1860s, after Charles Darwin's attribution of evolution to secular processes of natural selection, rather than divine ordering and control. Well before the century turned there must have been a familiar ring to the sort of musings Miriam Henderson engages in at one point in *Pilgrimage*:

> distinguished minds . . . thought Darwin was true . . . No God. No Creation . . . It was probably true . . . only old-fashioned people thought it was not. It was true. (I, pp. 169–70)

Nevertheless, from a twentieth-century point of view, the Victorian period seemed to possess, relatively at least, a kind of stability and certainty which later events made harder and harder to sustain. The 'enormous criticism going on of faiths upon which men's lives and associations are based',[30] which H. G. Wells saw around him in the early years of the twentieth century, was still further expanded by the shock to religious and moral certainty created by the First World War. Looking back from the perspective of the 1920s, Elizabeth Drew remarks on how 'solidly sure of itself' the Victorian age seemed, and on how 'the Victorian novel shared in the general self-confidence' (p. 32). John Carruthers, writing in 1928, finds that in comparison with the Victorians his time was 'riddled with disbelief', adding that 'the novels of to-day directly mirror the conditions of religious, moral and political instability in which we all perforce live' (pp. 24, 27).

As he suggests, some of the changes in the contemporary novel are appropriately seen as 'mirroring' an age of declining religious faith and moral certainty. The regular absence from early twentieth-century fiction of what Hillis Miller calls the 'stabilising presence' of an omniscient author can be seen to mirror loss of faith in an omniscient deity. Without this figure of ultimate authority, or associated assumptions about the coherence and meaning of life, the subjective vision of the individual became, increasingly, the only arbiter of experience. In Henry James's terms, the particular viewpoint of the 'first person singular' became as valid, as 'definite and responsible' as any other. Fiction in the early years of the century shows a new interest in such viewpoints: as discussed earlier, this appears not only in James's work, but in the novels of Ford and Conrad. Each author examines processes through which individual vision attempts to create coherence and meaning; through which a stabilising point can still be created in a universe that lacks absolute, overall principles of order and control.

A second, more particular aspect of Nietzsche's significance lies in his questioning not only religion, but the existence of coherence and meaning anywhere, certainly anywhere beyond the individual mind. His philosophy challenges ultimate authority or truth in any form: he denies not only that 'facts could explain anything', but that any facts or certainties exist meaningfully at all. He asserts that

there are *no eternal facts*, just as there are no absolute truths . . .

What are man's truths ultimately? Merely his *irrefutable* errors.[31]

Nietzsche sees the universe as structureless, irrational, and quite beyond the shapes and categories ascribed to it by human consciousness. This activity is undertaken merely in order to satisfy the mind's private craving for comprehension and order. 'The understanding does not draw its laws from nature,' Nietzsche believes, 'it prescribes them to nature' – a nature with which the mind can enjoy no authentic contact. Nietzsche suggests that

sense impressions naively supposed to be conditioned by the outer world are, on the contrary, conditioned by the inner world . . . we are always unconscious of the real activity of the outer world.[32]

Such views were supported elsewhere in the philosophy of the time. William James, for example, remarked in 1904 that 'the notion that even the truest formula may be a human device and not a literal transcript has dawned on us',[33] and Henri Bergson (whose work is further considered in Chapter 3) held some comparable views about the distorted connection between mind and the outer world created by 'human device'. The work of such philosophers, around the turn of the century, expresses the epistemological crisis or shift mentioned in the last chapter – a turning away, as the twentieth century began, from the stabler assumptions through which the external universe had most often been perceived in the vision of the nineteenth.

Radical doubt about the process or even the possibility of true perception, and a general questioning of how the mind could encounter a world alien to its categories and orders, show this epistemological shift developing in contemporary philosophy: such challenges to the validity of 'true formulae' and 'the laws of nature' also extended a scepticism towards the activities of science. Nietzsche remarks, for example, that

> it is perhaps just dawning on five or six minds that physics too is only an interpretation and arrangement of the world . . . and *not* an explanation of the world.[34]

Science offered the late Victorians what seemed an order, an authority, and a hope for progress which could at least partly substitute for religious faith. In the early years of the twentieth century, by contrast, the minds most ready to accept Nietzsche's sort of scepticism often belonged to the most advanced scientists themselves. Science at the time seemed enthusiastically ready to investigate and emphasise its own limitations and ultimate uncertainties. By 1923 Heisenberg's Uncertainty Principle had established, with all the rigour and logic of mathematics, the incapacity of science to establish anything about the physical universe with absolute rigour, logic or certainty. Heisenberg's work partly developed from the challenge to absolute laws or views of the universe expressed in Albert Einstein's Theories of Relativity: Einstein suggests that no law or observation can be universally reliable, but depends, among other factors, on the position of the individual observer. His conclusions not only interested scientists, but found a much wider appeal: as described in Chapter 1, ideas of relativity had reached and excited a huge audience by the early 1920s.

The appeal of Relativity was immediate enough to suggest to D. H. Lawrence that it summed up some general temper in the contemporary outlook. He remarked in 1923 that

Everybody catches fire at the word Relativity. There must be
something in the mere suggestion which we have been waiting for . . .
Relativity means . . . there is no one single absolute central principle
governing the world . . .

Really, an anarchical conclusion . . .

So, there is nothing absolute left in the universe. Nothing . . .

I feel inclined to Relativity myself . . . But I also feel, most
strongly, that in itself each individual living creature is absolute: in
its own being. And that all things in the universe are just relative to
the individual living creature . . .

There is only one clue to the universe. And that is the individual soul
within the individual being. That outer universe of suns and moons
and atoms is a secondary affair. (*Fantasia of the Unconscious*, pp.
177-9, 147)

As Lawrence helps to suggest, science as well as contemporary
philosophy, Einstein's work as well as Nietzsche's, left 'nothing
absolute in the universe'. Whether or not this was a conclusion the
age was 'waiting for', there is much evidence of its general
recognition at the time; in particular, in the work of modernist
novelists besides Lawrence himself. Joyce remarks in *Stephen
Hero*, for example, that 'it is a mark of the modern spirit to be shy
in the presence of all absolute statements' (p. 183). 'Science and
religion,' Virginia Woolf remarks, 'have between them destroyed
belief . . . all bonds of union seem broken, yet some control must
exist.' [35] In the passage quoted, Lawrence suggests where this sort
of vestigial control or stability might still be found – in 'the
individual soul in the individual being'. In an age of destroyed
beliefs and dismantled certainties, devoid even of authentic contact
with 'the real activity of the outer world', modernism inevitably
examined more deeply the contents and consciousness of individual
souls as the only remaining 'clue to the universe'. Proust's work also
stresses the inevitability of concentration on this 'clue'. Marcel
remarks in *A la recherche du temps perdu* that in

the current philosophy of the day . . . it was agreed that intelligence
was in direct ratio to the degree of scepticism and nothing was
considered real and incontestable except the individual tastes of each
person. (I, p. 304)

Since 'nothing was considered real' beyond individual taste or
vision, and little possibility seemed to exist for authentic contact

with 'the real activity of the outer world', what Marcel calls the 'realist . . . form of perception which places everything in the object' is not so much 'clumsy and erroneous' but simply impossible or invalid. Marcel emphasises this conclusion himself when he records the capacity of his thoughts to form a

> sort of recess, in the depths of which I felt that I could bury myself and remain invisible even while I looked at what went on outside. When I saw an external object, my consciousness that I was seeing it would remain between me and it, surrounding it with a thin spiritual border that prevented me from ever touching its substance directly; for it would somehow evaporate before I could make contact with it. (I, p. 90)

May Sinclair's heroine in *Mary Olivier* likewise considers the philosophical conclusion that

> all that is perceived in space or time, and with it all objects . . . have no existence grounded in themselves outside our thoughts. (p. 247)

The urge among modernist authors to 'look within' and place 'everything in the mind' thus mirrors and extends contemporary thinking, which considered there may have been nowhere else rewardingly or even possibly to look; little wholly sure or convincingly real beyond the individual mind. The 'outer universe' seemed drained of meaning and order by an increasingly secular age; no more than 'a secondary affair' for the shifting epistemologies of the early twentieth century; perhaps even, as Marcel suggests, beyond genuine contact of any kind. Inevitably, the envelope or recess of consciousness seemed the most natural, promising space for the novel to represent.

The promise of the recess of consciousness was confirmed by other factors, not just drawn from the science and philosophy of the early twentieth century, but inscribed in the everyday experience of modern life. Some of its pressures are made particularly clear in Lawrence's fiction, which shows even the individual soul as a precarious refuge from modern industrialism. The landscapes of his novels, in which the black coal pits stand out sharply against an open green background, help reflect the dark threats to nature imposed by the spreading industrialisation of 'the machine age'. Such threats to physical nature obviously extend to disturb human nature as well. Paul Morel, in *Sons and Lovers*, gloomily considers that 'he was a prisoner of industrialism . . . taken into bondage' (pp. 113–14) just as much as his father, a miner, had been. Ursula, in *The Rainbow*, resents and fears

> human bodies and lives subjected in slavery to that symmetric monster of the colliery . . .
> No more would she subscribe to the great colliery, to the great machine which has taken us all captives. In her soul, she was against it . . . she knew it was meaningless. (p. 350)

Lawrence's most sustained attack on the great machine of industrialism is focused on the figure of Gerald Crich, the colliery owner in *Women in Love*. Gerald's remorseless determination to extract more wealth from his workers leads him to reform the management of his mine and enthusiastically exploit technologies, newly available in the modern machine age, which help him to reject the liberal, paternalistic capitalism his father exercised in controlling the family's colliery. His new expertise makes Gerald 'the God of the machine' (p. 250), rationalising the pit on purely economic and technological principles. He unquestioningly subordinates the welfare of his work-force to improvements in efficiency and, ultimately, the creation of more wealth:

> He had conceived the pure instrumentality of mankind. There had been so much humanitarianism, so much talk of sufferings and feelings. It was ridiculous. The sufferings and feelings of individuals did not matter in the least . . . What mattered was the pure instrumentality of the individual. As a man as of a knife: does it cut well? Nothing else mattered . . .
>
> It was this inhuman principle in the mechanism he wanted to construct that inspired Gerald with an almost religious exaltation . . . he found his eternal and his infinite in the pure machine-principle . . . the substitution of the mechanical principle for the organic, the destruction of the organic purpose, the organic unity, and the subordination of every organic unit to the great mechanical purpose. It was pure organic disintegration and pure mechanical organisation . . .
>
> There was a greater output of coal than ever. (pp. 250–1, 256, 260)

Gerald's obsession with 'mechanical control' both arises from and adds to his alienation from his own feelings, with eventually disastrous results. As his lover Gudrun realises, Gerald's 'machine principles' are eventually thoroughly realised in himself. 'The Geralds of this world', she reflects, 'turn into mechanisms . . . become instruments, pure machines, pure wills' (p. 524). Machine-like and chillingly inert emotionally, Gerald dies an appropriately icy death, frozen in the snowy wastes of the Alps. Long before Gerald's actual death, however, real life has been drained out of his workers, forced themselves to become 'instruments, pure machines':

> the miners were reduced to mere mechanical instruments. They had to work hard, much harder than before, the work was terrible and heart-breaking in its mechanicalness.
> But they submitted to it all. The joy went out of their lives, the hope seemed to perish as they became more and more mechanized. (p. 259)

Similar anxieties about denaturing processes in industrialised society appear in *Lady Chatterley's Lover*, in which Lawrence laments that

> all vulnerable things must perish under the rolling and running of iron . . . [in] a world of iron and coal, the cruelty of iron and the smoke of coal, and the endless, endless greed that drove it all. (pp. 123, 149)

Lady Constance Chatterley flees with her lover Mellors this world of 'the mechanical greedy, greedy mechanism and mechanized greed' (p. 123) presided over by her husband Clifford. He considers the miners in the same terms as Gerald in *Women in Love*:

> he saw them as objects rather than men, parts of the pit rather than parts of life, crude raw phenomena rather than human beings. (p. 16)

Crippled literally by the First World War, Clifford is further figuratively presented as maimed by a commitment to profit and the industrialised machine. This leaves him less than fully human himself: Constance reflects that

> Clifford was drifting off to this other weirdness of industrial activity, becoming almost a *creature*, with a hard, efficient shell of an exterior and a pulpy interior, one of the amazing crabs and lobsters of the modern, industrial and financial world, invertebrates of the crustacean order, with shells of steel, like machines, and inner bodies of soft pulp. (p. 114)

So deeply inscribed in Lawrence's writing, anxiety about humanity becoming like machines – or disfigured by hard, efficient shells concealing pulpy or empty interiors – also appears elsewhere in modernist writing. In Conrad's *Chance* (1913), for example, the corrupt financier is said to be 'a mere sign, a portent. There was nothing in him' (p. 70), and is aptly named 'de Barral'. In *Heart of Darkness*, the central figure of Kurtz – another character who exploits humanity in the quest for 'something that is really profitable' (p. 98) – eventually appears to the narrator Marlow to be 'hollow at the core' (p. 83). T. S. Eliot takes from *Heart of Darkness* his epigraph for 'The Hollow Men', a poem that goes on to examine a kind of inner emptiness as a general condition of a spiritless modern humanity. It is a condition that Eliot also considers in 'Rhapsody on a Windy Night', in which the speaker records how

> . . . the hand of the child, automatic,
> Slipped out and pocketed a toy that was running along the quay.
> I could see nothing behind that child's eye.
> I have seen eyes in the street
> Trying to peer through lighted shutters,
> And a crab one afternoon in a pool,
> An old crab with barnacles on his back
> Gripped the end of the stick which I held him.[36]

Once again, the individual is shown as empty within – like Gerald, 'a hollow shell', with a 'dark void' at its centre (p. 363). There is apparently nothing behind the child's eye, and the speaker comes closer to genuine contact – almost a kind of handshake – with the crab than with any of the people in the poem, variously occluded behind doors and shutters. As human beings grow empty within a shell-like exterior, shelled creatures like the crab come to seem more nearly human. A similar reciprocal exchange of qualities occurs between machines and human beings. Machines and things are personified, taking on normally human attributes: it is the toy, rather than the child, that runs along the quay, while elsewhere in the poem streetlamps speak and doors seem to grin. Human beings are fragmented – presented only as eyes or hands rather than whole, integrated beings – and mechanical, empty behind their eyes and 'automatic' in their actions. While things are personified, people are reified, made 'thing-like'.

Reification, the portrayal of people as things or objects, is in the sense discussed above a literary device. In a comparable sense, however, in the view of Karl Marx, it is also a real condition of modern labour, forced to make itself into a usable commodity that can be exploited for wages. Marx suggests that

> within the capitalist system all methods . . . distort the worker into a fràgment of a man, they degrade him to the level of an appendage of a machine . . .

> *The means of production*, the *material conditions of labour*, are not subject to the worker, but he to them. This in itself . . . entails the personification of things and the reification of persons. (I, pp. 799, 1054)

Reification in economic terms is reflected in literary ones, in Lawrence's writing at least. The kind of industrialised world Gerald Crich creates – making people interchangeable with things, or treating 'a man as . . . a knife' – emphasises the denaturing, reifying conditions of modern industrial labour. Conrad's fiction (in *Nostromo*, another tale of the corruption of mining wealth, as well as in *Heart of Darkness*) and Eliot's poetry indicate that some of Lawrence's awareness of the effects of contemporary industrial and financial conditions was more widely shared. Lawrence's fiction, however, shares with Conrad and with modernism generally a disposition not only to reflect or show awareness of reifying forces in contemporary life, but to find means, at least in imagination, to compensate for them. The need for such compensation is a further, fundamental source of modernism's determination to 'look within'. The 'modern industrial and financial world' negates feeling in favour of instrumentality, reduces whole beings to the sum of their usable functions, or leaves people hollowed out and pulpy beneath a brittle surface. Such a world urgently requires some compensating enhancement and enlargement of the inner life to sustain for the individual a full, non-crustacean humanity and an integral sense of the self.

This compensatory function of modernist innovations is clarified by *The Political Unconscious: Narrative as a Socially Symbolic Act* (1981), in which the Marxist critic Fredric Jameson shows the reifying nature of what he calls 'social relations in late capitalism' (p. 42) informing modernism and its styles. 'Modernism and reification,' he suggests, 'are parts of the same immense process which expresses the contradictory inner logic and dynamics of late capitalism' (p. 42). Jameson, however, demonstrates with conviction that modernism is not simply a reflection of the reifying logic

of late capitalism, but an attempt to balance, even neutralise it. He
sees modernism as

> a revolt against . . . reification and a symbolic act which involves a
> whole Utopian compensation for increasing dehumanization on the
> level of daily life . . .

> modernism can . . . be read as a Utopian compensation for
> everything reification brings with it. (pp. 42, 236)

One example of such compensation is to be found in the work of
Henry James, Jameson seeing his insistence on 'polished perceivers'
and the subtleties of fine inner conscience as one of the 'more
desperate myths of the self' (p. 221) that modernism is forced to
generate. Many other examples of this sort of compensation might
be found: Miriam Henderson provides a kind of theory for it when
she muses in *Pilgrimage*:

> Everything's here, any bit of anything, clear in your brain; you can
> look at it. What a terrific thing a person is, bigger than anything. (II,
> p. 256)

Once narrative places 'everything in the mind', a sense of significance can be restored to individuals: it becomes once again possible
to consider 'what a terrific thing a person is' – regardless of how
diminished (or, in Miriam's case, severely financially constrained)
their actual lives in the modern industrial world may be. Appropriately it is Gerald, a character thoroughly committed to the
negative forces of industrialism, who is so shocked by the dark
reaches of a 'whole universe' of space beneath the visible surface of
experience. Like Miriam Henderson, other characters find this sort
of space more congenial. For modernist fiction generally, it offered
a welcome area in which to sustain a fuller sense of a self, freed
from the object world and a life reified by 'the logic and dynamics
of late capitalism'. An age that threatened to leave nothing behind
the eyes of its inhabitants inevitably encouraged literary strategies
which could reach some inviolable innermost flame of consciousness. Something had to be found to continue illumining a 'first
person singular' still 'definite and responsible' despite the disintegral forces which daily confronted it. D. H. Lawrence's letter to his
publishers in 1914 not only warns that 'the old stable *ego*' may be
harder to find than ever, but also promises a 'deeper sense than any

we've been used to exercise', one still able to reveal characters as 'the same single radically unchanged element'.[37] His views are representative of a whole phase of the modernist initiative, compensating, through deeper senses, formal shifts and subtler strategies, for the dehumanising, disintegral pressures of late capitalism on the self.

Fredric Jameson's understanding of modernism in relation to contemporary history also helps locate the movement within the wider evolution of literary history. In particular it allows modernism to be seen as a late extension of Romanticism, or perhaps a modified replacement for it. Modernism offers 'Utopian compensation' for the dehumanising nature of daily life in a late phase of industrialism: Romantic poetry undertook a comparable task in response to a much earlier phase, developing most strongly just after the Industrial Revolution at the end of the eighteenth century. When large sections of the population were being forced away from the land and into dismal factory employment in cramped, grimy cities, poetry that located humanity in a natural, green environment offered an ideal compensation for the actual denaturing that was taking place. In this and other ways, Romantic poetry provided a congenial vision of the status and significance of the individual at a time when in reality huge numbers of individuals were being reduced to insignificant units within the system of wage slavery. The Romantic vision not only placed individuals back in a natural environment; it showed them in empathetic, mutually signifying contact with this environment. As critics have often observed, the natural world functions for the Romantics as a kind of mirror, reflecting and enlarging the shape and the drama of the individual soul, and vice versa. Through such pastoral connection, the individual seemed neither dehumanised nor diminished, but a central, significant pulse of ego, drawing vision of a whole world around itself.

The post-Industrial Revolution, Romantic phase of the late eighteenth and early nineteenth centuries was followed by the further technological revolutions of the late nineteenth and early twentieth, which left nature and the external green world unable to offer the potential it had for the Romantics, and the population more than ever centred in the kind of complex, claustrophobic cities that often form the background of modernist writing. The proliferation of the black collieries that scar the green landscape of

Nottingham for D. H. Lawrence, or the spreading, rust-coloured suburban sprawl that threatens to overwhelm the world of E. M. Forster's *Howard's End* (1910), diminishes the possibility of finding any landscape empty enough, benign enough, safe enough from the modern industrial and financial world, to fulfil the needs of a consoling Romantic vision. The English landscape ceases to seem open, or a liberation of the soul, but crowded and restricting instead. On his nocturnal hunt in Lawrence's short story 'The Fox' (1923), for example, Henry finds a 'network of English hedges netting the view': as a result, 'suddenly it seemed to him England was little and tight, he felt the landscape was constricted . . . tight with innumerable little houses' (p. 121). Significantly, no English landscape can satisfy Virginia Woolf's requirement in *To the Lighthouse* for a setting unsullied by human activity – a setting of absolute loneliness for Mr Ramsay to walk and brood in – and she has to go as far as the island of Skye to find it.

Even a landscape of loneliness, however, is no longer consoling as it was for the Romantics. Particularly in the second part of the novel, Woolf's vision is firmly anti-pastoral and anti-Romantic. As discussed earlier, Woolf's style in this section brings to life a natural world which – far from demonstrating sympathy or connection with the individual soul – systematically diminishes and marginalises consciousness and human agency. The second section eventually makes completely explicit the impossibility of any longer discovering in external nature a viable space for consoling reflections of the self:

> the sea tosses itself and breaks itself, and should any sleeper fancying that he might find on the beach an answer to his doubts, a sharer of his solitude, throw off his bedclothes and go down by himself to walk on the sand, no image with semblance of serving and divine promptitude comes readily to hand bringing the night to order and making the world reflect the compass of the soul . . .

> those who had gone down to pace the beach and ask of the sea and sky what message they reported or what vision they affirmed had to consider . . . the silent apparition of an ashen coloured ship . . . a purplish stain upon the bland surface of the sea as if something had boiled and bled, invisibly, beneath. This intrusion into a scene calculated to stir the most sublime reflections and lead to the most comfortable conclusions stayed their pacing. It was difficult blandly to overlook them, to abolish their significance in the landscape; to

continue, as one walked by the sea, to marvel how beauty outside mirrored beauty within.

Did nature supplement what man advanced? Did she complete what he began? With equal complacence she saw his misery, condoned his meanness, and acquiesced in his torture. That dream, then, of sharing, completing, finding in solitude on the beach an answer, was but a reflection in a mirror . . . contemplation was unendurable; the mirror was broken. (pp. 146, 152–3)

Deprived of external space, finding the mirror of nature broken, modernist vision had little choice but to turn to inner space as a dimension in which to console and make significant the self – in which to bring the night to order and make the world reflect the compass of the soul'. This is very much the conclusion Woolf herself indicates in *To the Lighthouse* when instead of beauty and order outside she talks of

the vision within. In those mirrors, the minds of men . . . dreams persisted . . . good triumphs, happiness prevails, order rules . . . [there was] some absolute good, some crystal of intensity, remote from the known pleasures and familiar virtues, something alien to the processes of domestic life, single, hard, bright, like a diamond in the sand, which would render the possessor secure. (pp. 150–1)

It was suggested earlier that the preoccupation in *To the Light-house* with 'subject and object and the nature of reality' provided a kind of paradigm of modernist interests. Sections such as the above show the novel offering not only a paradigm but an explanation for the modernist imperative to 'look within'. Looking elsewhere, either at the natural world or at the objects constituting it, ceases to offer either happiness or order: only 'the vision within' offered anything to 'render the possessor secure'. Following this vision in its first and third sections, *To the Lighthouse* demonstrates the direction followed by modernist narrative in general as a compensation for the kind of new hostility and emptiness in the object world which Woolf dramatises in the novel's second part.

The first of the passages quoted above also indicates an immediate historical reason for finding 'the minds of men' a necessary refuge from an intractable, indifferent, fractured external reality. The 'ashen ship' and the 'purplish stain' on the surface of the sea bear to the watcher on the shores of Skye traces of the First World War, a final, previously unimaginable disaster of the modern industrial and financial world. This war was a time when, as John Carruthers puts it, there were 'a few million lives tossed away for no reason that . . . anyone . . . has yet been able to discover' (p. 25). It was a time when guns turned into machines and men took refuge from them within the hard shell of tanks; when, as Woolf remarks in *To the Lighthouse*, 'flesh turned to atoms which drove before the wind' (p. 150). The experience of such a time offered sharp confirmation of the effects of 'the logic and dynamics of late capitalism' in turning the individual into a meaningless, almost worthless commodity. Given the stresses of such a period, the simplest explanation of the movements of modernist narrative considered in this chapter can be provided by Andrew Marvell's suggestion in 'The Garden' (1681) – a poem also written in a period of great historical upheaval – that

> . . . the mind, from pleasure less
> Withdraws into its happiness;
> The mind, that Ocean . . .[38]

Confronted by a sea of troubles, stained by the destruction of war, the mind in the early twentieth century had obvious reasons to withdraw to the oceanic spaces within itself, and to pursue the streams of consciousness running through them. War and 'the modern industrial and financial world', however, had consequences not only for modernism's commitment to 'the vision within', but for the overall structure of its narratives. This aspect of modernism, and its sense of time and history, are considered in the next chapter.

# TIME

As there is a geometry in space, so there is a psychology in
time.
(Marcel Proust, *Remembrance of Things Past* (*A la
recherche du temps perdu*), 1913–27, vol. III, p. 568)

Time, unfortunately, though it makes animals and
vegetables bloom and fade with amazing punctuality, has no
such simple effect upon the mind of man. The mind of man,
moreover, works with equal strangeness upon the body of
time. An hour, once it lodges in the queer element of the
human spirit, may be stretched to fifty or a hundred times
its clock length; on the other hand, an hour may be
accurately represented on the timepiece of the mind by one
second. This extraordinary discrepancy between time on the
clock and time in the mind is less known than it should be
and deserves fuller investigation.
(Virginia Woolf, *Orlando*, 1928, p. 69)

## STRIKING CLOCKS AND NEW CHRONOLOGIES

The business of this chapter is to give the 'discrepancy' outlined
above in *Orlando* the fuller investigation Virginia Woolf suggests it
deserves. Disposed, as explained in Chapter 2, to place 'everything
in the mind', modernism might have been logically expected – in the
terms *Orlando* outlines – to favour 'time in the mind' rather than
'time on the clock'. There is, in fact, much evidence throughout
modernist fiction of just this sort of preference. Gudrun's views of
Gerald in *Women in Love* (1921) are worth considering at greater
length in this context. As suggested in Chapter 2, they are typical
of modernism's general concern about the reification and mechanisation of 'the modern industrial and financial world': they

also introduce a particular – possibly related – dislike of time on the clock. Gudrun reflects:

> Oh God, the wheels within wheels of people, it makes one's head tick like a clock, with a very madness of dead mechanical monotony and meaninglessness. How I *hate* life, how I hate it. How I hate the Geralds, that they can offer one nothing else . . .
>
> The thought of the mechanical succession of day following day, day following day, *ad infinitum*, was one of the things that made her heart palpitate with a real approach of madness. The terrible bondage of this tick-tack of time, this twitching of the hands of the clock, this eternal repetition of hours and days – oh God, it was too awful to contemplate . . .
>
> How she suffered, lying there alone, confronted by the terrible clock, with its eternal tick-tack. All life, all life, resolved itself into this: tick-tack, tick-tack, tick-tack; then the striking of the hour; then the tick-tack, tick-tack, and the twitching of the clock fingers.
>
> Gerald could not save her from it. He, his body, his motion, his life – it was the same ticking, the same twitching across the dial, a horrible mechanical twitching forward over the face of the hours . . . across the eternal, mechanical, monotonous clock-face of time. (pp. 522–3)

Gudrun's reflections sum up her horror of the machine-like nature of Gerald, here imagined as a clock – a 'pure will' that works 'like clockwork, in perpetual repetition' (p. 524). Her views also introduce a wider uneasiness about bondage to time, and a particular questioning of time as represented by the tick-tack and twitching fingers of the clock. Comparable anxieties, specifically about clocks and clockwork, appear with striking frequency in modernist writing. In James Joyce's *A Portrait of the Artist as a Young Man* (1916), for example, the image chosen to represent hell is of the unceasing 'ticking of a great clock' (p. 133). Clocks occupy an equally unpleasant and threatening role in Virginia Woolf's fiction. In *The Waves* (1931), one of the things which most upsets the sensitive Bernard is 'the stare of clocks' (p. 25), while in *Orlando* clocks are capable of striking 'like thunder', 'like a meteor' (pp. 226, 227). Woolf's central figure finds

> the clock ticking on the mantlepiece beat like a hammer . . . the clock ticked louder and louder until there was a terrific explosion right in her ear. Orlando leapt as if she had been violently struck on the head.

Ten times she was struck. In fact it was ten o'clock in the morning . . .

'Confound it all!' she cried, for it is a great shock to the nervous system, hearing a clock strike. (pp. 210–11, 216)

Clocks are also a shock to the 'nervous system' in Joseph Conrad's writing: a surprising number of crises in his fiction are superintended by them in one way or another. In *Under Western Eyes* (1911), Razumov finds that after the crucial encounter with Haldane in his lodgings, he is too unnerved to hold his watch long enough to find out the time: looking 'wildly about as if for some means of seizing upon time which seemed to have escaped him altogether' (p. 61), he hears for what he thinks must be the first time a town clock striking nearby. In *Nostromo* (1904), Captain Mitchell's interrogation by Sotillo's troops is strangely interrupted by Sotillo himself, first using his prisoner's 'sixty-guinea gold half-chronometer' (p. 278) as a means of threatening him, then becoming so mesmerised by the quality of its mechanism that he forgets Mitchell altogether. In *Lord Jim* (1900), the hero, while also briefly imprisoned, inexplicably finds that it is only while tinkering with 'a nickel clock of New England make' that the 'true perception of his extreme peril dawned upon him': he 'dropped the thing like a hot potato' (p. 192) to seek his escape. Earlier in the novel, another odd episode shows Captain Brierly carefully tying his gold chronometer, a reward for outstanding service, to the rail of his ship before jumping overboard to lose himself forever in the shapeless vastness of the sea.

Clocks turn up most frequently and sinisterly in Conrad's *The Secret Agent* (1907). They share with other machines in the novel the kind of readiness to take on human attributes which, as suggested in Chapter 2, modernist writing often shows accompanying the reifying transformation of people into things or machines. Many scenes in *The Secret Agent* resound to music produced entirely mechanically by a 'lonely piano', capable of moods of apparent cheekiness or grumpiness, or of 'aggressive virtuosity' in striking 'a few chords courageously' (pp. 72, 58). A clock in the Verlocs' house is likewise possessed of human attributes, suggesting by its 'lonely ticking' that it wants to steal into the bedroom 'as if for the sake of company' (p. 149). Later in the novel, just after Mrs Verloc's murder of her husband, a more sinister ticking suggests –

figuratively at least – that the clock's urge to take over a human place in the household has been violently, murderously realised:

> Nothing moved in the parlour till Mrs Verloc raised her head slowly and looked at the clock with inquiring mistrust. She had become aware of a ticking sound in the room. It grew upon her ear, while she remembered clearly that the clock on the wall was silent, had no audible tick. What did it mean by beginning to tick so loudly all of a sudden? Its face indicated ten minutes to nine. Mrs Verloc cared nothing for time, and the ticking went on . . . tic, tic, tic . . .
>
> Her fine, sleepy eyes travelled downward on the track of the sound, became contemplative on meeting a flat object of bone which protruded a little beyond the edge of the sofa. It was the handle of the domestic carving knife with nothing strange about it but its position at right angles to Mr Verloc's waistcoat and the fact that something dripped from it. Dark drops fell on the floorcloth one after another, with a sound of ticking growing fast and furious like the pulse of an insane clock. (pp. 213–14)

Characters in modernist fiction outwith the British context are often disposed, like Conrad's, to look at the clock with 'inquiring mistrust', or sometimes just to drop it altogether. In F. Scott Fitzgerald's *The Great Gatsby* (1926), for example, at the crucial moment when at last he meets Daisy again, Gatsby dislodges his host's 'defunct mantlepiece clock' (p. 93), which threatens to smash into pieces on the floor. In William Faulkner's *The Sound and the Fury* (1929), Quentin Compson actually does begin his final, fatal day at Harvard by smashing the glass of his watch and tearing off the hands, nevertheless remaining oppressed by 'the blank dial with little wheels clicking and clicking behind it' (p. 76).

It is not only characters in modernist fiction who are inclined to find the clock a shock to the nervous system, or to retaliate by trying to destroy it. At one stage of his study *Aspects of the Novel* (1927), the figure E. M. Forster holds responsible for having 'smashed up and pulverised [the] clock and scattered its fragments over the world' (p. 48) is not a character, but the novelist. Modernist characters' hostility to clockwork can be seen as a figuration, a symbolic focus, of a changed attitude to time more generally evident in the texts in which they appear – in their structure particularly. Hostility to clocks, within modernist texts, is matched by novelists' reluctance to rely on chronological sequence as the basis of their construction. Forster was on the whole a traditional rather than a modernist writer, relying on conventional rather than innovative forms: he therefore found the new, clock-pulverising attitudes potentially dangerous, as he considered the structure of the novel to depend, at least to some extent, on what he calls 'sequence in chronology' (p. 49) – on an element of story which he thought

> can be defined. It is a narrative of events arranged in their time sequence – dinner coming after breakfast, Tuesday after Monday, decay after death, and so on. (p. 35)

Modernist fiction rarely abandons the story altogether, or smashes up the clock entirely, but it does resist as far as possible the arrangement of 'events in their time sequence' – the kind of 'mechanical succession of day following day' Gudrun sees as part of the 'terrible bondage' of the clock. Virginia Woolf complains in her diary about a similar bondage, about the 'appalling narrative business of the realist: getting on from lunch to dinner: it is false, unreal, merely conventional'.[1] Her own programme for the novel, set out in her essay 'Modern Fiction' (1919), includes the view that 'life is not a series . . . symmetrically arranged' (*Collected Essays*, vol. II, p. 106). Much of her fiction in the years that followed, and modernist writing generally, gave up, amended or abbreviated the chronological sequence, the vision of life as a series, which had conventionally structured the novel in the nineteenth century. The progressive, sequential development of the *Bildungsroman*, for example – tracing its central figure's life, step by step, over many years from birth to maturity – is at a considerable remove from the work of Joyce or Woolf, following their protagonists through only single days in *Ulysses* (1922) or *Mrs Dalloway* (1925).

These and other novels of the 1920s show the final results of innovations in chronology and structure whose development – like the movements into interior monologue and stream of consciousness discussed in Chapter 2 – occurred more or less progressively throughout the earlier years of the century. In several ways Marcel Proust's *A la recherche du temps perdu* provides an ideal starting-point for an analysis of such developments. Proust, first of all, is as clear as any modernist author in rejecting conventional time and sequence in chronology. In *A la recherche du temps perdu*, he seeks explicitly to create a fiction which 'suppresses the mighty dimension of Time', one able to 'make visible, to intellectualise in a work of art, realities that were outside Time' (III, pp. 1087, 971). In undertaking this task, Proust's writing illustrates many of the techniques available to writers seeking to suppress or reshape the dimension of time – so many, in fact, that Gérard Genette, in *Narrative Discourse* ('Discours du recit', 1972), bases a whole theory of the novel on examples drawn from Proust, using *A la recherche du temps perdu* as a kind of inventory of narrative techniques and strategies.

One further advantage of Proust's work, and one emphasised by Genette, is that it shows that modernist techniques for suppressing time are not necessarily new inventions, but often extensions or adaptations of characteristics already existing in the novel form. Discussing the historical origins of the form itself, Mikhail Bakhtin suggests that 'The novel, from the very beginning, developed as a genre that had at its core a new way of conceptualising time' (p. 38). Gérard Genette likewise sees as a 'core' of the novel its potential to manipulate time. What he calls 'anachrony' – departure, in narrative, from the order in which events supposedly occurred – he defines as 'one of the traditional resources of literary narration . . . one of the constitutive features of narrative temporality' (pp. 36, 85). As these two theorists confirm, one of the most obvious appeals of narrative art in general is the possibility it offers of reshaping into desired or significant order the flow of life, which – in actuality's casual juxtapositions and bland successions – may offer of itself little particular shape or significance at all. Proust did not discover this capacity. His status as a precursor of modernism's escape from 'life as a series' is owed to the scale and dexterity, rather than any absolute novelty, with which this capacity is exploited.

A central basis for his anachronic tactics is, after all, the perfectly traditional device of first-person narrative. More or less by definition, narrators of novels in the third person are not involved personally in the events they relate. From a position of some objective distance and aloofness, they can be expected to present events in an orderly way, most often in the sequence in which they supposedly occurred; Tuesday following after Monday, decay after death, and so on. Fiction in the first person, on the other hand, may plausibly be arranged more idiosyncratically, particularly since most first-person narrators retain an awareness of two strands of time rather than one – of the time lived through while events are narrated, as well as of the time during which these events were experienced. What happens on Monday is recorded on Tuesday, and first-person narrators may well begin with Tuesday, with the time of writing, rather than with Monday.

They may further disrupt the chronology of events by following the order in which they are recalled, rather than the order in which they occurred. As Proust's narrator Marcel remarks,

> our memory does not as a rule present things to us in their chronological sequence . . .

> we relive our past years not in their continuous sequence, day by day. (I, p. 622; II, p. 412)

'Reality,' Marcel suggests, 'takes shape in the memory alone' (p. 201), and his narrative is shaped and ruled by the random ordering of memory at least as much as by chronological sequence. Proust adds to this disruption of chronology by investigating a form of memory able to exercise, with unusual power, a dislocating effect on experience, and on narrative – immersing the novel in a 'time in the mind' quite separate from what is happening in external reality. His narrator Marcel indicates the nature of this sort of memory when he remarks:

> the better part of our memories exists outside us, in a blatter of rain, in the smell of an unaired room or of the first crackling brushwood fire in a cold grate . . . Outside us? Within us, rather, but hidden from our eyes in an oblivion more or less prolonged. It is thanks to this oblivion alone that we can from time to time recover the person that we were, place ourselves in relation to things as he was placed . . . In the broad daylight of our habitual memory the images of the past turn gradually pale and fade out of sight. (I, p. 692)

'Habitual memory', or as it is called elsewhere, 'voluntary memory' (I, p. 47) – the memory of the intellect which deliberately, willingly *chooses* to think of certain past episodes – produces only the palest, the most desiccated vision of the past. Involuntary memory, on the other hand – the kind of association triggered almost automatically by a sound, a smell, a blatter of rain, or an otherwise random sensual experience in the present – does not simply or deliberately *call* to mind some remembered scene or detail. Instead, it so suffuses the mind with floods of old sensation that characters are left virtually transformed into earlier versions of themselves. This happens at several stages of *A la recherche du temps perdu*: when Swann's remembered passion for Odette is triggered by hearing the Vinteuil sonata, for example; or in Marcel's rediscovery of a continuity of present experience and past sensation when he catches his foot on a paving stone at Guermantes. Most famously, it transports him back into an 'identical moment' in his childhood in Combray when he tastes once again a 'petite Madeleine' cake dipped in tea. He discovers that

> all the flowers in our garden and in M. Swann's park, and the water-lilies on the Vivonne and the good folk of the village and their little dwellings and the parish church and the whole of Combray and its surroundings, taking shape and solidity, sprang into being, town and gardens alike, from my cup of tea. (I, pp. 50–1)

Here past time is shown continuing to exist not only in the recesses of the mind, but virtually in the body; digested, deeply engrained, within the physical structure of the self.

Neither the existence of this sort of 'involuntary memory', nor even its literary use, are wholly Proust's discovery. Charles Dickens, for example, points to much the same phenomenon when in *David Copperfield* (1849–50) his hero, remembering a stage of his courtship of Dora, remarks that

> the scent of a geranium leaf, at this day, strikes me with a half comical half serious wonder as to what change has come over me in a moment; and then I see a straw hat and blue ribbons, and a quantity of curls, and a little black dog being held up, in two slender arms, against a bank of blossoms and bright leaves. (p. 456)

As in *A la recherche du temps perdu*, a sensual stimulus, scent in this case, is sufficient to transport the narrator almost into reinhabiting the past. Such transport in Dickens, however, only briefly affects and disturbs the narrator, without much dislocating the narrative. The narrative continues to proceed throughout *David Copperfield*, for the most part chronologically, from David's birth, through his youth, towards the stability and maturity of the moment at which he writes. In the instance above, there is only the briefest of deviations into the moment of writing – 'at this day' – before a return to the account of his affair with Dora, resplendent in her straw hat and curls. And this memory of Dora itself occurs exactly in its proper place in the chronological sequence of episodes in David's life.

In *A la recherche du temps perdu*, on the other hand, memory has a central role not only in the emotional life of the narrator, but in structuring the text. This role is immediately apparent in the opening 'Overture' to *A la recherche du temps perdu*, which begins with a general reflection on dream, memory and sleep: their functioning is then examined in a variety of remembered episodes and scenes, ranging freely between childhood and adulthood. The narrator moves on to more general recollections of childhood in Combray, returning at the end of the 'Overture' to the 'one day', many years later, when he encounters the Madeleine and brings his childhood back to life. The next section of the novel, 'Combray', goes on to give a longer account of these early years. The first fifty pages of the novel thus confront the reader with what are called 'shifting and confused gusts of memory' (p. 7) recorded in a narrative which moves very freely between them. Even by the end of the 'Overture', consummated by the Madeleine's coalescence of past and present, *A la recherche du temps perdu* has thoroughly enacted its own title. Ruled by memory, with its powerful connections of past and present, Proust's novel constantly searches out past or lost times, and as the last section of *A la recherche du temps perdu* eventually demonstrates, largely recovers them in the 'Time Regained' created by the fiction itself.

As Genette suggests, Proust's tactics make *A la recherche du temps perdu*

> undoubtedly, as it proclaims, a novel of Time lost and found again,
> but it is also, more secretly perhaps, a novel of Time ruled, captured,
> bewitched, surreptitiously subverted, or better: *perverted.* (p. 160)

Opening up multiple, interweaving pathways into the past, Marcel's memory not only recovers lost times, but thoroughly frees his narrative from bondage to the tick-tack of clock or calendar time in general; from the mechanical succession of life as a series. As Genette shows at length in *Narrative Discourse*, Proust's multiplying anachronies go far beyond the simple alternations of a narrating present and a remembered past. Instead, Proust sets one memory on top of another, or allows a flashback to intermingle indistinguishably with a flash forward, or surreptitiously lets a narrative of remembered experience catch up with and overtake the point in time from which the memory began. Such tactics leave the temporality of any event fluid and difficult to specify, thoroughly realising the novel's ambition to 'suppress the mighty dimension of Time'. As Genette remarks, Proust 'made clear, more than anyone had done before him and better than they had, narrative's capacity for *temporal autonomy*' (p. 85) – an achievement which 'anticipates the most disconcerting proceedings of the modern novel' (p. 67).

Proust thus occupies a pivotal position between fiction of the nineteenth century and modernism. In several ways, in subject at least, *A la recherche du temps perdu* resembles the nineteenth-century *Bildungsroman*. Like *David Copperfield*, it is a highly personal story, almost an autobiography, following the development of a hero from childhood to adulthood, from naïvety to maturity. Yet at the same time, if *A la recherche du temps perdu* is not original in subject, its treatment of its subject moves towards modernism's characteristic commitment to change and innovation in form. As Genette suggests, by extending so widely and variously narrative's potential for 'temporal autonomy', Proust provides models for the 'disconcerting proceedings' of many later modernist writers. In particular, *A la recherche du temps perdu* demonstrates the full potential of memory in departing from the chronological sequence of narrative – in making the past of any character wholly recoverable, through deliberate or involuntary association, at any moment in the present time of the story. Marcel talks of memory's potential to lift a character out of the present moment almost like a rope: D. H. Lawrence uses much the same image to indicate the strength and completeness of memory's connection of past and present. He describes Gudrun, seeking sleep in *Women in Love*, as

> conscious of everything – her childhood, her girlhood, all the forgotten incidents . . . it was as if she drew a glittering rope of knowledge out of the sea of darkness, drew and drew and drew it out of the fathomless depths of the past, and still it did not come to an end, there was no end to it, she must haul and haul at the rope of glittering consciousness, pull it out phosphorescent from the endless depths of the unconsciousness. (p. 391)

Modernist narrative seeks to place 'everything in the mind': memory offers a means of including in it past as well as present experience. As modernist fiction, in the early years of the twentieth century, moves further within the consciousness of characters, and even towards their unconsciousness, the 'rope' of memory is increasingly employed to hold past and present together. Memory becomes for modernist narrative a central, structuring device in the creation of a 'time in the mind' which moves, through the randomness of recollection, away from 'mechanical succession' and the control of the clock.

Joseph Conrad's work provides an early example of this in the British context. Conrad's use of what Henry James calls 'a definite intervening first-person singular' ensures that it is partly the consciousness of a figure in the fiction, rather than only the more aloof vision of the author, that controls and structures the novel. Conrad's use of the narrator Marlow makes *Lord Jim* (1900), for example, into a first-person narrative, though of an unusual kind – in a way still freer than Proust's to move randomly among various episodes in the story. From the start of the fifth chapter to the end of the thirty-fifth, *Lord Jim* is supposedly Marlow's spoken narrative, a yarn spun out 'in detail and audibly' (p. 31) after dinner in some distant part of the world, with 'refreshments' of some kind to help him through what Conrad specifies as three hours or so of speech. Taking the form of a huge letter that Marlow subsequently writes to a privileged member of his circle of after-dinner listeners, the last ten chapters of the novel, from Chapter 35 to the end, contrast with and highlight the particular characteristics of the earlier oral narrative. With Marlow writing rather than speaking, this section of his narrative more or less follows the chronological order of events during Jim's adventurous life in Patusan. This relative straightforwardness – and the dominance of Jim's romantic imagination in shaping the life of his colourful new domain – leaves *Lord Jim* itself resembling in its closing stages the kind of 'light holiday literature' (p. 11) that initially turned Jim's mind towards the idea of an adventurous life at sea.

Earlier, Marlow's after-dinner monologue presents readers and listeners with something more challenging. First-person narrators with the leisure to write events down, as Marlow does in his concluding letter, have the opportunity to order them carefully, and chronologically if they choose. Narrators delivering a story orally, on the other hand, may be more plausibly expected to recount events simply in the order in which they occur to them – an order ruled by memory and associations between events possibly more powerful than any created by their simple successiveness in time. In this way, it is the process of Marlow's recollection of events, and of the ways in which he found out about them, that dictates the order of their presentation in his monologue, at times apparently regardless of the chronology of their actual occurrence. Details about the survival of Jim's ship the *Patna*, for example – which might have been expected to follow the account of its striking a submerged object at the end of Chapter 3 – are delayed until Chapters 12 and 13. This happens to be the point in his monologue when Marlow recalls meeting, 'a long time after' (p. 107), the French Lieutenant who was almost solely responsible for rescuing the ship as it drifted on the open seas. Drifting apparently randomly between episodes in this way, and perhaps increasingly influenced by 'refreshments' – ironically specified as 'a glass of mineral water of some sort to help the narrator on' – Marlow's narrative quickly becomes what Conrad calls 'a free and wandering tale' (p. 7).

The randomness of its movement between episodes, however, is of course only apparent. Departures from chronological order allow Conrad much opportunity to stress moral points in the story: in the above instance, for example, to enforce comparison or contrast of the French Lieutenant's supposed heroism with Jim's apparent disgrace in his trial, recounted in Chapter 14, immediately after the French Lieutenant's story. Mutual significance, rather than simple succession in time, dictates Conrad's juxtaposition and assemblage of episodes in *Lord Jim*. Like Proust, he is less interested in 'the mighty dimension of time' than in connections and patterns of association which transcend or suppress it. Just as Jim hastily gets rid of a clock while escaping imprisonment in Patusan, Conrad shows himself, in *Lord Jim* and elsewhere, disposed to get rid of conventional, serial construction for something freer, unconstrained by the 'mechanical succession' of chronology.

Some of the principles underlying this disposition were later summed up by Conrad's occasional collaborator, Ford Madox Ford. In *Joseph Conrad: A Personal Remembrance* (1924), Ford remarks of their work together:

> it became very early evident to us that what was the matter with the Novel, and the British novel in particular, was that it went straight forward, whereas in your gradual making acquaintanceship with

your fellows you never do go straight forward . . . To get . . . a man in fiction you could not begin at his beginning and work his life chronologically to the end. You must first get him in with a strong impression, and then work backwards and forwards over his past. (pp. 129–30)

Working 'backwards and forwards over the past' in this way is a tactic Ford employs extensively in his own fiction – for example in *The Good Soldier* (1915), a novel partly resembling *Lord Jim*, as was suggested in Chapter 2, in both theme and structure. Like Conrad, Ford shows a narrator perplexedly grasping at explanations, trying to assemble a coherent picture of a character who fascinates him. This sometimes involves associating and juxtaposing episodes separated by years in their actual occurrence. The 'free and wandering' aspect of the narrative that results is made to seem natural by almost the same device Conrad uses in *Lord Jim*. Though Ford's narrator, John Dowell, does not deliver his story to an actual circle of after-dinner listeners, he carefully stresses that he proceeds – and abandons chronological order – as if he did so:

I have, I am aware, told this story in a very rambling way so that it may be difficult for anyone to find their path through what may be a sort of maze. I cannot help it. I have stuck to my idea of being in a country cottage with a silent listener, hearing between the gusts of the wind and amidst the noises of the distant sea, the story as it comes. And, when one discusses an affair – a long, sad affair – one goes back, one goes forward. One remembers points that one has forgotten . . . one recognises that one has forgotten to mention them in their proper places . . . I console myself with thinking that this is a real story and that, after all, real stories are probably told best in the way a person telling a story would tell them. They will then seem most real. (p. 167)

In a way, Dowell's remarks raise once again '*the* question of all questions. What is reality in the novel?' which Chapter 2 quoted Hugh Walpole asking writers in the early twentieth century. Dowell acknowledges that there *are* 'proper places' for episodes in a story, presumably in the chronological order in which they occurred. But he also suggests that 'real stories' do not ideally follow this order. Realism – 'what will seem most real' – may not be created by following it. Typically of the feelings and tensions underlying the development of modernism, Dowell indicates a gap between 'proper' or established conventions of fiction, and what is real; between the novel's traditional strategies and devices for representing the world, and a world that seems to have outgrown them, or to be out of step with them. Like Virginia Woolf, Ford and Conrad find the stuff of fiction ideally 'a little other than custom would have us believe it', and the custom of 'going straight forward', representing 'life as a series', particularly to be avoided. The way they do so in *Lord Jim* and in *The Good Soldier* shows them occupying, as in another way does Proust, a transitional role in the growing 'temporal autonomy' of modernist narrative. In one way, their departures from serial, chronological order create highly unconventional novels. On the other hand, these departures are also carefully explained, as in the passage above: they are sanctioned as natural, even conventional, aspects of oral narrative; a legitimate, plausible source of such effects. In this way, Conrad and Ford simultaneously serve both propriety and novelty, convention and innovation.

Both authors went on to experiment further, and in some ways more radically, with fictional structure and chronology. In Conrad's *Nostromo* (1904), a spoken narrative does appear briefly, in Captain Mitchell's garrulous account of the revolution in the imaginary South American republic of Costaguana. His story, however, actually provides what is called a 'more or less stereotyped relation of the historical events' (p. 389) – one shown to represent these events distortingly and inadequately. It is elsewhere in the novel, without the sanction of a narrator, that Conrad decisively departs from chronological order. This departure could nevertheless still be seen as plausible enough in another way – as a response to a South American history considered too lacking in logic, obvious consequence or coherent progress to be easily reduced to any conventional order, logical or chronological. This is after all a view of their history sometimes shared by later South American novelists themselves, notably Gabriel García Márquez and Mario Vargas Llosa.

Conrad's *The Secret Agent* (1907), on the other hand, is set firmly in London, yet, as in *Nostromo*, its third-person narrative extensively interrupts and warps chronological sequence. Conrad's policeman, Chief Inspector Heat, is described at one stage as rising above 'the vulgar conception of time' (p. 78), and the novel itself often follows him in this direction. When Heat encounters the anarchist Professor, for example, the narrative interrupts their conversation to loop back and fill in many details Heat recalls about the earlier part of his day, and about how he was informed of the attempted bombing of Greenwich Observatory. As Genette points out in discussing Proust, such flashbacks – and anachronies in general – are not new in fiction, but part of the traditional resources and appeal of narrative. Yet there is a certain novelty in the extravagance with which they are employed in *The Secret Agent*. Heat's conversation with the Professor is interrupted, between a single question and answer, by seven pages of his retrospection, as if deliberately demonstrating his conclusion that 'ages . . . could be contained between two successive winks of an eye' (p. 79). More generally, the novel acts out Heat's view that there may be 'unexpected solutions of continuity, sudden holes in space and time' (p. 76). Characters' retrospections, such as occur in the case of Heat's conversation with the Professor, repeatedly create startling anachronies, dissolving the conventional continuity of fiction and leaving it riddled with holes – or at least gaps and loops – in its sense of time. Continuities are thus dissolved in *The Secret Agent* not, as in *Lord Jim*, through the fickle associations made in a narrator's monologue, but by following the mental processes of a character within the story, whose thoughts often depart in voluntary or involuntary memory from the moment it has reached. *The Secret Agent* is in this way closer than *Lord Jim* to later modernist devices, disrupting chronology through the idiosyncrasies of characters' inner consciousnesses rather than their speech or storytelling. In Conrad's *Heart of Darkness* (1902), Marlow concludes that 'the mind of man is capable of anything – because everything is in it, all the past as well as all the future' (p. 52). *The Secret Agent* shows Conrad relying, actually more than in *Heart of Darkness* or *Lord Jim*, on the infinite capability of inner consciousness to coalesce past and present, to incorporate earlier experience into present thought.

Heat's thoughts, however, are still reported in the third person. As later narrative entered more and more fully into the minds of individual characters, through devices such as stream of consciousness, it became more and more free to abandon serial chronology and pursue random associations within mind and memory. This development can be illustrated by comparing *The Good Soldier* with Ford's later *Parade's End* (1924–8). As suggested in Chapter 2, *Parade's End* shares the increasing inwardness of fiction in the 1920s in moving through Free Indirect Style and interior monologue into the inner space of characters' minds. Mental processes are much more central in *Parade's End* than in *The Good Soldier* or in Conrad's fiction, effecting at times more thorough-going disruptions of serial chronology; more frequent and minute insertions of past events into the story's present. The sort of recursive, looping tactic Conrad uses to insert past events into the present of Heat's conversation with the Professor is employed more frequently and at still greater length throughout *Parade's End*. Ford's protagonist Christopher Tietjens provides what is almost a theoretical description of his author's tactics when he suggests to his lover Valentine:

> You cut out from this afternoon, just before 4.58 . . . I heard the Horse Guards clock. . . . To now. . . . Cut it out; and join time up. . . . It *can* be done. . . . You know they do it surgically; for some illness, cut out a great length of the bowel and join the tube up. (p. 285)

The possibilities Tietjens outlines are demonstrated by the chapter in which his suggestion is made. It begins, and ends, with his return home at 3.30 a.m., and his subsequent departure for the trenches. Between, the narrative goes back, through Tietjens's recollections, to events earlier in the evening, and earlier in the day, including those around 4.58 p.m., tracing them in fragments of Free Indirect Style, reported thought and memory. Some of these events are in any case already familiar from their recollection by Valentine in the previous chapter. Throughout *Parade's End*, by entering char-acters' thoughts in this way, whole sections are cut from the slack bowel of time and reshaped through memory into loops that return into the past and proceed forward again until they have caught up with the moment of consciousness at which the retrospection began.

Several characters in *Parade's End* comment with surprise on the fascinatingly anachronous nature of thought and its capacity to warp or telescope time – perhaps incidentally indicating something of Ford's own relish for his new techniques. Tietjens's wife, for example, remarks to herself after an elaborate set of reflections, 'Good God! . . . Only one minute. . . . I've thought all that in only a minute' (p. 417). After a wide-ranging reflection of her own, Valentine is likewise surprised to realise that 'she had thought all that in ten seconds . . . that was what thought was' (pp. 518-19). Such sections emphasise the kind of conclusion reached by Virginia Woolf when she remarks in *Orlando* that 'an hour may be accurately represented in the timepiece of the mind by one second'. Demonstrating and reflecting on 'what thought was' in this way, *Parade's End* largely shares the full, modernist 'temporal autonomy' developed in the work of Woolf and Joyce – the capacity, if not to suppress altogether the mighty dimension of time, at least to represent principally 'time in the mind' rather than only 'time on the clock'.

Virginia Woolf herself, throughout the 1920s, established her own ways of cutting and stitching up time again; of escaping 'the appalling narrative business of the realist' in proceeding straightforwardly from lunch to dinner. In the same diary entry in 1928 she resolves 'I will read Proust I think. I will go backwards and forwards.' Much of her fiction reflects Proust's emphasis on memory and his conclusion that 'we relive our past years not in their continuous sequence'. In the novel finished shortly before her diary entry was made, *Orlando*, she suggests:

> Memory is the seamstress, and a capricious one at that. Memory runs her needle in and out, up and down, hither and thither. We know not what comes next, or what follows after. Thus, the most ordinary movement in the world, such as sitting down at a table and pulling the inkstand towards one, may agitate a thousand odd, disconnected fragments . . . our commonest deeds are set about with a fluttering and flickering of wings, a rising and falling of lights. (p. 55)

Like Proust, Woolf finds past associations triggered powerfully yet almost arbitrarily by events in the present: powerfully enough to ensure that, in *Mrs Dalloway*, for example, 'people . . . came back in the middle of St James's Park on a fine morning – indeed they did' (p. 9). Memory functions equally strongly in *To the Lighthouse* (1927). While painting her picture Lily Briscoe turns over in her mind a sudden memory of Mrs Ramsay sitting on the beach and asks:

> D'you remember? . . . Why, after all these years had that survived,

ringed round, lit up, visible to the last detail, with all before it blank and all after it blank, for miles and miles? (p. 194)

However inexplicable this sort of involuntary connection seems, it is also inescapable: while continuing with her painting in the present, Lily is simultaneously almost physically carried back into the past:

at the same time, she seemed to be sitting beside Mrs Ramsay on the beach . . . as if a door had opened, and one went in and stood gazing silently about. (pp. 194–5)

Such moments, Lily reflects, are 'extraordinarily fertile . . . like a drop of silver in which one dipped and illumined the darkness of the past' (p. 195). They are certainly extraordinarily useful in Woolf's fiction, as in modernism generally. Like Proust, she uses the memory as a seamstress to cut and reshape sections taken out of the ordinary, sequential passage of time. 'Fertile moments' in the present offer a door through which the past experience of characters can be illumined, allowing a full sense of their earlier lives to be presented within the single days of consciousness she concentrates on in *Mrs Dalloway*, and in a way in *The Waves* (1931); or the two days in *To the Lighthouse*. Concentrating on the 'myriad impressions', memories included, daily passing through the mind, Woolf achieves her ambition of going back as well as forwards, firmly rejecting 'life as a series' yet managing to retain a full sense of the life of her characters.

Something similar is achieved by Joyce in *Ulysses*. Joyce's narrative progresses steadily enough through Bloom's day in Dublin, 16 June 1904, but it also ranges widely over Bloom's remembered earlier life, freely exploiting the mind's capacity to stray in imagination or memory far from the actual external events unfolding around it. His stream of consciousness continually recovers past events to juxtapose or associate with present ones. Chapter 6, 'Hades', for example, finds Bloom a mourner at Paddy Dignam's funeral, yet also moving back in memory to the suicide of his father long before; to the burial of his infant son Rudy, ten years previously; to earlier times with Molly, living in Lombard Street West. Such past details are included in sufficient quantity to provide a picture of a life more or less as complete as in any Victorian *Bildungsroman*, yet very differently presented;

constantly, immediately illumined through the fertile movements and moments of Bloom's mind in his single day in Dublin.

The potential of this sort of illumination of the past is perhaps most fully realised at the end of *Ulysses*, in the freewheeling movements of Molly Bloom's mind, turning over and mixing events on the edge of sleep in 'Penelope', the last chapter. In its concluding pages, Molly's memory associates with the present not a single recollection, but two different eras of earlier experience. Her mind moves back, first of all, to Bloom's proposal to her, '16 years ago my God' – i.e. in 1888 – and to the way she 'wouldnt answer first only looked out over the sea and the sky thinking of so many things he didnt know' (p. 643). These things include memories of another earlier phase of her life, her youth in Gibraltar, a location which helps to create a sense of universality at the end of *Ulysses*. Certain versions of the story of Odysseus (which Joyce of course follows carefully throughout *Ulysses*), tell of a final voyage taking him beyond the rock of Gibraltar – in myth, the Pillars of Hercules, which marked the point at which the known world opened out into chartless, unknowable, oceanic infinity. Moving in his last chapter towards a point that marked the end of knowable space, Joyce also goes as far as possible beyond specific or specifiable time. Molly's memories of accepting Bloom's proposal in 1888 are interfused with an earlier saying 'yes' to a lover in Gibraltar; perhaps also with a reaffirmation of her relationship with Bloom in the present of 1904. But in moving between Ireland, Gibraltar and the open sea beyond, and between 1904, 1888 and earlier, Molly's mind so interweaves memory and recollection, even remembered recollection, that it creates for the novel an affirmative, comedic conclusion largely beyond particular time as well as space. Molly's concluding 'yes' is spoken to no single man, nor at any specific moment, but to all human relationships. In his various plans for *Ulysses*, which he later allowed to be made public, Joyce indica≳s a particular time of day for each of the novel's chapters except the last, for which he either – in one plan – stipulates no particular time, or – in another – inserts in place of an hour of the day the symbol $\infty$ to represent infinity.[2]

Rather than bringing the action of *Ulysses* firmly to a close at the end, Joyce thus opens it out beyond the constraints of geography or chronology. If, in Gérard Genette's view, *A la recherche du temps perdu* is a novel of 'temporal autonomy' – of 'time ruled, captured, bewitched, surreptitiously subverted' – then so is *Ulysses*. Molly Bloom's soliloquy consummates the modernist desire, discussed in Chapter 2, to 'look within' at inner consciousness: it also realises as fully as possible the disposition discussed in this chapter, to rule rather than be ruled by the hours, to rely on the timepiece of the mind rather than the mechanism of the clock. Obviously, the two movements, towards inner consciousness and away from clocks and mechanical succession, are related. When modernist fiction recognised, in Marlow's terms, that 'the mind of man is capable of anything' it also acquired a method for structuring 'all the past' into present experience, using the 'rope' of memory to escape sequence in time. Streams of consciousness and interior monologues offer a fluent entry not only to the mind's present movement, but to the depths of past experience, revitalised by association with immediate impressions. Some of the contemporary pressures discussed in the last chapter, that encouraged fiction to develop strategies to 'look within' are thus also relevant to the restructuring of fiction examined above. There were also, however, some factors in the life of the early twentieth century that may be more particularly related to the hostility to the clock which this chapter began by outlining, and to modernism's consequent quest for 'temporal autonomy' and 'time in the mind'. These factors are discussed in the next two sections.

## THE TIME PHILOSOPHY

By far the most prolific contemporary commentator on the issue, Wyndham Lewis, had no doubt about the factors responsible for a new concern with time in the life and art of the 1920s. In his huge, 480-page assessment of contemporary culture, *Time and Western Man* (1927), Lewis explains that the new conception of time which he sees as such a distinctive feature in the writing of his period directly resulted from 'what was originally a philosophic theory used currently in the practice of the arts of expression, and become a second nature for the practitioners' (p. 149). The philosophic theory Lewis believed so universally (and, in his view, damagingly) influential was the 'philosophy of *psychological time*' (p. 102), as he called it, expounded in the work of Henri Bergson. Lewis considered Bergson more than any other single figure . . . responsible for the main intellectual characteristics of the world we live in, and the implicit debt of almost all contemporary philosophy to him is immense. (p. 166)

In Lewis's view, 'practitioners' of Bergson's thinking in the literary sphere included, among others, Proust, Gertrude Stein and, above all, James Joyce. In his extended 'Analysis of the Mind of James Joyce' in *Time and Western Man*, Lewis remarks:

I regard *Ulysses* as a *time-book*; and by that I mean that it lays its emphasis upon, for choice manipulates, and in a doctrinaire manner, the self-conscious time-sense, that has now been erected into a universal philosophy. This it does beneath the spell of a similar creative impulse to that by which Proust worked . . .

Without all the uniform pervasive growth of the time-philosophy starting from the little seed planted by Bergson, discredited, and now spreading more vigorously than ever, there would be no *Ulysses*, or there would be no *A La Recherche du Temps Perdu*. There would be no 'time-composition' of Miss Stein; no fugues in words. In short, Mr. Joyce is very strictly of the school of Bergson-Einstein, Stein-Proust. He is of the great time-school they represent. His book is a *time-book*, as I have said, in that sense. He has embraced the time-doctrine very completely. (pp. 100, 106)

The question of whether Joyce or others actually need be seen as 'practitioners' in a *school* established by Bergson can be left aside for the moment. Lewis is right at least in pointing out the extent to which Bergson's philosophy bears comparison with aspects of modernist fiction; in particular with the views of time outlined in the last section. Like modernist writers, Bergson resists, as a core of his thinking, views of time or life as a series, a succession of separate events or divisible phenomena. Such views he considers covertly, misleadingly based on habits of mind appropriate only for conceptualising space. He suggests in *Time and Free Will* (*Essai sur les données immédiates de la conscience*, 1889) that

time, conceived under the form of a homogeneous medium, is some spurious concept, due to the trespassing of the idea of space upon the field of pure consciousness. (p. 98)

This 'spurious concept' leads to the error of supposing that time is a quantity, one that can be divided up and parcelled out like a piece of material. A principal agent – or really villain – in making such divisions is of course the clock, magisterially dissecting time into lumps and units. It is a natural focus for Bergson's criticism, an obstacle to the true, mental experience of time which he calls 'duration'. He remarks:

> When I follow with my eyes on the dial of a clock the movement of the hands . . . I do not measure duration . . . Outside of me, in space, there is never more than a single position of the hand . . . Within myself a process of organization or interpenetration of conscious states is going on, which constitutes true duration . . .
>
> . . . states of consciousness, even when successive, permeate one another, and in the simplest of them the whole soul can be reflected. (pp. 107–8, 98)

Bergson saw the trespass of space into thinking about time further assisted by the activity of the intellect, by its disposition to define, divide and categorise. Time could be truly understood not through the divisive intellect, but by means of intuition, able to apprehend the permeation of conscious states; the seamless flow of creative evolution and becoming. Such views of continuity and duration also create in Bergson's work a central role for memory: in the evolving flow of conscious states, past ones do not disappear but coexist with and interpenetrate present ones:

> Behind the memories which crowd in upon our present occupation and are revealed by means of it, there are others, thousands on thousands of others, below and beneath the scene illuminated by consciousness. Yes, I believe our past life is there, preserved even to the minutest details; nothing is forgotten; all we have perceived, thought, willed, from the first awakening of our consciousness, persists indefinitely.[3]

Bergson's view that 'nothing is forgotten' coincides with Gudrun's realisation in *Women in Love* that 'everything . . . all the forgotten incidents' are actually still available to present consciousness, able to be drawn back by the 'glittering rope' memory reaches into the fathomless depths of the past. Bergson's explanation of present occupation inevitably revealing and recovering past memories likewise offers a philosophic version of Lily Briscoe's discovery, in *To the Lighthouse*, that 'fertile moments' in the present open doors upon the past; or of Marcel's experience with the Madeleine in *A la recherche du temps perdu*. Like Proust, Bergson considers present sensual stimuli automatically opening up powerful, complete entries to the past: in *Time and Free Will*, he offers as his own example of the association of past and present:

> I smell a rose and immediately confused recollections of childhood come back to my memory . . . I breathe them in with the very scent; it means all that to me. (p. 161)

Bergson's belief that time exists truly as duration, within the self, and that the conscious states constituting this duration are seamlessly continuous, also coincides with some more general modernist principles. It matches both the assumption that the truest experience is found by looking within, and that this mental experience is stream-like and continuous in nature. Though the phrase 'stream of consciousness' belongs to William James, the idea that consciousness is not a chain of separate items, but a constant flow of memories and impressions, is equally Bergsonian. Molly Bloom's final soliloquy gives an example of the sort of conscious activity, eliding distinctions between separate thoughts and between past and present, that Bergson saw as the true life of the mind (at least as far as it is possible to transcribe this in language). In this way, *Ulysses* or other modernist novels could indeed be seen as '*time-books*', as Lewis suggests. Bergson certainly shares the hostility to clockwork and the reactions made against it that appear in modernist fiction. In *Time and Free Will*, he asks directly for 'some bold novelist', able to show the 'infinite permeation of a thousand different impressions' by 'tearing aside the cleverly woven curtain of our conventional ego' (p. 133). His request seems directly answered by modernism's movements beyond what Lawrence calls 'the old stable *ego*' [4] and by its development of techniques able to record the 'myriad impressions' Woolf sees daily passing through the mind.

Bergson's potential appeal, and relevance, for the modernists also went some way beyond his views of time. His preference for apprehending experience through intuition, rather than intellect or rational analysis, is further developed throughout his philosophy, and widely shared and echoed in modernism. Throughout the modernist period trends can be seen away from the rational, logical and deductive, towards the intuitive, the unconscious, and the emotional. This tendency appears fairly generally in D. H.

Lawrence's writing, and particularly in the complaint in *Lady Chatterley's Lover* (1928) that 'the mind can only analyse and rationalize', leaving humanity 'over-conscious' and 'on the spontaneous, intuitive side dead' (pp. 39, 159). Proust similarly prefers spontaneous, automatic memory to 'the memory of the intellect'. A character in Richard Aldington's *Death of a Hero* (1929) remarks that it is 'so much better to trust to the deeper instincts than to talk about things with "the inferior intelligence" ' (p. 25). Intellect and cleverness are likewise not much approved in *To the Lighthouse*. Part of Mrs Ramsay's virtue is that 'her simplicity fathomed what clever people falsified' (p. 34): part of her husband's limitation is his inveterate inclination to rationalise, categorise and define.

While Bergson's interest for modernism thus extended well beyond his ideas of time (other relevant phases of his thinking are considered in Chapter 4), his appeal was also widened by the way his ideas were communicated, and by their particular status in the early years of the twentieth century. Philosophy might seem too abstract and esoteric to have much direct contact with popular or even literary thinking. Yet Bergson's views are expressed unusually accessibly, often even poetically, and at the turn of the century they reached an audience much wider than the usual one for formal philosophy. At the time, Bergson occupied a position comparable to those of Roland Barthes or Jacques Derrida in the later twentieth century – complex, challenging thinkers, the originality and range of whose ideas nevertheless extend their influence into popular culture as well as academic circles, making them almost figures of fashion. Bergson's lectures at the Collège de France in the 1890s were very well attended, almost society occasions, and his published work rapidly ran through several editions, both in the original and in English translation. There is plenty of evidence that his ideas were widely disseminated at different levels of society in the years that followed – Bergson turns up, for example, as a promising subject for tea-time chat among Princeton undergraduates in F. Scott Fitzgerald's *The Beautiful and Damned* (1922). There is also evidence that contemporary authors were more or less directly in touch with his ideas: William Faulkner, for example, remarked that he agreed with 'Bergson's theory of the fluidity of time'.[5] Even Wyndham Lewis attended Bergson's lectures, despite his hostility. So did Marcel Proust, a distant cousin of Bergson's by marriage. Bergotte, a significant character in the early part of *A la recherche du temps perdu*, is sometimes said to be modelled on Bergson: Marcel certainly ponders at some length the validity of Bergson's theories of memory in the 'Cities of the Plain' section of the novel (II, pp. 1016–17). Joyce, too, can be deciphered as showing a familiar interest in Bergsonian ideas. The sixth section of *Finnegans Wake* (1939) mentions 'the sophology of Bitchson' in the course of a debate about psychological time and the relation of time to space – figured as the 'dime-cash' problem, of much concern to 'Windy Nous' (pp. 56, 149).

As well as the 'sophology of Bitchson', *Finnegans Wake* also discusses the 'theorics of Winestain' (p. 149). In the view of Windy Nous, or Wyndham Lewis, the 'theorics' of Einstein were probably partly derived from Bergson's work,[6] and certainly served to reverse any falling away in popular interest in Bergson himself. Even though Bergson's own fame and fashionableness may have slightly faded, Einstein's popularity in the 1920s reinvigorated a 'time-school' which Lewis saw including several other contemporary philosophers, such as Samuel Alexander and A. N. Whitehead, as well. Lewis explains the continuing influence of 'the school of Bergson-Einstein' by remarking that

> The philosophy of the space-timeist is identical with the old . . . bergsonian philosophy of *psychological time* (or *durée*, as he called it). It is essential to grasp this continuity between the earlier flux of Bergson, with its Time-god, and the einsteinian flux, with its god, Space-time. (p. 102)

In one way this assumption of identity, or 'great orthodoxy' (p. 218), among all these contemporary thinkers is simply wrong. Bergson's insistence that ideas of space must be kept separate from concepts of time differs quite clearly from the views of later thinkers. Einstein, in particular, encouraged the habitual hyphenation 'space-time' in the 1920s, establishing the idea of a unified medium in which time figures as a fourth dimension alongside the three of space.

Such differences between Bergson and the space-timeists of the 1920s were carefully pointed out by Bertrand Russell, and ought to have been clear enough in philosophic circles in any case. Nevertheless, Lewis was not the only one to ignore them, and they may have been still more easily overlooked in the popular mind. Bergson himself, after all, attempted to find a resemblance between Einstein's ideas and his own, in his study *Durée et simultanéité* (1922), though he did later acknowledge that the attempt had not been altogether successful. And Einstein's public pronouncements might easily have encouraged a feeling that his work followed from and confirmed other recent theories of time, Bergson's in particular. Einstein once remarked, for example, that

> The really important factor is ultimately intuition . . .
>
> The subjective sensation is a reality.
>
> There is only a psychological time, different from the time of physicists.[7]

With all the supposed weight of scientific truth, this sort of pronouncement offered – actually rather as Lewis suggests – powerful substantiation of psychological or durational time, rather than time on the clock or the time of physicists, as the true measure of experience.

Einstein's views carried into the 1920s a huge wave of popular excitement and interest in such issues. After his theories had apparently been confirmed by observations carried out during the solar eclipse of May 1919, as one contemporary commentator, Alexander Moszkowski, expressed it,

> a wave of amazement swept over the continents . . .
>
> During that time no name was quoted so often as that of this man. Everything sank away in face of this universal theme which had taken possession of humanity . . . Relativity had become the sovereign password. (pp. 13–14)

Difficult as Einstein's ideas were to grasp, there soon appeared a huge literature of explanations and introductions – such as Moszkowski's *Einstein the Searcher* (1921) or Bertrand Russell's *The ABC of Relativity* (1926) – to ensure that, as Lewis put it,

> within a few years of the arrival of Einstein upon the European scene, the layman, I suppose, knows more about Relativity physics than any layman has ever known about the newtonian cosmology. (p. 11)

Lewis, therefore, had some reason to suggest in *Time and Western Man* that Einstein's influence may have revived Bergson's; certainly that Relativity kept new ideas of 'psychological time' in the forefront of general interest in the 1920s. *Time and Western Man* could have gone even further in considering how one or two other recent thinkers might have contributed to this interest. Lewis might have examined more thoroughly some of the figures concerned in the epistemological shift – the radical challenge to the validity, even the possibility, of human understanding of the universe – whose appearance in the late nineteenth and early twentieth centuries was discussed in Chapter 2. A suspicion of conventional views of time was bound to figure in a shift of opinion that questioned – as mere 'human device', without universal validity – any means by which consciousness envisages and establishes its place within nature. Nietzsche's radical scepticism inevitably includes questioning of the conventional meaning of time, which he sees lacking natural or absolute existence, and simply prescribed upon the world for human convenience. Nietzsche particularly attacked the erroneous assumption of the existence of 'divisible time spans' and 'divisible spaces', part, in his view, of a more generally misleading 'presumption of eternal truths, and space, time, and causality as absolute and universally valid laws'. Rather than some divisible medium, Nietzsche considers that 'in truth we are confronted by a *continuum* . . . a flux'; a 'course of *becoming*'. This continuum Nietzsche sees submitted to 'arbitrary division and dismemberment' by the habits of the intellect.[8] Such views place his thinking quite close to Bergson's concept of time as a continuous, durational evolution of consciousness and experience. The assertion that time is an invented, arbitrary category, rather than an absolute or universal one, also coincides with Einstein's views, at least as they were summed up by Bertrand Russell in *The ABC of Relativity*:

> The time-order of events is in part dependent upon the observer . . .

> The universal cosmic time which used to be taken for granted is thus no longer admissible. (pp. 44, 50)

Conventional temporal ordering of events was challenged in another way, around the turn of the century, by the work of Sigmund Freud. In Freud's view, past and present are crucially connected, though hardly in chronological sequence. The past not only continues to exist – though mostly buried in unconscious memories – it is largely the expanding effects of past psychic events that continue to shape and structure present personality. Distant events, especially those in childhood, are often more influential in this way than more recent ones: pain or pleasure thirty years ago may be more important, and in some ways closer to the present, than the events of yesterday. The origins of such distant but inescapable influences can also be recovered in the present. At least occasionally, in 'fertile moments', or pulled up on the right 'glittering rope', the past can be exhumed – allowed to 'reappear in the light',[9] in Freud's view, principally through the agency of dreams. Freud's thinking suggests the past can be recovered through dreams almost as powerfully as Bergson thought it might by means of memory. Freud suggests in *The Interpretation of Dreams* (1899):

> What we have long ceased to think about, what has long since lost for us all importance, is constantly recalled by the dream . . .

> Nothing which we have once psychically possessed is ever entirely lost. (pp. 11, 15)

In *Women in Love*, when Gudrun finds that 'everything . . . her childhood, her girlhood, all the forgotten incidents' still exist in 'the sea of darkness . . . the fathomless depths of the past . . . the endless depths of the unconsciousness', her discovery belongs as much with the idea of a rope of dreams outlined by Freud as to the faculty of memory stressed by Bergson. It may be significant that several of the moments in modernist writing when chronological order is most comprehensively abandoned or transcended occur, as in Gudrun's case, when characters hover on the edge of sleep or dreams. Marcel is in this condition throughout the time-wandering Overture to *A la recherche du temps perdu*; Molly Bloom shares it in the time-denying conclusion to *Ulysses*; and when rising furthest above 'the vulgar conception of time' in *The Secret Agent* it is of 'long and terrifying dreams dreamed in the instant of waking' (p. 78) that Chief Inspector Heat finds himself thinking. Writing in *Aspects of the Novel* in 1927, E. M. Forster particularly indicates dreamers, as well as artists and lovers, as 'partially delivered from . . . tyranny' exerted by 'Father Time' (p. 36). By the late 1920s, and probably before, there was widespread belief and interest in this capacity of dream to escape from the tyranny of time, allowing the dreamer to wander freely and apparently at random in the past, or even in the future. Further evidence of this appears in the publication of J. W. Dunne's *An Experiment with Time* in 1927. From his experience of several dreams that seemed to predict the future,

Dunne elaborated a whole theory of the existence of a fourth dimension, free from the ordinary passage of time. It could be entered in dream or visionary states, allowing visits to things past or yet to come. Dunne's work was sharply satirised by Wyndham Lewis, but it was widely respected elsewhere at the time.[10] Dunne was invited to speak at Oxford by the philosopher A. J. Ayer; Joyce knew and seems to have admired his work; and *An Experiment with Time* was popular enough to remain in print almost sixty years after its first publication.

Sixty years or so after the first publication of *Time and Western Man*, Lewis's criticism remains a fascinating assessment – too often overlooked by later critics – of the new habits of mind appearing in his period. Lewis's views carry the authority of a contemporary eye-witness, an artist and novelist at work in the age he describes, and they are also extraordinarily eclectic in examining this age, ranging far beyond literature and philosophy. At one stage, for example, *Time and Western Man* talks of 'the association of Einstein with Miss Stein, of Swann and Stein, of Bergson and Bloom, of Miss Loos, Charlie Chaplin and Whitehead' (p. 218). Yet the immediacy of Lewis's contact with his age, and in some ways his eclecticism, also set some limits to the validity of his conclusions. Discussing his own priorities, particularly as a painter, Lewis talks of a preference for anything 'nobly defined and exact, as opposed to that which is fluid', and for the 'definition and logical integrity that, as a graphic artist, I require'.[11] Contrary to this requirement, he saw the art and writing of his time apparently dissolving into streams of consciousness or in various other ways denying definition and exactness, temporal or otherwise. Not unnaturally, Lewis was inclined to suppose that such a general disposition in the age, and one so contrary to his own, could hardly have appeared of its own accord, but must be the result of some powerful influence; a 'great orthodoxy'; almost a kind of conspiracy. Finding 'fluidity . . . the life-blood of the philosophy of Bergson',[12] Lewis chooses to see this influence and orthodoxy arising principally from his work. The choice is in one way an obvious one, since Lewis does show successfully that contemporary literature, philosophy and many other contemporary phenomena are much preoccupied with new ideas of time which are largely analogous to Bergson's. As suggested in Chapters 1 and 2, however, such analogy or parallelism is not a necessary or sufficient basis for assuming causality.

Lewis is too ready to turn correlation into cause, coincidence into conspiracy. Fredric Jameson provides a necessary warning about *Time and Western Man* when he remarks of it that

> as a neutral description of the originality of modern consciousness it is surely unexceptionable – but rather its form is fundamentally problematic. The theme of time is here an instrument of analysis and descriptive explanation which is then called upon to function as a causal hypothesis.

As Jameson suggests, *Time and Western Man* as a description of contemporary consciousness is 'unexceptionable': Jameson himself confirms of Lewis's period that

> contemporary consciousness . . . also modern art, and the modern sensibility in all its manifestations, are saturated by an original and historically new sense of temporality.[13]

One of the principal values of *Time and Western Man* is that it shows how thoroughly a new sense of temporality did imbue the whole age, not only in literature and philosophy but throughout 'the modern sensibility' in all the manifestations – from Bergson to Charlie Chaplin – which Lewis piles helter-skelter into his argument. To explain this new temporality simply as the *result* of Bergson's work, however, supposes that the intellectual contours of an age derive from philosophy rather than, equally possibly, vice versa. The popular impact of Bergson and Einstein may have been owed not only to their genius in generating and persuading people of totally new ideas, but to their formulation within scientific or philosophic discourse of concepts already colouring popular thought, or at least congenial to it. This is the view D. H. Lawrence takes in the passage, quoted in Chapter 2, in which he remarks that if 'everybody catches fire at the word Relativity', it is because 'there must have been something in the mere suggestion which we have been waiting for'. Likewise, Dorothy Richardson once remarked of the question of Bergson's influence:

> I was never consciously aware of any specific influence . . . No doubt Bergson influenced many minds, if only by putting into words something then dawning within the human consciousness: an increased sense of the inadequacy of the clock as a time-measurer.[14]

Richardson's remarks suggest a worthwhile place for Bergson and other philosophers in the study of modernist fiction. Their work puts into words, makes explicit and directly accessible – in some of the passages quoted above, for example – priorities more implicitly informing fiction. Philosophy may not cause, but it can clarify. It may be tempting to go further and follow Lewis's conveniently complete explanation of modernist writing as simply the result of Bergson's persuasive philosophy, but it would not be logical to do so, even in Lewis's own terms. If there could be no *Ulysses* without the 'tiny seed' planted by Bergson, then presumably without some other seed or set of factors there would be no Bergson, either. This set of factors, however, cannot always, as Lewis supposes, just be looked for in other writers or philosophers. If the sense of temporality he saw so widely disseminated in the early years of the twentieth century was, as Jameson suggests, 'historically new', then it is in the new conditions of contemporary history that its origins must also be sought. Wyndham Lewis's enquiry in *Time and Western Man* needs to be extended into a still wider scrutiny of pressures on Western Man in the late nineteenth century and the first decades of the twentieth. Why should a hostility to clocks and a preference for 'time in the mind' have appeared so widely throughout the sensibility of this particular period?

## MEAN TIME

A certain resentment or suspicion of the clock is of course not unique to the period, nor altogether new in literature. The *carpe diem* theme common in poetry for centuries, for example, partly depends on such thinking. So do many of Shakespeare's sonnets, and the celebration in *As You Like It* of the fact that 'there's no clock in the forest' (III, ii) sums up a widespread sense of the unnaturalness – even the actual hostility to nature – of the clock as a time-measurer. Like any other, however, this general sense can be focused by specific historical circumstances: by the end of the nineteenth century several factors had coalesced to intensify and particularise it. Perhaps most obviously, the nineteenth century saw large sections of the British population move away from clock-free forests, or rural labour, towards life centred around the factory as a place of work, in the kind of huge, complex cities which later provide the setting of much modernist fiction. As the nineteenth century went on, factory work and city life created conditions increasingly unlike the more casual rhythms of the country and of agricultural labour, shaped by sunrise, sunset and season. Eventually shift-work made interchangeable even the activities of night and day. And as tasks were increasingly divided up among separate individuals, each completing a particular phase in the assembly of some product, machines recording every individual arrival and departure from the factory became necessary, replacing the hooters and whistles used to summon whole shifts of workers earlier in the century. By 1890 this ritual of 'clocking-in' and 'clocking-out' came to establish the beginning and end of each day's work, the clock now exactly controlling each entry to and exit from the workplace.

During the working day, from the end of the nineteenth century onwards, labour was increasingly organised by what Frederick W. Taylor called 'rules, laws, and formulae, which replace the judgement of the individual workman'. These were eventually codified by Taylor in *The Principles of Scientific Management*, published in 1911. 'Scientific management' depended on the belief that, as Taylor puts it, 'in the past the man has been first; in the future the system must be first' (pp. 22, 8). To create the system of scientific management, time and motion studies were introduced to establish an exact duration for all tasks: like entry to the factory, each piece of work was now intensely regulated by the clock. It is this kind of new attitude created by Taylorism and Scientific Management that D. H. Lawrence reflects in Gerald Crich's development of the mines in *Women in Love*. Gerald's modernisation creates

> the great reform. Expert engineers were introduced in every department . . . New machinery was brought from America, such as the miners had never seen before, great iron men, as the cutting machines were called, and unusual appliances. The working of the pits was thoroughly changed, all the control was taken out of the hands of the miners, the butty system was abolished. Everything was run on the most accurate and delicate scientific method, educated and expert men were in control everywhere.
>
> There was a new world, a new order, strict, terrible, inhuman . . . a great and perfect system that subjected life to pure mathematical principles. (pp. 259–60)

Strict, minute regulation of the kind Lawrence describes, submitting everything to careful chronological control, allowed management to treat individual workers more and more as wheels and cogs, mere components, within the greater machine of the whole factory. Scientific management made human nature increasingly subordinate to the machinery workers had to serve, or often virtually interchangeable with it. Its spread from the United States to Britain in the early years of the twentieth century played a significant part in the anxieties about the reification of humanity, in a late capitalist age, discussed at the end of Chapter 2 – the kind of anxieties that Leopold Bloom sums up in *Ulysses* when he reflects that 'Machines. Smash a man to atoms if they got him caught. Rule the world today' (p. 98); or that Lawrence reflects in *Lady Chatterley's Lover* in the comment 'soon there'll be no use for men on the face of the earth, it'll be all machines' (p. 109).

Within such anxieties, the clock occupied a unique position, a symbolic as well as an actual focus for concern. Entirely regulating working life, the clock functioned as a crucial agent of the new rule of the machine; it also provided an appropriate emblem of the result of such increasingly stringent regulation. As humanity in the twentieth century increasingly risked taking on the mechanical nature of its new 'rulers' – or was increasingly forced to do so – it could be more and more appropriately represented by the clock, an intricate, ever-moving machine with a face and hands. In *Women in Love*, Gudrun turns immediately and naturally to this metaphor to sum up her horror of both the industrial master, Gerald, and the men he has subordinated to his will:

> the wheels within wheels of people, it makes one's head tick like a clock, with a very madness of dead mechanical monotony and meaninglessness . . .
>
> Let them turn into mechanisms . . . perfect parts of a great machine . . . the miner, with a thousand wheels, and then the electrician, with three thousand, and the underground manager, with twenty thousand, and the general manager with a hundred thousand little wheels working away to complete his make-up, and then Gerald, with a million wheels and cogs and axles.
>
> Poor Gerald, such a lot of little wheels to his make-up! He was more intricate than a chronometer-watch. (pp. 522, 524–5)

Even outside the factory the early years of the twentieth century saw conditions of leisure made almost as firmly subject to control by the clock as those of work. Pressures on production during the

First World War, concern about bad time-keeping in crucial industries, and an obvious need to avoid accidents in munitions factories led to attempts to eliminate drunkenness by controlling the opening hours of pubs, through licensing laws introduced under the Defence of the Realm Act.[15] Resounding across the 'Game of Chess' section of *The Wasteland*, the pub-closing cry 'HURRY UP PLEASE IT'S TIME' – sounding almost like a warning about time itself – was still a relatively new addition to the spiritlessness of the urban landscape when T. S. Eliot published his poem in 1922. In other ways, too, the First World War enforced more immediate concern with time and its measurement. Conditions of combat made exactly timed co-ordination of troop movements essential: waves of attacking soldiers required even stricter synchronisation than shifts of workers. So army officers increasingly adopted the use of easily consulted wrist-watches: before the war, these had been thought an affectation, a rather flamboyant alternative to the leisured consultation of a fob watch. During the war such leisure ceased to exist, as did millions of the men who might have enjoyed it. The regulative apparatus bound to each wrist began to dictate the organisation and timing not only of work and leisure, but of death.

Material production and military organisation – the working life and death of 'the modern industrial and financial world' – thus helped make the clock master rather than servant of humanity. A particular aspect of Gudrun's fears about 'the terrible clock' indicates other factors which, reaching even beyond factories or the trenches of the First World War, ensured the clock's complete mastery of the population as a whole. Thinking of Gerald and modern industrialised man, she finds that

> she could never escape. There she was, placed before the clock-face of life. And if she turned round as in a railway station, to look at the bookstall, still she could see, with her very spine, she could see the clock, always the great white clock-face . . . the eternal, mechanical, monotonous clock-face of time. (p. 523)

It is appropriate that during her chilling vision of the clock it is in a railway station that Gudrun thinks of standing. Throughout the nineteenth century, the spread of railways did at least as much as the expansion of factory work to put the clock firmly in control of everyday life – to make time mean, and be Mean, for everyone.

Until the great advance of the railways in the 1840s, most British towns lived in little local time zones of their own – the time on clocks in Bristol, for example, was eleven minutes different from those in London. Strange as this now seems, it was in one way both sensible and perfectly natural, as the sun and stars, markers of true or astronomical time, rise and set at different times in different parts of the British Isles. Such differences in local times, however, created at one extreme the disturbing possibility that – at least on a fairly short journey – a train might apparently arrive somewhere at a time before it had set out. Such confusions had to be eliminated: in general, a homogeneous, nationwide time was essential if passengers everywhere were to know when to turn up for their journeys, and railwaymen when to commence them. As the railway historians Jeffrey Richards and John M. MacKenzie remark,

> Trains had to leave on time for the railway system to make sense in both passenger and goods terms. For the system to work efficiently this had to be standard national time and not solar time. So God's time, or natural time, the time dictated by the sun's progress through the heavens and the countryman's age-old rhythm of life, was superseded by Man's time. (p. 94)

In some areas, such as Bristol, where the station clock had an extra hand to indicate local time as well as the time used by the railway company, God's time held out for a while. Increasingly, however, it was the railway's clocks that came to define the time for the whole population, with particular effects on the life and thinking of the age. As Richards and MacKenzie suggest, 'the life of Victorian man [came] to be programmed, conditioned, and disciplined by the railway's demand for punctuality in its customers' (p. 96). In *A la recherche du temps perdu*, Marcel likewise records that

> since railways came into existence, the necessity of not missing trains has taught us to take account of minutes, whereas among the ancient Romans . . . the notion not only of minutes but even of fixed hours barely existed. (II, p. 853)

Such 'taking account of minutes', as Marcel reflects, had consequences for the imagination as well as the practicalities of time. He talks of the

> 1.22 train, whose hour of departure I could never read without a palpitating heart on the railway company's bills or in advertisements

for circular tours: it seemed to me to cut, at a precise point in every afternoon, a delectable groove, a mysterious mark. (I, pp. 418–19)

The kind of changes in the sense of time effected by railways in the nineteenth century continued in various ways to influence the imagination of the twentieth. Writing as late as 1934, for example, Joyce's friend Frank Budgen suggests that, where the 'social time sense' is concerned,

> discoveries of the astronomer and the mathematician have less immediate effect . . . than the electrification of the suburban lines. Light and the heavenly bodies are doing what they always did, but the wheels of mechanical civilisation are ever accelerating. (p. 132)

In Budgen's view, in other words, railway timetables and contemporary changes in forms of transport were more responsible than the thinkers Wyndham Lewis identifies, such as Einstein, for the new sense of time in Western Man – a view Budgen epigrammatically summarises in remarking 'spacetime came in with the taximeter, which is by petrol engine out of clockwork' (p. 132).

Further changes in the 'social time sense' in the late nineteenth and early twentieth centuries resulted from further systematisation of national and international time-measurement. For much of the nineteenth century Britain's standard national time was known colloquially (and distinguished from local time) as 'Railway Time'. The 1880s saw a change in name and an increase in the influence of this national standard: evidence of interest in the new arrangement appears, for example, in Arthur Wing Pinero's *The Magistrate*, first performed in 1885. Reassuring another character about the time, Pinero's hero remarks, 'Hurray! Just half-past ten. Greenwich mean, eh Guv?' (I). The comment is not only assured, but topical. A year earlier, in 1884, as Stephen Kern explains, the Prime Meridian Conference had

> establish[ed] Greenwich as the zero meridian, determined the exact length of the day, divided the earth into twenty-four time zones one hour apart, and fixed a precise beginning of the universal day. (p. 12)

Though Greenwich Mean Time thus became the standard within Britain, it was not immediately accepted world-wide. In *A la recherche du temps perdu*, Marcel records the continuing use, elsewhere on the Continent, of Central European Time and the Eastern calendar, for example. New forms of electronic communication, however, quickly spread Greenwich's influence. *Ulysses* shows Leopold Bloom pondering in 1904 the Dublin time-signal that 'falls at Greenwich time. It's the clock is worked by an electric wire from Dunsink' (p. 137). Just as the spread of railways made national standard times essential, still faster communications, telegraphy particularly, strongly encouraged the introduction of an international, centrally controlled, world time. As Stephen Kern explains in *The Culture of Time and Space 1880–1918*, the International Conference on Time in Paris in 1912 firmly established a world-wide, homogenised time system, centred on Greenwich, and prepared for the first world time-signal to be broadcast in July 1913.

As Kern's study suggests, it was principally in the period 1880 to 1918 – or, more exactly, 1884 to 1913 – that the world moved from the charms and idiosyncrasies of local time zones to a system that ensured, globally, that time and space were rationally divided, ordered and defined. This period of radical change in the world's whole sense of time, the era of the clock's final triumph in ordering life, also coincides quite exactly with the formative years of most modernist authors. Joyce and Woolf were born in 1882, and Lawrence in 1885. For anyone growing up around the 1880s, new systems of time were an occasional subject of conversation, as Pinero's play suggests, and inevitably of general interest and influence. The passage about the Dublin time-signal shows Joyce recalling this interest when he came to write *Ulysses*: a character pondering 'time ratified by Greenwich' (p. 113) in *Mrs Dalloway* suggests the same continuing awareness in the work of Virginia Woolf.

New precisions, new powers in dividing space and time inevitably interested the modernists, but did not necessarily seem wholly agreeable, or as 'delectable' as Marcel finds the cutting of his afternoon into grooves by the 1.22 train. Some uneasiness about the new dispensations can be traced, obliquely at least, in Conrad's *The Secret Agent*, centred on Verloc's attempt to blow up Greenwich Observatory with the help of his half-idiot brother-in-law Stevie. Verloc's sinister paymaster, Vladimir, makes clear that it is the observatory's role in defining a new world order that is to be attacked. Verloc is not supposed to be 'having a go at astronomy', but is told instead that – since 'the whole civilised world has heard of Greenwich' – he is to 'go for the first meridian' (pp. 37, 39).

Conrad records basing the novel on true events, which he describes in his introductory note as the

> old story of the attempt to blow up the Greenwich Observatory; a blood-stained inanity of so fatuous a kind that it was impossible to fathom its origin by any reasonable or even unreasonable process of thought. For perverse unreason has its own logical processes. But that outrage could not be laid hold of mentally in any sort of way. (p. 9)

In one way, of course, *The Secret Agent* is itself an attempt to gain hold mentally of this outrage, and it is appropriate that in his introduction Conrad allows for a certain logic even in unreasonable processes of thought. Much of Conrad's fiction is concerned with attempts by reasonable, orderly figures to 'lay hold of' more unreasonable, aberrant or anarchic characters, or to discover what possible meaning or logic may be offered by them. With his 'belief in a few simple notions' (p. 39) – of 'fidelity to a certain standard of conduct' (p. 44) – Marlow tries to fathom Jim's 'subtle unsoundness' (p. 72) in *Lord Jim*, and Kurtz's orgiastic abandon in *Heart of Darkness*. This sort of conflict of reason with disorder, unreason or anarchy is also figuratively embodied in the repeated image in Conrad's writing – perhaps most clearly presented in *Typhoon* (1903) – of the orderly microcosm of shipboard life threatened by the vast turmoil of waters around it. Set almost exclusively in London and on dry land, *The Secret Agent* considers the same sort of conflict in political and social rather than elemental terms. Conrad shows it occurring between agents of law and order such as Chief Inspector Heat and his governmental superiors, and forces ranged against them which include strange anarchist elements such as the Professor, Ossipon and Verloc, and also – in some ways – the new, bewildering complexity and anonymity of twentieth-century city life itself. In a more abstract, figurative way, the conflict extends into the contrasts between, on the one hand, the rational, world-ordering and time-defining meridians which circle the globe, officially centred on Greenwich, and, on the other, Stevie's habitual, half-mad, drawing of

> circles, circles; innumerable circles, concentric, eccentric; a coruscating whirl of circles that by their tangled multitude of repeated

curves, uniformity of form, and confusion of intersecting lines
suggested a rendering of cosmic chaos . . .

the pastime of drawing those coruscations of innumerable circles
suggesting chaos and eternity. (pp. 45–6, 192–3)

Stevie's cosmic chaos of circles almost parodies Greenwich's drawing of world-circling, universally ordering lines around the globe. It
certainly opposes it symbolically, and it is in some ways appropriate
that Stevie is destroyed, literally blown into fragments, in the
course of an actual assault on the Observatory – which itself,
Conrad records, 'did not show as much as the faintest crack' (p. 9).
It is equally appropriate that after attacking the universal clock at
Greenwich Verloc dies (in the passage quoted towards the beginning of this chapter) to the sound of 'ticking growing fast and
furious', as if attacked in turn by an enraged clock.

Conrad's irony throughout *The Secret Agent* is directed against
Verloc and his friends, leaving little affection for him in either life
or death. Stevie, however, is a different matter. He is a centre of
sympathy and human feelings throughout the novel – an innocent,
idealistic, if barely coherent opponent of 'injustice and oppression'
(p. 18), whether exercised against poor people, cab-horses, or in
general. And it is not only chaos or anarchy that Stevie's scribblings
oppose against the universal system of Greenwich. His circles
represent chaos but also eternity; a relic in the novel of a time
without beginning, end or division; God's time beyond the systems
of man's time or Mean Time. Stevie's actual fragmentation, exactly
on the first meridian, figuratively embodies in *The Secret Agent*
some sense of the menace to humanity of the new system of
organisation and power centred on Greenwich – to borrow
Lawrence's term, 'a great and perfect system that subjected life to
pure mathematical principles'. As his introductory note suggests,
consciously or explicitly Conrad had little liking for forces attempting to destroy this system. Yet at other levels, unconscious or
figural, Conrad remains fascinated, even sympathetically interested
in such forces. He would hardly, otherwise, have spent a whole
novel trying to 'lay hold of mentally' what he took to be beyond
reason; or examined so frequently in his fiction as a whole conflicts
between reason and its opposite; or made of Stevie, the character
most given to unreasonable processes of thought, his most
sympathetic figure in *The Secret Agent*. Like Mrs Verloc after the

murder of her husband, and more secretly than overtly, Conrad's novel looks with 'inquiring mistrust' at the clock, and at the new systems of power it had recently come to exercise so widely over modern life.

Conrad's interest in Greenwich can also be related to the 'inquiring mistrust' with which, at some stages of his fiction, he looks at the new systems of power brought into existence by the spread of empire at the end of the nineteenth century. The critic Edward Said describes imperialism as 'an act of geographical violence through which virtually every space in the world is explored, charted, and finally brought under control'.[16] The Prime Meridian Conference constituted just such an act of 'geographical violence', the meridians centred on Greenwich throwing across the world a grid insidiously confirming its domination from London – significantly described in *The Secret Agent* as 'the very centre of the Empire on which the sun never sets' (p. 174).

Other modernist writers shared Conrad's scepticism about empire: more generally, as suggested earlier, they were often disposed against ordinary reason and what could be, in Conrad's terms, 'laid hold of mentally', or at any rate by means of the intellect. Such a disposition was scarcely likely to welcome Greenwich's new control and systematisation, however sensible it seemed to anyone from railway travellers to explorers or scientists. Quoted at the end of Chapter 2, Lawrence's short story 'The Fox' shows his hero finding 'a network of English hedges netting the view', leaving England 'little and tight'. After the Prime Meridian Conference, a network of imaginary lines also spread beyond England, invisibly netting and tightening control of the whole world – further encouragement to the movement undertaken by modernism, discussed in Chapter 2, from a restrictive external reality to the freer, private spaces of the mind.

The new system left time as fragmented as space, the 'age-old rhythm of life' and 'the sun's progress through the heavens' dissected as firmly as Marcel's 1.22 train cut a groove through his afternoon, and much more universally and inescapably. Such divisions – along with the 'rules, laws, and formulae' that Taylor's scientific management erected upon them – completed by the early twentieth century a historically new commodification of time. More than ever before, time could be exactly and officially counted; bought and sold for wages; used to control the minutely measured movements of workers or machines. No wonder the kind of gold chronometer used to reward Captain Brierly in *Lord Jim*, or Captain Mitchell in *Nostromo* – or a cheaper equivalent – had become by the end of the nineteenth century the standard retirement present for faithful employees. Such instruments celebrated the precision of mechanical ingenuity achieved by the machine age: they also counted the commodity most recently and successfully brought under its control. They were even emblematic of the likely nature of the employees so rewarded, reified and drained of vitality – reduced, in Gudrun's assessment to 'so many little wheels' – by prolonged servitude to the modern industrial and financial world. A further summary image of the effects of such servitude occurs not in fiction but in film – in the scene in *Modern Times* (1936) showing Charlie Chaplin so trapped by intricate cogs and wheels of industrial machinery it is as if he were being mangled by the workings of a monstrous clock.

No wonder D. H. Lawrence found that by the 1920s 'the mere suggestion' of Relativity was one which his contemporaries had all been waiting for. An age so subject to new rules, laws, formulae and precisions in its everyday life was naturally ready to 'catch fire', as he suggests, at something that offered to dissolve the whole basis on which they were made, making time once again relative, local, idiosyncratic, rather than rigidly exact. Along with much of the philosophy of the time, modernist writing shares in this sort of reaction against such new systematisation of life – in Mean Time, clocking in for factory work, and synchronised death in the trenches. It was suggested in Chapter 2 that modernism's increasing location of narrative perspective within consciousness was an attempt to sustain a full sense of individuality in a domain partly beyond the grasp of 'the modern industrial and financial world'. Modernism's disposition against time on the clock, and its structuring of narrative to reject it in favour of time in the mind, can be similarly construed – in Fredric Jameson's terms, as a further 'Utopian compensation' for 'the logic and dynamics of late capitalism'. When confronted by 'true perception of . . . extreme peril' some of Conrad's characters drop the clock 'like a hot potato'. Consciously or unconsciously aware of the increasing peril of 'great and perfect systems', of 'rules, laws, and formulae' in an increasingly complex late industrial age, modernist writing likewise drops the clock. Moving away from serial chronology, it recreates in a past recovered in memory, in streams of consciousness, or in a time in the mind otherwise established in the ways discussed earlier, some of the organic continuity that had been divided, subdivided and sliced out of contemporary public life. The 'temporal auto-nomy' Joyce creates at the end of *Ulysses*, or Proust throughout *A la recherche du temps perdu*, shows modernism freeing narrative as far as possible from time on the clock in an era – and as a *result* of an era – that had used the clock to make time less than ever free. Similarities in the work of Bergson, Joyce, Woolf and the other figures discussed above did not necessarily arise, as Wyndham Lewis claimed, from influence or mutual relations of cause and effect. They can be seen as the consequence of an age whose new, highly specific, sense of temporality inevitably created reactions of a comparable nature in a variety of areas of contemporary art and life.

## FRAGMENT OR FLOW

Modernist fiction's 'temporal autonomy', its reshaping of structures and styles, may free narrative as far as possible from time on the clock, but such freedom could neither be absolute nor altogether continuously sustained. The old clock ticked on within modernism's new chronologies. This leaves in modernist literature a conflicting, double awareness; of two separate, even antithetical views of time and life – a double awareness shared by other phases of contemporary culture, and in some ways by the age as a whole. Stephen Kern sums up dual allegiances in the period he examines when he remarks that 'the introduction of World Standard Time had an enormous impact on communication, industry, war, and the everyday life of the masses' – but also adds that a further feature of the age was

> the assault on a universal, unchanging, and irreversible public time . . . the metaphysical foundation of a broad cultural challenge to traditional notions about the nature of the world and man's place in it. (pp. 313–14)

Developments in contemporary science provide a good example of the contradictory movements Kern indicates. Einstein's ideas, denying the existence of an absolute time – 'the time of physicists' – were finally formulated in his General Theory of Relativity in 1916. The kind of thinking on which they were based, however, originated some time before, at least as early as Ernest Mach's suggestion that the idea of absolute, universal time and space, as outlined by Isaac Newton in the late seventeenth century, was no more than an 'idle metaphysical conception'.[17] Mach's claim was made in *The Science of Mechanics*, published in 1883. The period in which, as the last section discussed, international conferences were determining Prime Meridians and firmer-than-ever ways of measuring universal time – from 1884 to 1913 – therefore coincides almost exactly with the period – 1883 to 1916 – during which science and mathematics dissolved time more and more towards indefiniteness or even non-existence. *The Times* for 7 November 1919 offers a perfect indication of the simultaneous, antithetical imperatives that were a consequence in thinking about time by the end of the First World War. A column on the right of page 12 is headlined 'Revolution in Science. New Theory of the Universe. Newtonian Ideas Overthrown.' It reports the challenge to conventional ideas of space and time mounted by Einstein's theories, whose confirmation had been announced at a meeting of the Royal Society the previous evening. Meanwhile the extreme left-hand column of page 12 explains details of how the entire country is to be simultaneously immobilised – trains, factories, traffic, even pedestrians, arrested in mid-stride – at precisely 11 a.m., Greenwich Mean Time, on 11 November, at the request of the King, to mark the first anniversary of the armistice at the end of the war. Just as time measured by the clock was finally being denied any absolute significance by scientists, it was being employed more uniformly and absolutely than ever to rule ordinary life.

Other factors in contemporary life similarly confirmed contradictory aspects in contemporary thinking about time. New technologies of communication, for example, required increasing systematisation of time in public life, but also created an increasing fluidity and amorphousness for time in private experience. Telephones, telegraphy and rapid transport by road, rail or eventually air, all required firm, standardised time systems for their effective operation. By performing almost immediately tasks or journeys previously hugely prolonged they also, however, seemed to deny the power of time in life fairly completely. In *A la recherche du temps perdu*, Marcel records with admiration the 'instantaneous speed' (III, p. 96) of the telephone. He also suggests that 'distances are only the relation of space to time and vary with it' (II, p. 1029), adding that they had been 'habitually shortened by speed . . . today' (III, p. 413).[18] At many other points *A la recherche du temps perdu* further praises the ability of new forms of transport, cars in particular, to undermine and reshape the old, firm assumptions about distance, time and space. As was discussed in Chapter 1, these were changes that seemed particularly significant to the Futurist F. T. Marinetti, the basis for his conclusion in 'The Founding and Manifesto of Futurism' (1909) that 'Time and Space died yesterday . . . because we have created eternal, omnipresent speed'.

The continuing power of time, as well as of attempts to escape it, was also more evident in contemporary philosophy than Wyndham Lewis suggests in *Time and Western Man*. His distress about the apparent popularity of ideas of time's flexibility, fluidity or non-existence led him to exaggerate the uniformity of contemporary philosophic support for them. Views quite contrary to Bergson's were hardly unheard of at the time. Although some of Nietzsche's views are close to those of Bergson, there are others which are far from seeing mental processes as stream-like: at one stage of his philosophy, Nietzsche suggests, for example, that 'every successive phenomenon in consciousness is completely atomistic'. Even among philosophers more consistently close to Bergson, ideas of the fluidity of time and the incompetence of the clock figure as a matter of debate rather than certainty. One symptom of this uncertainty is the regularity with which contemporary philosophy re-examines the problems raised by Zeno of Elea. Like some of Marcel's musings in *A la recherche du temps perdu*, Zeno's paradoxes question relations of distance, time and space, and the divisibleness or continuity of each medium. The Eleatic paradoxes suggest, for example, that a flying arrow cannot really be supposed to traverse space at all, since at any single specific instant it must be imagined static, frozen in mid-flight at a single specific point. Such paradoxes are examined at one stage or another in the work of Nietzsche, Bergson, A. N. Whitehead, Bertrand Russell and Samuel Alexander as well as Wyndham Lewis himself. Naturally each of them uses Zeno to advance his own point of view: Nietzsche, for example, to emphasise further the unbridgeable gap between life and knowledge, reality and mind; Bergson to stress the obvious fallacies created by conceiving time as divisible or made up of individual parts.

Views of reality similarly divided between the frozen and the fluid, fragmentation and continuity, also preoccupied mathematics and physics in the last decades of the nineteenth century and the early part of the twentieth. Mathematical calculus, for example, depends on Zeno-like techniques of imaginatively immobilising a moving body, for purposes of computation, by subdividing the space and time through which it travels. The theoretical grounding of calculus developed rapidly in the early years of the twentieth century, as did its use. Silvanus R. Thomson's guide, *Calculus Made Easy*, for example, went through fourteen printings between 1900 and 1922 – though possibly only because ballistics and the study of the flight-path of projectiles, which calculus facilitates, was made a priority by the First World War.

In physics, by 1887 enough experimental evidence had accumulated to support James Clerk Maxwell's view of radiation as continuous and wave-like in form. From then on, however, anomalies in experiment and observation led to new theories suggesting that radiation and energy existed primarily in quanta: individual, separate units. The award of the Nobel Prize to Max Planck in 1918 confirmed general acceptance of this new idea. Writing two years later, Einstein's acquaintance Alexander Moszkowski suggested the wider relevance for the wave–particle debate within the general outlook of the age:

> The absolute continuity of events was one of the generally accepted canons of thought . . . but deep down in the consciousness of man there has always been an opposition to it, and when the French philosopher Henri Bergson set out to break up this line of continuity by metaphysical means in ascribing to human knowledge an intermittent, cinematographic character he . . . made no new 'discovery', he felt his way intuitively into a new field of knowledge and recognised that the time was ripe for the real discovery. This was actually presented to us in our day by the eminent physicist Max Planck, the winner of the Nobel Prize for Physics in 1919, in the form of his 'Quantum Theory' . . . a discontinuous, intermittent sequence, an atomistic structure, was proved by means of the weapons of exact science, to be true of energies which, according to

current belief, were expected to be radiated regularly and connectedly. This was probably not a case of the accidental coincidence of a new philosophical view with the results of reasoning from physical grounds, but a demand of time, exacting that the claims of a new principle of thought be recognised. (pp. 91–2)[19]

Moszkowski usefully confirms how widely the age demanded consideration of conflicts between continuity and intermittency, though any correlation between Bergson and Planck is of a different form from the one he suggests. Moszkowski partly misread Bergson, who did not 'break up the line of continuity', or 'the absolute continuity of events', by metaphysical or any other means. On the contrary he thoroughly supported the idea of continuity, but complained that the nature of knowledge left little opportunity for its proper appreciation. Typical of his philosophy, Bergson's view of knowledge finds the intellect impeding rather than assisting true contact with experience. In *Creative Evolution* (*L'Evolution Créatrice*, 1907), he warns that

> instead of attaching ourselves to the inner becoming of things . . . we take snapshots, as it were of the passing reality . . . perception, intellection, language . . . set going a kind of cinematograph inside us . . . the *mechanism of our ordinary knowledge is of a cinematographic kind.* (pp. 322–3)

Knowledge, for Bergson, distorts the continuous evolution of life, freezing it into static, conveniently graspable units.

Bergson explains at some length in *Creative Evolution* how the cinematograph creates an impression of continuous movement out of what is actually a series of static images. This explanation was probably necessary not only for philosophic purposes, but on account of the novelty and possible unfamiliarity of the apparatus he uses for his metaphor. The cinematograph had only recently reached a final, fully effective stage in its development. This development can be seen as beginning in the 1870s, when Eadweard Muybridge recorded multiple pictures of a galloping horse, which triggered each of a series of cameras in its passing. In the 1880s, E. J. Marey's 'chronophotography' used rapidly successive exposures to record multiple images, expressive of movement. By the later nineteenth century popular entertainments extended such techniques: 'bioscopes', for example, or the 'Mutoscope pictures . . . for men only. Peeping Tom' that Bloom remembers in *Ulysses*

(p. 301). These used a series of photographs falling rapidly on top of each other to create the impression of motion out of still pictures. But it was only with the work of the Lumière brothers in 1896 that the cinematograph was established in the form Bergson refers to – hardly long enough before his lectures on 'the mechanics of ordinary knowledge', at the Collège de France in 1902, for him to be sure his audience would be quite familiar with the new invention.

Appearing simultaneously but independently in France and America, this new invention might itself be seen as a further manifestation of 'the demands of the time'. An age so divided between looking upon reality as fragmentary or as continuous naturally welcomed, perhaps even inspired, a technology able to create the impression of continuity and movement out of actually separate, individual images. At any rate, the cinematograph and the mechanics of its operation quickly caught the imagination of artists and writers, though their interest was sometimes tempered with suspicion. The Italian Futurists were generally excited by the new technologies, but one of their number, Anton Bragaglia, complained rather like Bergson that

> cinematography . . . merely reconstructs fragments of reality, already coldly broken up, in the same way as the hand of a chronometer deals with time even though this flows in a continuous and constant stream.

Bragaglia went on to work out a new technique of his own, 'Photodynamism': a sort of continuous time exposure creating a blurred image suggestive of movement, rather than a series of static ones. Bragaglia explains that

> chronophotography could be compared with a clock on the face of which only the quarter-hours are marked, cinematography to one on which the minutes too are indicated, and Photodynamism to a third on which are marked not only the seconds, but also the *intermovemental* fractions existing in the passages between seconds.[20]

Other Futurists, however, were more content to exploit the tactics of chronophotography or cinematography. In paintings such as 'Dynamism of a Dog on a Leash' (1912) or 'Little Girl Running on a Balcony' (1912), for example, Giacomo Balla follows Marey's work, using multiple, superimposed images to suggest the dynamics of a moving object.

Among contemporary novelists, Proust shows himself to be as interested as Bergson in the mechanics and metaphoric potential of cinematography and the earlier stages of its technical development. Discussing in the opening section of *A la recherche du temps perdu* the overall effect of 'shifting gusts of memory', Marcel suggests that he

> did not distinguish the various suppositions of which it was composed any more than, when we watch a horse running, we isolate the successive positions of its body as they appear upon a bioscope. (I, p. 7)

Later Proust investigates further a fundamentally fragmentary quality underlying the apparent continuity of life and experience. Though Marcel suggests that 'Nothing is further from what we have really perceived than the vision that the cinematograph presents' (III, p. 917), after the death of his lover Albertine he recalls her in cinematographic, almost chronophotographic terms:

> In order to enter into us, another person must first have assumed the form, have adapted himself to the framework of time; appearing to us only in a succession of momentary flashes, he has never been able to reveal to us more than one aspect of himself at a time, to present us with more than a single photograph of himself. A great weakness no doubt for a person, to consist merely of a collection of moments ... he is a product of memory ... this moment which it has recorded endures still, lives still, and with it the person whose form is outlined in it. And moreover, this disintegration does not only make the dead one live, it multiplies him or her. In order to be consoled I would have to forget, not one, but innumerable Albertines ...
>
> It was not Albertine alone who was a succession of moments, it was also myself ... I was not one man only, but as it were the march-past of a composite army. (III, pp. 487, 499)

Marcel outlines a similar view of the emotions in general:

> What we suppose to be our love or our jealousy is never a single, continuous and indivisible passion. It is composed of an infinity of successive loves, of different jealousies, each of which is ephemeral, although by their uninterrupted multiplicity they give us the impression of continuity, the illusion of unity. (I, p. 404)

The mechanics of cinematography, of multiplicity giving the impression of continuity, also provide a summary image for Wyndham Lewis's views of time and reality. In *Time and Western Man* he discusses, as a symptom of contemporary thinking about time, the idea of a

> domestic cinematograph . . . The mechanical photographic reality . . . somewhat that sense of things laid out side by side, of the unreality of time, and yet of its paramount importance. (p. 266)

Lewis was impressed by the Italian Futurists at an early stage of his career and was obviously, as *Time and Western Man* lengthily explains, generally disposed against any idea of time as fluidly continuous. His own early fiction accordingly creates an innovative prose style which does lay things out side by side, creating a series of static fragments that diminish any sense of time's flowing. This is immediately apparent in the striking opening paragraphs of Lewis's first published novel, *Tarr* (1918):

> Paris hints of sacrifice.=But here we deal with that large dusty facet known to indulgent and congruous kind . . .
> Inconceivably generous and naïve faces haunt the Knackfus Quarter.=We are not however in a Selim or Vitagraph camp (though 'guns' tap rhythmically the buttocks).=Art is being studied.=Art is the smell of oil paint, Henri Murger's 'Vie de Bohème,' corduroy trousers, the operatic Italian model. But the poetry, above all, of linseed oil and turpentine.
> The Knackfus Quarter is given up to Art.= Letters and other things are round the corner.=Its rent is half paid by America.[21]

Inventing the curious, emphatic punctuation mark '.=', Lewis sharply separates his sentences, framing them as discrete, autonomous units. Such devices do in a way make *Tarr* into a 'domestic cinematograph' of the kind Lewis later describes in *Time and Western Man*. Lewis probably began writing *Tarr* as early as 1909, and – like Bergson in 1902 – he might well have had the mechanics of the recently invented cinematograph in mind. References in these cryptic opening paragraphs to Selim and Vitagraph help suggest this – Selig and Vitagraph were early, pioneering cinema production companies. At any rate, consistently with his antipathies to the 'time-school' expressed in *Time and Western Man*, and to Joyce as a particular exemplar of it, Lewis's early writing moves as far as possible from any idea of time as stream-like. So strangely and heavily punctuated, the prose of *Tarr* offers a complete contrast to the unpunctuated stream of Molly's soliloquy at the end of *Ulysses*. These opening paragraphs from *Tarr*, and the closing chapter of *Ulysses*, stand at opposite ends of the spectrum of new prose styles that modernism developed in its reflection of different conclusions about the divisibility or the stream-like continuity of time.

Not all of *Ulysses*, of course, is written in the style of Molly's soliloquy. Much as this section shows time as a stream – even, in the end, time transcended or time denied – the clock and the divisions of its hours by no means disappear from the novel as a whole. In the early pages of *Ulysses*,

> the bells of George's church . . . tolled the hour: loud dark iron.
>
> > *Heigho! Heigho!*
> > *Heigho! Heigho!*
> > *Heigho! Heigho!* (p. 57)

and towards the end of the novel the sound recurs:

> the sound of the peal of the hour of the night by the chime of the bells in the church of Saint George . . . (p. 578)

Between these two references to the bells, across the 'flowing . . . stream of life' (p. 126), there often falls the iron voice of the clock. Even Molly keeps consulting the 'unearthly hour' (p. 642) as she lies awake at the end. In this way, *Ulysses* is not just a stream of consciousness, but a 'dance of the hours . . . morning hours, noon, then evening coming on, then night hours' (p. 57). Other aspects of the novel add to a sense of discontinuity as much as of fluidity. Joyce's plans for the novel not only indicate a separate hour of the day for each chapter: they also – among many other distinguishing aspects – often specify a different style. Such stylistic differences ensure that, however stream-like individual sections of *Ulysses* seem, the novel overall reads very discontinuously. Discussing Joyce's work, the critic Hugh Kenner rightly emphasises 'the pains he takes to impede the notion of linear narrative: *Ulysses* is as discontinuous a work as its author can manage'.[22] Passing between Chapters 13, 'Nausicaa', and 14, 'Oxen of the Sun', for example, is almost like passing between novels by different writers, and some of the other styles used in individual chapters are equally sharply contrasted. Even the transcription of consciousness within them is not always as completely stream-like as in the final chapter.

Much of Bloom's thought is in the form of telegrammatic, fragmentary sentences – 'Cup of tea soon. Good. Mouth dry.' (p. 45) – reflecting as much an atomistic as a fluid view of the movement of consciousness. Such sections, and the radical shifts in style (further discussed in Chapter 4), create in *Ulysses* as much a sense of fractured multifacetedness as of seamless, homogeneous flow.

Other modernist fiction exhibits a similar duality of allegiance. Dorothy Richardson's narrative in *Pilgrimage* (1915–67), for example, however fluently it moves into the unfolding thoughts of Miriam Henderson, also remains at times sharply fractured. Large gaps in the text's layout on the page are used to indicate transitions of time or locale, and are all the more marked since conventional exposition – explaining changes of time or place between different scenes, or offering brief summaries of intervening events – is generally missing from *Pilgrimage*. Chapter divisions occur even more arbitrarily in Proust, who passes over natural breaks in his story in favour of extending chapters at great length, then ending them more or less in the middle of episodes.

Division and continuity likewise compete in Virginia Woolf's construction of *The Waves* (1931), which alternates between characters' freely associative thoughts or memories and sections which intrude upon them to reflect the passage of time throughout a single day in the natural world. Such distinctions between fluidity and division, atom and flux, preoccupy Woolf throughout her writing. She asks in her diary:

> is life very solid or shifting? I am haunted by the two contradictions. This has gone on for ever; will last for ever; goes down to the bottom of the world – this moment I stand on. Also it is transitory, flying, diaphanous. I shall pass like a cloud on the waves. Perhaps it may be that though we change, one flying after another, so quick, so quick, yet we are somehow successive and continuous we human beings. (*A Writer's Diary*, p. 140)

Woolf's 'Modern Fiction' essay likewise considers relations between the successive and the continuous – between 'myriad impressions . . . the incessant shower of innumerable atoms' and the 'luminous halo' into which they seem to form themselves. In *To the Lighthouse*, Mrs Ramsay ponders the 'little separate incidents which one lived one by one' and which – almost in a wave–particle duality of her own – she then thinks of as becoming 'curled and whole like a wave' (p. 55). *To the Lighthouse* further contrasts the intuitive wholeness of Mrs Ramsay's mind with the 'little separate incidents' of her husband's. Mr Ramsay creates a whole alphabet of separate philosophical concepts, running from A to Z, or sometimes A to Q – another device of 'the masculine intelligence, which ran up and down, crossed this way and that, like iron girders spanning the swaying fabric' (p. 122). Across the 'swaying fabric' of the novel itself, the 'eternal passing and flowing' (p. 183) of its characters' thoughts and memories, there falls both the beam of the lighthouse, with its clock-like rhythm of recurrence, and the shadow of time and history, intruding in the middle section of the novel, 'Time Passes', to shatter the hopes and trouble the memories outlined in the first and third parts.

Time's passage intrudes similarly divisively and persistently into *Mrs Dalloway*. The 'irrevocable . . . leaden circles' (p. 6) of Big Ben's chimes fall across the novel's fabric of thoughts as firmly as the 'loud dark iron' of the clock in *Ulysses*. *Mrs Dalloway* frequently shows how much harder than at present (even in an age of beeping digital watches) time's passage must have been to ignore in the early years of the twentieth century, when so many clocks, public or private, routinely chimed. 'Flooding' characters' minds, sometimes between single lines of conversation, the deafening intrusion of Big Ben's chime is backed up by an extraordinary number of other vociferous clocks in *Mrs Dalloway*, forcing characters to consider, for example, how

> Shredding and slicing, dividing and subdividing, the clocks of Harley Street nibbled at the June day, counselled submission, upheld authority, and pointed out in chorus the supreme advantages of a sense of proportion, until the mound of time was so far diminished that a commercial clock, suspended above a shop in Oxford Street, announced genially and fraternally, as if it were a pleasure to Messrs Rigby and Lowndes to give the information gratis, that it was half-past one.
>
> Looking up, it appeared that each letter of their names stood for one of the hours; subconsciously one was grateful to Rigby and Lowndes for giving one time ratified by Greenwich; and this gratitude . . . naturally took the form later of buying off Rigby and Lowndes socks or shoes. (pp. 113–14)

Woolf's view of 'the clocks of Harley Street' is in several ways exemplary – first of all of the new sense, in the early twentieth century, of a 'time ratified by Greenwich' and also closely connected with commerce: of time commodified and turned into saleable socks and shoes, in fact. The passage is also typical of Bergson's – or others' – views of time in the mind as something whole or continuous; time as a 'mound', but one which is shredded and divided up by time on the clock. Such distinctions underlie much of Woolf's view of time in the rest of her writing. They also appear, for example, in the passage from *Orlando* quoted at the start of this chapter, or in Bernard's conclusion in *The Waves* that, in a kind of separate world, there is an 'unlimited time of the mind, which stretches in a flash from Shakespeare to ourselves'. He adds, however, that when 'suddenly one hears a clock tick. We who had been immersed in this world became aware of another. It is painful' (p. 235).

Such 'pain', such tension between 'worlds' separated by different concepts of time, appears not only in Woolf's writing, and in modernist fiction generally, but also in modernist poetry. Awareness of distinct worlds, or ways of seeing the world, are highlighted and contrasted with particular clarity in T. S. Eliot's 'Rhapsody on a Windy Night'. In passing a succession of bright streetlamps, the speaker establishes a regular, drum-like rhythm, which includes precise recording of the hour of the night, and the voice of the lamp itself, often directing attention to the more reified, mechanical aspects of humanity depicted in the poem. Between the lamps, darker 'reaches of the street' are infused with the subtler illumination of the moon, helping to 'dissolve . . . clear relations . . . divisions and precisions', partly by stirring the memory and the subconscious into throwing up throngs of imaginative images. In Chapter 2, it was suggested that 'Rhapsody on a Windy Night' exemplifies modernist anxieties about reification: the poem's different areas, different illuminations and different priorities are also paradigmatic of other – related – tensions and antitheses central to art and literature in the early twentieth century. On the one hand there is precise, orderly, proportioned, intellectual division and categorisation of life; life viewed as a 'series of gig-lamps' – or streetlamps – 'symmetrically arranged'. On the other hand there is a preference for darker, less measured entry into memory, intuition, movement away from exactness – measured by the clock or otherwise – and even away from the waking consciousness towards deeper, more inward reaches of the mind.

Though Wyndham Lewis and other commentators, at the time and since, rightly see modernism principally favouring the latter set of priorities, the other side could not be and never was ignored. 'Rhapsody on a Windy Night' wholly favours neither set of the possibilities it outlines, but simply presents and contrasts them. Even writers apparently following Bergson in favouring 'time in the mind' could not ignore 'time on the clock', and indeed became – like Woolf in *Mrs Dalloway* – all the more painfully aware of it because of their own antithetical disposition. However much 'Zeit's sumonserving' (p. 78), as Joyce calls it in *Finnegans Wake*, might have been disliked, especially now that it was equipped with all the authority of Mean Time and World Standard Time, it remained stubbornly a part of life. Even while complaining in *Women in Love* about 'the terrible bondage of this tick-tack of time . . . oh God . . . too awful to contemplate', Gudrun acknowledges that 'there was no escape from it, no escape' (p. 522). Though Quentin Compson twists off the hands of his watch in *The Sound and the Fury*, 'the watch ticked on . . . the blank dial with little wheels clicking and clicking behind it' (p. 76).

Critics have long pointed to both the stream of consciousness and also, on the other hand, the representation, even celebration, of a fragmentary, disjointed quality in modern life as characteristic of modernism's innovatory views of the world. Though this seems contradictory, the contradiction is not in the criticism but in the phenomenon itself. Michael Levenson talks of 'the modernist urge towards dualistic opposition and radical polarities' (p. ix): one of the best examples of this is in modernism's contrasts or reconciliations between fragment and flow, between atom and wave, between the divisions of the clock and the continuity of consciousness. Such antitheses and tensions run through and structure not only modernist fiction, but with unusual intensity the whole age in which it was written, evident in it from Bergson to Bloom, as Wyndham Lewis might have said, and from quantum theory to cinematograph. Another factor contributed to them, not so much in daily life and the measurement of its passage, but in the whole sense of the evolution of history itself. That factor was the age's greatest crisis, the First World War.

## CRACKS AND CHASMS: TIME AND THE WESTERN FRONT

The effects of the war on contemporary life and writing were, obviously, immense and inescapable. J. B. Priestley, for example, himself a combatant in the trenches, later remarked,

> No intelligent and sensitive European – and writers can hardly succeed without intelligence and sensitivity – could escape the terrible impact of these four years . . . the war was there, all around them. (p. 322)

Destruction, loss and sorrow seemed to have entered the world on a scale unknown before. Sigmund Freud, who worked out his principle of *thanatos*, the death wish, during the war, believed that his contemporaries might never again see a joyous world. He even thought it possible that the human race might be replaced by a more tractable species – an idea that 'man is a mistake, he must go' which D. H. Lawrence also ponders in *Women in Love* (p. 142), written at the time of the war. Ironically, the war actually helped the dissemination of Freud's ideas, because of their usefulness in the treatment of its shell-shocked victims.

One such victim, Septimus Warren Smith in *Mrs Dalloway*, functions partly as a symbol of a whole society, non-combatants included, in a state of shock not readily curable by any treatment, even after the war has been over for some time. The novel remarks of Septimus's state:

> such things happen to everyone. Everyone has friends who were killed in the War . . .
>
> this late age of world's experience had bred in them all, all men and women, a well of tears. (pp. 74, 12)

Though never directly mentioned, this late experience is in a way even more strongly marked in Woolf's *Jacob's Room* (1922), from the moment the protagonist's name, Jacob Flanders, begins to resound in the novel its anticipatory echo of the geography of the trenches. Named as a figure of doom, Jacob is destined to leave behind the empty room towards which the desires and memories of the novel are fruitlessly directed. The tormenting emotional vacuum left among those who loved him typifies an experience of the 1920s generally; of hollow men and women surviving in a sad decade. D. H. Lawrence also points out that the deep emotional effects of the war lasted long after its actual conclusion. In *Lady Chatterley's Lover* (1928) he talks of

> the bruise of the war . . . creating the great ache of unrest, and stupor
> of discontent. The bruise was deep, deep, deep . . . the bruise of the
> false inhuman war. It would take many years for the living blood of
> the generations to dissolve the vast black clot of bruised blood, deep
> inside their souls and bodies. (p. 52)

Fiction always offers an opportunity to recreate or inhabit the past imaginatively, and is often strongly shaped by nostalgia. Largely because of the war, however, memory and nostalgia were more than usually important for the modernists. The ache of unrest in the years after 1914 offered a particular reason to let down ropes of memory into orderly earlier times, untroubled by the explosions of contemporary history. It was suggested in Chapter 2 that the uncongenial public world of the 1920s encouraged withdrawal into the private domain of the individual mind. Withdrawal into memory existed concurrently with this urge. Writers in the 1920s had every reason to look at the war with what Ford Madox Ford might have described as a wish to 'cut it out and join time up' – to find ways of connecting the present, through memory, with the Edwardian period before the war, one which offered the kind of coherence and security contemporary public life lacked. When considered in retrospect during the 1920s, or indeed many later phases of the twentieth century, the pre-war years seemed, or could be made to seem, an especially splendid age – even the years after 1910, when Virginia Woolf thought 'human character changed'. Richard Aldington writes in *Death of a Hero* (1929) of 'the feeling of tranquil security which existed, the almost smug optimism of our lives' (p. 199) at this time. In his *Letter to Mrs. Virginia Woolf* (1932), Peter Quennell invites his readers to remember

> the placid pre-war universe – how tranquil and how olympian it must
> have been! Was the pound really worth twenty shillings, and were
> there parties every night and hansom cabs? . . . then the War to End
> Wars and so good-bye. (p. 17)

Confronted by an imminent second war in *Coming up for Air* (1939), George Orwell looks back all the more fondly on the years before the first:

> 'before the war' ? I *am* sentimental about it . . . It's quite true that if

you look back on any special period of time you tend to remember the pleasant bits . . . But it's also true that people then had something that we haven't got now.

What? . . . It isn't that life was softer then than now. Actually it was harsher. People on the whole worked harder, lived less comfortably, and died more painfully. The farm hands worked frightful hours for fourteen shillings a week and ended up as worn-out cripples with a five-shilling old age pension . . . And yet what was it that people had in those days? A feeling of security, even when they weren't secure. More exactly, it was a feeling of continuity . . . things would go on as they'd known them . . . a settled period, a period when civilization seems to stand on its four legs like an elephant . . . their way of life would continue . . . they thought it was eternity. (pp. 106–9)

Sentimentally or otherwise, modernism looks back to recover in fiction what has vanished in fact. In *Ulysses*, written between 1914 and 1922, Joyce meticulously re-creates the life and geography of Dublin in 1904, partly destroyed in the Easter Rising of 1916. Woolf, in the first section of *To the Lighthouse*, revisits one of the tranquil summer afternoons of the 'placid pre-war universe'. Ford Madox Ford, in the opening of *Parade's End*, looks back ironically to the belief that 'a war is impossible' (p. 20), and regretfully to the 'perfectly appointed . . . luxuriant, regulated . . . admirable' pre-war world (p. 3). Its decay and loss is charted in the thousand pages that follow. As his title *A la recherche du temps perdu* ('In Search of Lost Time') emphasises, Proust seeks in memory experiences now otherwise lost. The landscape of his childhood so fondly and frequently recalled by Marcel has in reality been utterly obliterated by the battles of the First World War. As a letter from Gilberte informs him, it is now a

ravaged countryside, where vast battles are fought to gain possession of some path, some slope which you once loved . . . they have become for ever a part of history . . . The battle of Méséglise lasted for more than eight months; the Germans lost in it more than six hundred thousand men. (III, p. 778)

In the process of writing the novel, Proust changed the location of *A la recherche du temps perdu*, setting its childhood scenes in what became the battlefields of the First World War in order to emphasise how completely the times recalled in its early stages had vanished. Rather like his contemporary Alain-Fournier, in *The*

*Lost Domain* (*Le Grand Meaulnes*, 1913), Proust shows that in the French context as much as the British, the years before the war seemed a *belle époque*, of alluring tranquillity, but a lost domain only art or memory could re-enter. For Proust, the years before the war seemed like an

> epoch from which it is now the convention to say that we are separated by centuries – for the philosophers of the war have spread the doctrine that all links with the past are broken. (III, p. 811)

Richard Aldington likewise suggests that 'pre-war seems like pre-history' (p. 199).

Stephen Kern confirms how far this sense of disjuncture from the lost times of the past influenced the post-war period. He remarks that 'the restlessness . . . of the "lost generation" ' in the 1920s resulted from a desire for *temps perdu* and from a frustrated wish for 'reintegration in the flow of time' (p. 298). As Kern suggests, the ache of unrest in the 1920s arose not simply from a vain, nostalgic wish somehow to re-enter earlier, happier times, but from an uneasiness with the sense of time itself. The war's enormous violence not only swept away a style of life, a *belle époque*: it extinguished a form of thinking, a sense of integration in the flow of time. It destroyed a 'feeling of continuity' which Orwell particularly ascribes to the Edwardian age, but which had actually existed, influentially, for much longer. A sense of some security within history, and a belief in the attractive qualities of the future to which it probably led, had sustained a good deal of thinking – and fiction – at least since the later part of the Victorian period. Rapid developments in science and technology, as well as a long period of relative peace and advancing imperial power for Britain, sometimes allowed a faith in material progress to replace declining religious faith in the later nineteenth century. Some of the thinkers who most seriously challenged religious belief still held strongly to ideas of a progress logically and naturally, if not divinely, ordained. Charles Darwin, for example, outlined processes of natural selection which he saw leading step by step, over millennia, to the development of creatures best adjusted to their environment and fittest for survival in it.

Victorian fiction, if not exactly demonstrating the 'survival of the fittest',[23] often follows characters who progress through time to realise their own potential, and fit in with society, as fully as possible. This process is central to the *Bildungsroman* form, following individual life sequentially through its day-by-day, year-by-year development. Within and beyond the *Bildungsroman* form, as Virginia Woolf remarks, 'peace and prosperity were influences that gave the nineteenth-century writers a family likeness'.[24] As she goes on to suggest, part of this likeness was their shared assumption of the meaningfulness of history, public or personal; of the coherence of development through time. The survival of this assumption into the early years of the twentieth century is suggested, for example, by H. G. Wells (a firm believer in utopian progress through technology) choosing for his 1910 novel the title *The History of Mr Polly*. Relative stability in political history encourages faith in the possibility of stability in private life, and in fiction. In what Orwell calls 'a settled period, when civilization stands on its four legs like an elephant', straightforward progress in time naturally offers a structuring basis for fiction. Victorian or Edwardian novels certainly show moral, emotional or other problems disturbing private or social life, but they also, almost always, offer and fulfil the promise that these problems would be ordered and resolved – coherently, if not necessarily happily – in the end.

The First World War changed all that. After its outbreak H. G. Wells abandoned his utopianism and turned to writing his history of the world, as if attempting to re-create some order for public events, at least in a text, or to find in the past some explanation of how present hopes could have been so dashed. The philosophies of time that Wyndham Lewis saw proliferating in the 1920s, and added to in his own work, may have resulted from a comparable response to the shock of the war. Such a radical break in the life of Western man encouraged reconsideration of what principles of evolution, or of coherent life in time, if any, could be thought to remain valid. Oswald Spengler's work is symptomatic of this new phase of uncertainty. His huge study *The Decline of the West* (*Der Untergang des Abendlandes*, 1918–22) establishes from its title onwards a flat contradiction to any surviving faith in progress. Within a day of the war's outbreak Henry James saw how completely it had invalidated such faiths. In a letter of 5 August 1914, he remarks of the war that

> the plunge of civilisation into this abyss of blood and darkness . . . is
> a thing that so gives away the whole long age during which we have

supposed the world to be, with whatever abatement, gradually bettering.

In a later letter, James writes of the war's 'violence of rupture with the past', adding 'what a breach must it all not make with the course of history'. The war not only destroyed ideas of progress, but almost the idea of history itself, certainly as a coherent 'course'. As early as September 1914, in the war's second month, Wyndham Lewis remarked that 'we have got clean out of history . . . we are not to-day living in history'.[25] In his study *The Great War and Modern Memory* (1979), the critic Paul Fussell likewise suggests that 1914 may have been virtually the last moment when events could be

> conceived as taking place within a seamless, purposeful 'history' involving a coherent stream of time running from past through present to future. (p. 21)

Rupturing the sense of the stream of time in this way, the First World War added very powerfully to tendencies, discussed in the last section, to conceive time as divided or fractured rather than – or sometimes as well as – seamlessly flowing. The war sliced across time and history as sharply, as absolutely, as its trenches cut across space. It is repeatedly figured in this divisive, cutting role in modernist fiction. D. H. Lawrence opens *Lady Chatterley's Lover* by remarking that 'The cataclysm has happened . . . there is now no smooth road into the future' (p. 5). Using almost the same image, Virginia Woolf remarks that in 1914, 'Suddenly, like a chasm in a smooth road, the war came' and 'cut into' contemporary lives.[26] In *Parade's End*, Ford Madox Ford similarly describes the war as a 'crack across the table of History' (p. 510). Like Proust, in his First World War story *All Our Yesterdays* (1930) H. M. Tomlinson writes of looking back into a lost pre-war landscape and finding 'a summer dubious with its immemorial aspect of continuity, yet suggesting bleakly a subtle yet disastrous interruption in the life of the earth'.[27] In *Death of a Hero*, Richard Aldington describes trench combat as a 'timeless confusion' that 'made a cut in . . . life and personality' (p. 323). He adds that in general 'adult lives were cut sharply into three sections – pre-war, war, and post-war' (p. 199).

This cutting of life into three sections is also strongly reflected in

*To the Lighthouse* as a feature of the novel's structure. The novel begins on a summer's day with a strong aspect of continuity, an almost untroubled expectation of continuing holiday time. Woolf moves on to show in the short, sharp middle section the disastrous interruption that cuts into or destroys altogether the lives of Mrs Ramsay and several of the figures central to the first part. *To the Lighthouse* ends with a third section in which there sometimes seems little left except a looking back on lost time, to the sound of forlorn voices crying 'Mrs Ramsay! Mrs Ramsay!' (p. 229) across the 'field of death' (p. 206) created by the war. The middle section is the sharpest, saddest indication in modernist fiction of the effects of a time emphatically not in the mind, but part of a world in which, as was suggested in Chapter 2, the mind can find no reflection, echo or sympathy for itself in a landscape irretrievably stained and broken by the war. Human disasters scarcely impinge on such a world: like his mother's, Andrew Ramsay's death merits only a casual parenthesis:

> [A shell exploded. Twenty or thirty young men were blown up in France, among them Andrew Ramsay, whose death, mercifully, was instantaneous.] (p. 152)

Laying such cracks and chasms across the previously 'smooth road' of history, the war also dictates the structure and sentiments of other modernist novels, though in ways sometimes less immediately visible than in *To the Lighthouse*. Some of them can be illustrated by looking in detail at D. H. Lawrence's project *The Sisters*. In the course of his writing during the First World War, Lawrence decided to split this long projected novel into two separate works, *The Rainbow* (1915) and *Women in Love*, eventually published in 1921. Differences in tone, structure and vision between the two finished novels are worth examining closely: they not only exemplify the effects of the war, but further illustrate some of the pressures which dictated modernism's departures from Victorian fiction, and its mood in general.

The opening of *The Rainbow* shows the steady, almost timeless situation of the Brangwen family, as much adapted to the cyclic life of t ie seasons as to forward progress in time or history:

> The Brangwens had lived for generations on the Marsh Farm . . . they felt the rush of the sap in spring, they knew the wave which cannot halt, but every year throws forward the seed to begetting,

and, falling back, leaves the young-born on the earth. They knew the intercourse between heaven and earth, sunshine drawn into the breast and bowels, the rain sucked up in the daytime, nakedness that comes under the wind in autumn, showing the birds' nests no longer worth hiding. Their life and interrelations were such; feeling the pulse and body of the soil. (pp. 7–8)

In examining 'Forms of Time and Chronotope in the Novel', Mikhail Bakhtin sums up the characteristics of this 'agricultural stage in the development of human society'. He considers that, at this stage,

Time is collective, that is, it is differentiated and measured only by the events of *collective* life . . .

Human life and nature are perceived in the same categories. The seasons of the year, ages, nights and days (and their subcategories), copulation (marriage), pregnancy, ripening, old age and death: all these categorical images serve equally well to plot the course of an individual life and the life of nature (in its agricultural aspect) . . . Time here is sunk deeply in the earth, implanted in it and ripening in it. Time in its course binds together the earth and the labouring hand of man . . .

The mark of cyclicity, and consequently of cyclical repetitiveness, is imprinted on all events occurring in this type of time. Time's forward impulse is limited by the cycle. (pp. 206, 208, 210)[28]

This 'immanent unity' (p. 217) of individual life, society and nature does not last, however. 'The time of personal, everyday family occasions' becomes

individualized and separated out from the time of the collective historical life of the social whole, at a time when there emerged one scale for measuring the events of a *personal* life and another for measuring the events of *history*. (p. 208)

*The Rainbow* charts this process of gradual fragmentation in the organic, agricultural community; the gradual emergence of a significance and a scale of events oriented around an individual who is increasingly separated from nature and from the full unity of a society. The apparently immutable, integral continuity of the Brangwens' life – an immemorial quality emphasised, early in *The*

*Rainbow*, by the biblical vocabulary and rhythms of Lawrence's prose – is first of all ruptured by the effects of the Industrial Revolution:

> About 1840, a canal was constructed across the meadows of the Marsh Farm, connecting the newly-opened collieries of the Erewash Valley. A high embankment travelled along the fields to carry the canal . . .
>
> Then, a short time afterwards, a colliery was sunk on the other side of the canal, and in a while the Midland Railway came down the valley . . .
>
> The Brangwens were astonished by all this commotion around them. The building of a canal across their land made them strangers in their own place, this raw bank of earth shutting them off disconcerted them. As they worked in the fields, from beyond the now familiar embankment came the rhythmic run of the winding engines . . . Then the shrill whistle of the trains re-echoed through the heart, with fearsome pleasure, announcing the far-off come near and imminent . . .
>
> The farmers of the land met the blackened colliers trooping from the pit-mouth. As they gathered the harvest, the west wind brought a faint, sulphurous smell of pit-refuse burning. As they pulled the turnips in November, the sharp clink-clink-clink-clink-clink of empty trucks shunting on the line, vibrated in their hearts with the fact of other activity going on beyond them. (pp. 11–13)

Throughout the novel, the canal is called, appropriately, 'the Cut'. The canal cuts off the Brangwens, in space, from a part of their land: along with the other effects of the Industrial Revolution and the encroaching machine age, it also cuts them off in time, separating them from the older, settled continuities of life in nature. The Cut destroys one of the last survivors from this old life, Tom Brangwen, who drowns when it overflows and floods the land. The new rhythms of the engine, the shriek of whistles 'announcing the far-off come near and imminent', force the other Brangwens to look beyond their old life at a world of history now developing beyond the reach of their old existence. Change increasingly impinges upon their lives. Each succeeding generation moves on into new sets of circumstances, rather than – in the old, natural, cyclic rhythm – only reliving the experience of its predecessors.

Some possibilities nevertheless remain for seeing human life and nature whole and unified, and for remaining in touch with the old, cyclic movement of time – 'still it was there, even if it were faint and inadequate. The cycle of creation still wheeled in the Church year' (p. 280). The year still moves through its seasons, and its religious festivals, Christmas and Easter, with all the strange awe and wonder that Lawrence shows surrounding them. Lawrence also shows traces of a cyclic movement within human affairs, of recurrence and continuity despite change. Portraying three genera- tions of Brangwens, *The Rainbow* shows each encountering new challenges, but within the same basic, recurrent pattern of marriage and procreation, and often with substantial repetition of the moods and attitudes associated with them.

Yet these patterns, too, grow insecure and unsettled in the end. The last of the Brangwens Lawrence considers, Ursula, remains – at least at the end of *The Rainbow* – outside the established cycles. The concluding phase of the novel finds her uncertain and alone, her relationship with a lover having ended unfulfilled, with a miscarriage after it has been broken off. She experiences the painful necessity of forging an individual existence, bereft of shared values and a sustaining community. At the moment of her deepest depression, 'in an ache of utter weariness', she remarks,

> I have no father nor mother nor lover, I have no allocated place in the world of things, I do not belong to Beldover, nor to Nottingham, nor to England, nor to this world, they none of them exist, I am trammeled and entangled in them, but they are all unreal. (p. 493)

Unlike members of any earlier generation in *The Rainbow*, Ursula is eventually lost, alone and unsure of anything except her own subjective sensations. Her experience at this point provides a final term in Lawrence's tracing, from around 1840 to the early years of the twentieth century, a process of ejection from a secure society and a 'collective historical life'. Ursula's life and situation at this point share many of the stresses characteristically examined in modernist and later twentieth-century fiction, following the lives of isolated, alienated protagonists; outsiders in a confusing world; individuals lonely and anonymous even in huge, crowded cities.

Ursula's weariness, however, does not quite end the novel. Instead, at the moment of her maximum loneliness and distress, Lawrence once again re-establishes a way of finding unity between the individual, nature and society. Once again, human life and nature are 'perceived in the same category' – at least at a level of vision and hope, if not in the raw real world which Ursula finds so uncomfortable:

> And again, to her feverish brain, came the vivid reality of acorns in February lying on the floor of a wood with their shells burst and discarded and the kernel issued naked to put itself forth. She was the naked, clear kernel thrusting forth the clear, powerful shoot, and the world was a bygone winter, discarded . . . whilst the kernel was free and naked and striving to take new root, to create a new knowledge of Eternity in the flux of Time. (p. 493)

Ursula's vision relocates her in an organic space of Eternity, of cyclic recurrence and growth beyond the destructive forward movement of historical time hitherto shown in the novel. This optimism – almost mysticism – Lawrence extends into hopes of a 'new germination' for Ursula's society as a whole. These hopes largely depend upon belief in the redeeming power of relationships, emphasised throughout the novel by symbolism attached to rainbows and arching shapes of all kinds. These represent the potential for mutual equilibration, secure support and joy, which can be achieved in balanced, complete union of man and woman. In her final vision of a rainbow, this potential offers Ursula a promise of redemption from the dreary tide of industrialisation that has flooded across the countryside and her family's land:

> She saw the stiffened bodies of the colliers, which seemed already enclosed in a coffin, she saw their unchanging eyes, the eyes of those who are buried alive: she saw the hard, cutting edges of the new houses, which seemed to spread over the hillside in their insentient triumph, a triumph of horrible, amorphous angles and straight lines . . . And then, in the blowing clouds, she saw a band of faint iridescence colouring in faint colours a portion of the hill. And forgetting, startled, she looked for the hovering colour and saw a rainbow forming itself . . .
>
> And the rainbow stood on the earth. She knew that the sordid people who crept hard-scaled and separate on the face of the world's corruption were living still, that the rainbow was arched in their blood and would quiver to life in their spirit, that they would cast off their horny covering of disintegration, that new, clean, naked bodies would issue to a new germination . . . She saw in the rainbow the earth's new architecture, the old, brittle corruption of houses and factories swept away. (pp. 495–6)

The miners, entombed in their industrial thraldom, or the scaly, empty shells of people – the hollow men Lawrence later examined in the figures of Gerald Crich and Clifford Chatterley – all seem redeemable in *The Rainbow* by this 'new germination', able to restore the spirit and nature of a whole civilisation from its ravaging by the modern machine age.

No such optimism or redeeming mysticism appears in *Women in Love*, which shows a society, and many individual lives, disintegral to an extent beyond the power or promise of any relationship or rainbow to redeem. In Gudrun and Gerald, physical attraction and passion function largely destructively, while Birkin and Ursula's relationship and marriage, far from having any wider effect on the society around them, is mostly an act of individual refuge and escape. They are tempted to flee altogether (as Lawrence himself did, later in life) from a drab, declining, industrialised Britain, seeking less sullied civilisation elsewhere. Like many modernist authors and their characters – Ursula at her worst moments in *The Rainbow* – they consider the possibility that they 'do not belong to Beldover, nor to Nottingham, nor to England'. Though Gerald's death forces them to return at the end, any possibility of 'new germination' even within their private relationship is questioned by Birkin's denial, at the end of the novel, that Ursula is really, finally enough for him. Such questioning leaves the nature and future of their relationship uncertain, and the ending of the novel unresolved.

A disintegral, uncertain quality in the characters' lives, throughout *Women in Love*, is reduplicated and emphasised by the disintegral aspect of the novel's structure. Lawrence once remarked 'I don't want a plot' and warned:

> don't look for the development of the novel to follow the lines of central characters; the characters fall into the force of some other rhythmic form.[29]

This 'rhythmic form' abandons straightforward, consecutive progress. Individual chapters exemplify a range of what Lawrence might have called 'allotropic states'[30] in his central characters, rather than always showing how such states follow from or logically relate to each other. Though some chapters do continue directly and clearly from others, many begin only with a mention of habitual action, or some other inspecific indication of time – 'A School Day'; 'Every Year'; 'One morning'; 'One day at this time'; and so on. Especially in its early stages, *Women in Love* seems almost like a collection of short stories about the same group of characters, rather than a conventional novel about them. This fragmented narrative makes *Women in Love* as different from *The Rainbow* structurally as it is in vision. *The Rainbow* is a connected, chronological novel, showing events following one another more or less in causal sequence, one set of family circumstances setting off consequences and emotional patterns which Lawrence traces into the next generation. In this way at least, *The Rainbow* is largely a conventional novel, resembling the kind of saga or chronicle novel of family life, popular in the Victorian period, which continued to be written in the early twentieth century by authors such as John Galsworthy. In showing Ursula's anguished exile from a supporting society Lawrence does hesitate towards an alienated modernist vision, but the novel's optimistic conclusion postpones full consideration of this state, and leaves *The Rainbow* fairly firmly and satisfactorily resolved at the end. The implications of Ursula's kind of autonomy and isolation are examined throughout *Women in Love*, which not only ends unresolved, but challenges the very possibility of convincing or satisfactory resolution, in life or in the novel. Birkin's scepticism about marriage not only questions a social institution, but a literary one: marriage, at least until the uncertainties of the twentieth century, provides one of the standard – usually comedic – conclusions of narrative.

Radically different in structure, vision and conclusion, *Women in Love* is only, as Lawrence himself suggests, 'more or less a sequel' to *The Rainbow*.[31] Small but inescapable clues in the later novel help account for its difference from its predecessor. These are apparent in the description of the corpses at the end of the 'Water Party' chapter, found lying sodden in 'raw banks of clay . . . raw rottenish water' (p. 141). They are also visible in Birkin's earlier conclusion that

> What people want is hate – hate and nothing but hate. And in the name of righteousness and love, they get it. They distil themselves with nitro-glycerine. (p. 141)

A more certain hint is given towards the end of the novel when Birkin looks at Gerald's corpse, after his death in the snow:

> 'I didn't want it to be like this – I didn't want it to be like this,' he cried to himself. Ursula could but think of the Kaiser's: '*Ich habe es*

*nicht gewollt.*' She looked almost with horror on Birkin . . . he watched the cold, mute, material face. (p. 539)

Ursula recalls here the disillusioned remark made by Kaiser Wilhelm II about the First World War.[32] In a letter of 1917, Lawrence confirms this connection between *Women in Love* and the destructiveness of contemporary history, indicating factors which coloured his imagination while he worked on *Women in Love* in the years following the publication of *The Rainbow* in 1915:

> About *The Rainbow*: it was all written before the war, though revised during Sept. and Oct. 1914. I don't think the war had much to do with it – I don't think the war altered it, from its pre-war statement . . . alas, in the world of Europe I see no Rainbow. I believe the deluge of iron rain will destroy the world here, utterly . . .
>
> There is another novel, sequel to *The Rainbow*, called *Women in Love* . . . This actually does contain the results in one's soul of the war: it is purely destructive, not like *The Rainbow*, destructive-consummating.[33]

The shadow cast upon his imagination by the war thus accounts, in Lawrence's own view, for the differences between *The Rainbow* and *Women in Love*. The war provides the final, catastrophic term to a phase of history of increasing uncertainty, traced in the two novels from the aftermath of the Industrial Revolution in the 1840s. This phase begins with organic community, 'time sunk deeply in the earth', and 'human life and nature in the same categories'. It leads on through the supposedly progressive history of the Victorian period. It ends with the cataclysm of the machine age, humanity reduced to 'material', to be diluted with high explosives and left as 'flesh turned to atoms which drove before the wind', as Virginia Woolf suggests in *To the Lighthouse* (p. 150). The first 'cut' across landscape and history made by the Industrial Revolution thus initiates a period terminated by the second – the crack, cut or chasm in the life of the times made by the trenches. The first cut still leaves it just possible, in *The Rainbow*, to find 'a rhythm of eternity in a ragged, inconsequential life' (p. 280). 'God's time' or natural time still tenuously exists in the cycles of events wheeling in the seasons and the church year. After the second cut, in *Women in Love*, Gerald

> found his eternal and his infinite in the pure machine-principle . . .

complex, infinitely repeated motion, like the spinning of a wheel . . .
this is the God-motion . . . and the whole productive will of man was
the Godhead. (pp. 256-7)

Time passes from God or nature to the possession of the machine;
from the wheeling seasons to the spinning of a factory wheel; from
the sun and stars to the laws and formulae which rule the age of
Frederick Taylor – the epoch of Man's time, of Mean Time, of 'the
logic and dynamics of late capitalism'.

Such transformations in views of history and the life in time in
Lawrence's two novels are representative of wider changes in the
thinking of his age. Differences between *The Rainbow* and *Women
in Love* are likewise paradigmatic of structural and other changes
that distinguish modernist from Victorian or Edwardian fiction.
Still holding to some sense of organic community and to the
possibility of the individual's integration in society, *The Rainbow*
retains an organic, developmental form, an arrangement of events
in coherent and progressive historical sequence. In *Women in Love*,
fragmentation and disintegration, accepted as fundamental in
modern society, are also installed in Lawrence's disconnected form
of fictional construction. More generally apparent in fiction at the
time, such changes are summed up, as aptly as anywhere, by the
Italian novelist Italo Calvino. He remarks of the development of
the novel:

Long novels written today are perhaps a contradiction: the
dimension of time has been shattered . . . We can rediscover the
continuity of time only in the novels of that period when time no
longer seemed stopped and did not yet seem to have exploded, a
period that lasted no more than a hundred years.[14]

Before the Industrial Revolution, in the sort of immemorial
agricultural life the Brangwens once enjoyed on the Marsh, time did
seem to have stopped, or at any rate to be at least as much cyclic as
progressive. While change and development dominated the
nineteenth century, long, sequential novels rested easily on what
seemed the continuing forward progress of history. With the First
World War, the dimension of time finally cracked, shattered or
exploded, leaving it 'one livid final flame', and history itself, as
Stephen Dedalus also suggests in *Ulysses*, 'a nightmare' (pp. 20, 28).

Writing about *Ulysses* in 1923, T. S. Eliot – rather like Calvino –
talks of the genre of the novel as the expression of an age that had

not 'lost all form'. What Eliot calls the 'futility and anarchy which is contemporary history' left the novel 'a form which will no longer serve'.[35] Given history as nightmare, futility or anarchy, and time as a livid final flame or the 'terrible bondage' Gudrun finds it to be in *Women in Love*, novelists by the 1920s could no longer find form and structure for their fiction simply in 'life as a series'. Two other possibilities remained. Firstly, narrative could in various ways reproduce the fragmented, discontinuous aspect of contemporary history – more or less the option chosen by Lawrence in *Women in Love*, or by Aldous Huxley in, for example, the fractured, contrasted narratives of *Point Counter Point* (1928). Or fiction could try to smooth over or escape from the cracks and chasms in contemporary life through streams of consciousness, recovered memory and loops in time. If time in the world became intolerable, in other words, narrative could celebrate and expand upon its capacity for 'temporal autonomy', creating an independent imaginative dimension of 'time ruled, captured, bewitched, surreptitiously subverted'. Or ruled and subverted, at any rate, as far as possible: as was suggested in the last section, since the ticking of the world's Mean Times could never entirely be ignored, modernist fiction is most often divided between the fluid and the fragmentary.

Movements into time as vision, time in the mind rather than time on the clock or in the world, are visible throughout modernist novels: in several cases – *Ulysses*, for example – they are most clearly marked at the end. Conclusions of modernist texts often provide a point of maximum contrast with Victorian fiction. The latter finds points of stability to resolve uncertainty in social or individual life, and bring its development firmly to a close – most often in marriage, if the story is to end happily, or death, if it is tragic. Modernist fiction more often ends in openness and uncertainty. In a disintegral society, as in *Women in Love*, marriage scarcely provides a secure or certainly stable conclusion. Even the conclusiveness of death diminishes in the early twentieth century. In *To the Lighthouse*, the perfunctory recording of the killing of Andrew Ramsay, along with twenty or thirty other young men, suggests that the scale of slaughter in the First World War hardly left death with sufficient significance or decency to resolve or conclude anything. Faced with this unresolvable turbulence in the actual social world, modernist fiction's endings are often forced to move altogether beyond it in one way or another. Individual marriages or relations may fail, but there is still scope for ecstatic vision of their potential, or transcendent memory of their ecstasies, at the end of *The Rainbow* or *Ulysses*, for example. This need for transcendence, however – though a consequence of the 'futility and anarchy which is contemporary history' – also relates to a more general modernist characteristic, its concern with vision and art itself. This central modernist concern is further considered in the next chapter.

# — 4 —

# *ART*

Real life, life at last laid bare and illuminated – the only life
which in consequence can be said to be really lived – is
literature.
(Marcel Proust, *A la recherche du temps perdu*, vol. III, p. 931)

Art and Life were to them the Reality and the Unreality.
   'Of course,' said Gudrun, 'life doesn't *really* matter – it is one's
art which is central.'
(D. H. Lawrence, *Women in Love*, p. 504)

## ART AND THE NOVEL

If art or literature are not always shown in modernist fiction, as
Proust suggests, as the only 'real life', they at least begin to figure very
frequently, in one way or another, as central subjects and concerns.
*Women in Love*, for example, itself demonstrates some of Gudrun's
views about the importance of art. Art or other processes of shaping
and moulding reality into models and pictures are activities
emphasised from the beginning of the novel, which shows Ursula
embroidering while Gudrun sketches. Art is also central to the
'Crème de Menthe' and 'Totem' chapters, in which Gerald discusses
and broods over the statuettes that he finds in Halliday's London
flat. Later, Gudrun's attraction for Loerke – finally, fatally excluding
Gerald from her life – is shown growing up largely through
discussions of Loerke's sculpture, and other conversations, such as
the one quoted above, about artistic priorities in general.

   Discussions of this sort reappear repeatedly, not only in
Lawrence's work, but throughout modernist fiction. In Lawrence's
*Sons and Lovers* (1913), Paul Morel believes firmly in the importance of his drawing and painting, and sometimes talks over its
conduct and aims at some length with his girlfriend Miriam.

*155*

Painting is the profession of Wyndham Lewis's hero in *Tarr* (1918) – his name a near-anagram of 'art' – and a regular subject of arguments with girlfriends and others. Like Joyce's Stephen Dedalus in *A Portrait of the Artist as a Young Man* (1916), May Sinclair's heroine in *Mary Olivier* (1919) often ponders or discusses the art and writing through which she finds an escape from some of the constraints of her society. Such interests also figure in Dorothy Richardson's *Pilgrimage* (1915–67), which records at an early stage Miriam Henderson's feeling that 'she wanted to "write a book" ' (I, p. 80). In Woolf's *The Waves* (1931), Bernard more or less shares this urge, finding it necessary to spend a lifetime making 'phrases and phrases' (p. 25) and reflecting on their nature and worth. Similar reflections on what Marcel calls 'the way in which artistic impressions are formed' and on 'the perspective of imagination and art' (I, p. 544; III, p. 50) appear at some stages on almost every page of Proust's *A la recherche du temps perdu* (1913–27). Marcel's acquaintanceships with a novelist, Bergotte, as well as the painter Elstir and the composer Vinteuil, ensure that such issues are examined widely, and in relation to a range of artistic forms. A similar range of artistic concerns, and of artists and writers – sometimes fictional portraits of actual modernist novelists such as Lawrence – also appears in Aldous Huxley's *Point Counter Point* (1928).

Such frequent and substantial discussion of art and writing, within the novel, is in one way an extension of growing debate in the early twentieth century about the novel *as* art, as a genre with its own specific formal and structural properties. This new consciousness began with Henry James, one of whose complaints about the state of the novel was that such thinking ought to have begun much sooner. Discussing the novel in 1914, James pointed to 'the scant degree in which that field has ever had to reckon with criticism'. James had long complained that the novel's lack of what he calls 'a theory, a conviction, a consciousness of itself behind it' left

> a comfortable good-humoured feeling about that the novel is a novel, as a pudding is a pudding, and that your only business with it could be to swallow it.[1]

This uncritical 'swallowing', however, had already begun to be challenged by 1914 by the many prefaces James wrote for his own fiction, discussing his priorities in form and style. James was virtually the first novelist writing in English to articulate a strong critical position around the practice of his own fiction, making him one of the first theoreticians of the novel of any sort. Other critics and commentators, however, soon extended his initiative. Percy Lubbock's *The Craft of Fiction* (1921) offered the novel 'a theory, a conviction' based fairly firmly around James's reasoning, and other studies of the novel continued to appear throughout the 1920s (some of them referred to in Chapter 2) by authors such as Elizabeth Drew, John Carruthers, Gerald Bullett, Edwin Muir and Edith Wharton. Several modernist authors also followed James in discussing the theory and priorities of novel-writing. D. H. Lawrence and Virginia Woolf were frequent writers of essays on fiction, sometimes advocating for it the kind of firmer aesthetic favoured by James. Woolf, for example, held a 'grudge against novelists . . . that they select nothing' [2] and felt that all literature should aspire to the density of poetry. Such ideas informed a critical output extensive enough to have made Woolf at some stages almost as influential a writer *on* fiction – especially in her celebrated arguments with the style of Arnold Bennett – as she was a writer *of* fiction. Wyndham Lewis certainly made himself into more of a critic and commentator than a purely creative writer in the 1920s, when huge volumes such as *The Art of Being Ruled* (1926) and *Time and Western Man* (1927) far outstripped his writing of novels.

From the scant beginnings indicated by James, the early decades of the twentieth century, and the 1920s in particular, were thus a period in which the novel rapidly acquired a theory and a framework for critical debate, and a new consciousness of its status as art and not 'pudding'. This development partly originated, as the critic Peter Keating has recently shown, in more flexible conditions of publishing and the great expansion in the reading public in the late nineteenth and early twentieth centuries. These changes made it financially possible for novels to address specific tastes within the novel-reading public, rather than trying, more or less, to reach it all. From the time of James, authors found it more possible – and in some cases more desirable – to concentrate not on the likely popular appeal of their work but on its particular status as an artistic form. As the novel came in this way to envisage and value itself more specifically as art, so art came to be more valued and discussed within it.

Another symptom of this shift of values and interests, and of the increasing centrality of art in fiction generally, appears in a gradual change away from the *Bildungsroman* and towards the *Künstler-*

*oman* – the novel which follows growth towards maturity as an artist rather than only as an individual. In the early years of the century, the *Bildungsroman* remained a popular, frequently used form – in Somerset Maugham's *Of Human Bondage* (1915); Arnold Bennett's *Clayhanger* series (1910–18) or D. H. Lawrence's *Sons and Lovers*, for example. In the latter, however, reflection on Paul's artistic inclinations appears alongside the central examination of his attempt to free himself from the influence of his family, making it a novel at least partly concerned with development in art as well as life. Compton Mackenzie's *Sinister Street* (1913–14) is a similarly transitional work, showing in Michael Fane a hero divided between allegiances to life, religion and art.

For modernist authors, growth came to be considered more and more exclusively in terms of artistic rather than personal maturity. Modernist fiction often follows central characters who move towards a point at which, however orderly or otherwise their actual personal lives, they can at least make of their experience something coherent in terms of vision, if not in fact. This form of development is central to *A la recherche du temps perdu*. Proust's narrator Marcel announces early in the first volume that he 'wished some day to become a writer' (I, p. 188), and he subsequently shows and discusses the many stages through which his ambition is realised and he finally discovers means whereby 'a life . . . can be realised within the confines of a book' (III, p. 1088). In a sense the novel shows Marcel chasing his own tale: it follows his development to the point at which he is finally able to write the narrative in which he appears – able at last to recover in art all the times he has in reality lost in the past. Similar processes of development, and comparable discussions of art and its principles, run through Joyce's *A Portrait of the Artist as a Young Man*. Joyce's change from his original title, *Stephen Hero*, indicates an increased emphasis on art since the draft novel was begun early in the century. Stephen Dedalus's name indicates from the start that he will become a 'fabulous artificer': throughout, Joyce follows the thinking through which – particularly in Stephen's lengthy artistic conversations with Lynch – he works out a 'theory of esthetic' (p. 214) of his own. By the end Stephen can declare himself ready

> to encounter for the millionth time the reality of experience and to forge in the smithy of my soul the uncreated conscience of my race. (p. 253)

Certain stages in Stephen's development indicate a factor which

encouraged early twentieth-century narrative's increased interest in
the orders of art. It was pointed out in Chapter 3 that by the late
nineteenth century religious belief came to be partly replaced by faith
in the potential of science and technological progress. In its own way
art also provided a kind of substitute faith or system of values at the
time. Especially in the 1890s – and in the life and work of Oscar Wilde
in particular – aestheticism and the doctrine of art for art's sake
offered a kind of alternative code of conduct, a substitute for
conventional morality. Stephen's experience partly reflects this shift
from the spiritual to the aesthetic. However much his name may
propel his flight from the reality of experience into the realms of art,
his first steps are towards a different transcendence of the immediate
world, not in art but in religion. It takes some time and anguish
before he rejects the 'grave and ordered and passionless . . . the
inhuman voice that had called him to the pale service of the altar'
(pp. 160, 170) in favour of working in the

> name of the fabulous artificer . . . the artist forging anew in his
> workshop out of the sluggish matter of the earth a new soaring
> impalpable imperishable being. (p. 169)

Though Stephen eventually reaches a conclusion in favour of art
rather than religion, the terms in which he does so remain highly
charged with the 'soaring impalpable imperishable' rhetoric of the
spiritual: the art he embraces seems partly interchangeable with
religion rather than altogether separate from or opposed to it.

Some of his conclusions, and some of his conflicts, are shared both
by Michael Fane in *Sinister Street* – a novel which also looks back
strongly to the aestheticism, dandyism and decadence of the 1890s –
and by May Sinclair's heroine in *Mary Olivier*. At various stages each
is divided between the demands of religion and of an art which
apparently offers more or less equivalent consolations. Other novels
similarly equate art and religion. Bernard, for example, remarks in
*The Waves* that 'some people go to priests; others to poetry . . . I to
seek among phrases and fragments something unbroken' (p. 229). *To
the Lighthouse* also suggests something of this equation between the
powers of priests and of poetry, of religion and art. When in the last
chapter of the novel Mr Ramsay reaches the lighthouse and Lily
completes her painting, her repeated comment, 'It is finished' (pp.
236–7), echoes Christ's 'consummatum est'. Some connection between
the two is further suggested by Lily's age when she begins her painting

in the first section, 33, the same as Christ's at the end of his life.

The ending of *To the Lighthouse* helps confirm a new sense in the early twentieth century – at a time when faith declined still more sharply than in the late nineteenth century – of a power in art in some ways equal to that of religion in escaping 'the sluggish matter of the earth' and finding a pattern or meaning for life. Often concerned with art throughout, Woolf's novel is worth looking at in further detail, as it offers some more general indications of how and why art came to figure as centrally as it did in the fiction of the early twentieth century. Rather like Proust at some stages of *A la recherche du temps perdu*, Woolf concentrates her interest on Lily's painting as a figuration of wider interest in the powers and possibilities of art. At one point in *A la recherche du temps perdu*, Marcel describes a painting as a 'little square panel of beauty which Elstir had cut out of a marvellous afternoon' (II, p. 436): cutting panels out of life, asking how art is framed from reality, or permanence out of change, is also a frequent practice in *To the Lighthouse*. It even extends, in one way, into the novel's use of square brackets, sometimes to frame its sadder or darker passages, such as the description in the third section of a character who

> [ . . . took one of the fish and cut a square out of its side to bait his hook with. The mutilated body (it was alive still) was thrown back into the sea.] (p. 205)

Elsewhere, shapes are cut and framed less painfully from life. The novel's first section, 'The Window', opens with Mrs Ramsay helping her little boy to cut out pictures from an illustrated catalogue, while remembering that she must remain carefully framed herself, sitting in the window, in the allotted place Lily has chosen for her in her painting. Mrs Ramsay not only remains aware of her place in Lily's picture, she sometimes shows an ability to share in other ways – part of a general affinity with Lily – something of her painterly preoccupation with 'the relations of masses, of lights and shadows' (p. 62). During the latter stages of her triumphal dinner party, for example, Mrs Ramsay mentally assembles a kind of still life out of the contents of the fruit bowl:

> her eyes had been going in and out among the curves and shadows of the fruit . . . putting a yellow against a purple, a curved shape against a round shape . . . until, oh, what a pity that they should do it – a hand reached out, took a pear, and spoilt the whole thing. (p. 125)

After the dinner party is over, she performs a kind of framing of her own, turning and pausing in the doorway as she leaves to look back over the happy scene in the hope that she can find a way to make 'Life stand still here . . . making of the moment something permanent' (p. 183).

For all her artistic proclivities with the doorframe or the fruit bowl, however, Mrs Ramsay's ambitions to still life and somehow make it permanent depend in the end upon people, not paint. She is a shaper of society, of individuals and their relations, and not – except in occasional moments of reflection – of Lily's abstract masses, lights and shadows. Mrs Ramsay still believes order and pattern can be found in the social world, and that marriage and stable relationships create sufficient security and coherence for individual and social life. The first part of *To the Lighthouse* closes with this sort of stable conclusion – with the news Mrs Ramsay has hoped for about Paul and Minta's engagement; with the elegant social integration of the dinner party; with the Ramsays' own marriage once again drawn together into one of its moments of wonderful concord after their numerous bright, promising children have been soothed to sleep upstairs.

But *To the Lighthouse* does not end there. In some ways it is two novels in one, the vision of its third part, 'The Lighthouse', differing from the first for reasons that appear in the middle section, 'Time Passes'. This section shows how war and the lapse of time intervene to destroy the coherence, even the principles of coherence, that Mrs Ramsay sustained with temporary success in the first part. In 'Time Passes', death – Andrew Ramsay's death in the war, Prue's in childbirth – carries away the brightest and best of Mrs Ramsay's children, and also Mrs Ramsay herself. The novel comments on

> Mrs Ramsay making of the moment something permanent . . . as in another sphere Lily herself tried to make of the moment something permanent. (p. 183)

Death and decay in 'Time Passes' show the failure of Mrs Ramsay's strategies for securing order, permanence or stability. Her own death leaves the third part of the novel as Lily's sphere, one from which she often looks back critically on Mrs Ramsay and her priorities in the first. Like Mrs Ramsay, Lily seeks stability and permanence, but her methods and her medium differ: Lily's commitment to art highlights some of the limitations of Mrs Ramsay's allegiance to life, and the inevitability of eventual failure in her attempts to shape it. Mrs Ramsay even knows herself that the wish to make 'life stand still' at her dinner party is unrealisable:

> the scene . . . was vanishing even as she looked . . . it changed, it shaped itself differently, it had become, she knew, giving one last look at it over her shoulder, already the past. (p. 128)

The marriage she believes in establishes nothing more durable than her dinner party. As Lily reflects in 'The Lighthouse', Paul and Minta's union, which Mrs Ramsay so hoped for and encouraged, turns out rather badly, declining into dreary adulteries. Looking back on Mrs Ramsay's efforts, Lily concludes that her principles – such as 'Marry, marry!' were 'limited, old-fashioned ideas' and that 'life has changed completely' in ways that have left them 'dusty and out of date' (p. 198). Lily's views share the conclusion reached in Chapter 3 – that the violence of the war and the cynicism of the years that followed it made apparently 'old-fashioned' both marriage and other points of finality or stability which once provided a fitting sense of an ending in life, or in fiction. As Lily also suggests, after the scale and arbitrariness with which it had occurred in the war, even death retained hardly any more decisive significance than marriage. 'Oh the dead!' Lily reflects, 'one pitied them, one brushed them aside, one even had a little contempt for them. They are at our mercy' (p. 198).

Such changes in outlook and experience leave coherence and permanence available to Lily only in art, rather than in life. Life will not stand still: art may. ' "You" and "I" and "she" pass and vanish; nothing stays; all changes; but not words, not paint,' she concludes. Only in art is it possible to find 'in the midst of chaos . . . shape; this eternal passing and flowing . . . struck into stability' (pp. 204, 183). In the life of sadness and disappointment 'The Lighthouse' shows following the First World War, Lily therefore finds 'a brush, the one dependable thing in a world of strife, ruin, chaos' (p. 170). The ending of *To the Lighthouse* further endorses her views. The penultimate chapter shows the lighthouse finally reached, and the expectation set up by the novel's title and much of its first section at last fulfilled. Yet this achievement in reality is not a sufficient conclusion, fading into the impalpable: for Lily, 'the Lighthouse had become almost invisible, had melted away into a blue haze' (p. 236). Instead it is Lily's decisive gesture – the final line 'there, in the centre' which completes her painting, allowing her to lay down her brush and conclude 'I have had my vision' (p. 237) – that actually brings *To the Lighthouse* to a close.

Only through art, through vision, this ending suggests, can 'eternal passing and flowing' be finally transcended or an action, however complete in itself, be endowed with significance. This suggestion, and the general interest in art throughout the third section, make *To the Lighthouse* paradigmatic of changes that occurred between Victorian and modernist fiction. Still believing in the possibility of finding shape and meaning within life and society, Mrs Ramsay rather resembles a Victorian novelist, and the first part of *To the Lighthouse*, with its apparently stable, happy ending, is not unlike a Victorian novel. The second and third parts show how twentieth-century life, especially after the First World War, seemed 'changed completely', and the sense of coherence in individual or social life much diminished. A world characterised by 'strife, ruin and chaos', in Lily's view – or 'futility and anarchy' in T. S. Eliot's – lacked the kind of substance on which the order and significance of fiction had conventionally been founded. In default not only of faith in religion, but in many other certainties – in society, history or the world in general – art offered a last possibility of finding 'in the midst of chaos, shape'. Art and artists begin to figure centrally in modernist fiction because apparently they, almost alone, offered a possibility of dealing with or escaping from the futile and anarchic history their authors surveyed.

Art and artists appear in modernist fiction, however, not only as representatives of this possibility, but also of the difficulty of realising it. Art may have seemed more than ever desirable as an almost unique, surviving domain of order in the early twentieth century, but at the same time this sort of order seemed more than ever difficult to create out of a reality increasingly shapeless and fragmentary in itself. Modernism's whole initiative – the general, radical reshaping of styles and structures considered in Chapters 2 and 3 – can be seen as a result of the need to find new and subtler strategies to contain new, radical challenges in the life of the early twentieth century. Stephen Spender sums up this view of modernism when he talks of the need to 'invent a new literature' for an age 'in many respects unprecedented and outside all the conventions of past literature and art'.[3] Modernist writers, after Henry James, were obliged not only to reject the novel as 'pudding', but to establish a whole new cuisine. This obligation made technique and style not only the tools of creation, but pressing enough matters also to force their way into the novel as themes: sometimes the artist likewise became the subject rather than only the agent of artistic creativity.

This kind of self-consciousness appears in a number of ways in modernist fiction – firstly, in the number of novels concerned with art which are also autobiographies. The movement towards the *Künstlerroman* discussed above is also a move towards self-examination: portraits of an artist are most often self-portraits. In *A la recherche du temps perdu*, for example, as his name implies, Marcel is a figure close to Proust himself. Many of his long speculations on how to construct a fiction which 'suppresses the mighty dimension of Time' (III, p. 1087) reflect his author's problems in constructing the novel in which he appears – Proust chases his own tale in showing Marcel pursuing his. Joyce's title implies a similarly autobiographical aspect in *A Portrait of the Artist as a Young Man*. Joyce draws on details of his own early life and uses Stephen's lengthy speculations about art to work out a 'theory of esthetic' also partly his own. Other modernist works are still more explicitly self-portraits. *Mary Oliver*, for example, was described by May Sinclair as being 'as autobiographically accurate as I can make it'. In a letter written at the time *Tarr* was being serialised in *The Egoist* – immediately following its publication of *A Portrait of the Artist as a Young Man* – Wyndham Lewis acknowledges that 'I make Tarr too much my mouthpiece . . . Tarr has just a trifle too many of my ideas to be wholly himself'.[4] As he suggests, most of Tarr's opinions could be taken directly out of Lewis's *Time and Western Man* – for example, his conviction that

> Anything living, quick and changing, is bad art, always . . . No restless, quick, flame-like ego is imagined for the *inside* of it. It has no inside. This is another condition of art; *to have no inside*. (p. 295)

Such views anticipate Lewis's antipathy to Joyce, in particular; to a stream-of-consciousness method that constantly traces fluid movements inside the ego. They also explain some of the style of *Tarr* itself, unusually resistant, in the ways examined in Chapter 3, to the 'quick and changing', and almost exclusively attentive to characters' external appearance and manner rather than their inner thoughts.

In this way *Tarr* is typical of another aspect of modernist fiction's artistic self-consciousness: opinions about art not only reflect the views of the author, but relate directly to the novel in which they are expressed. Self-consciousness and a habit of self-portraiture extend into a kind of self-reflexiveness in which texts talk about their own methods, or artists discuss or demonstrate problems and priorities that also figure in the construction of the novel in which they appear. A clear example of this is offered by the ending of *To the Lighthouse* described above. Lily's comment 'It was done; it was finished. Yes, she thought . . . I have had my vision' (p. 237) could be shared by the novelist, who concludes *her* vision and the novel itself, in this last sentence, at the same moment Lily completes her painting. Simultaneous conclusions are appropriate for phases of creativity, in paint and fiction, significantly correlated throughout *To the Lighthouse*. Several of the problems confronting Lily as an artist, and some of the solutions she finds for them, are analogous to decisions and strategies that shape Woolf's construction of the novel. Lily wonders, for example,

> how to connect this mass on the right hand with that on the left . . .
> the danger was that . . . the unity of the whole might be broken. (pp. 62-3)

Her doubts are ones Woolf herself might have considered in structuring a novel unusually split into parts reflecting single, separate days, with a lapse of ten whole years between. The device Lily uses to complete her painting – 'a line there, in the centre' (p. 237) – looks very much like the structural solution Woolf finds for the novel, placing the short, bleak middle section between the more expansive human visions of the first and third parts.

Woolf uses Lily's vision, Wyndham Lewis examines Tarr, and Lawrence follows some of the ideas of Gudrun and Loerke in *Women in Love* to reflect on the nature and construction of their own art. Modernist fiction often turns in this way to visual art and painting for figurative self-examination of its own techniques. Nevertheless, such self-reflexiveness also, inevitably, finds a specifically literary focus – an attention to words and language, since the medium of fiction, obviously, is words and not paint. Awareness of words and language, of how they 'paint' reality, inevitably formed a central part of the increasing artistic self-consciousness of modernism. This general modernist concern is first clearly apparent in two novels that consider literary rather than only visual art, *A la recherche du temps perdu* and *A Portrait of the Artist as a Young Man*.

## THE REVOLUTION OF LANGUAGE

In *A Portrait of the Artist as a Young Man*, Stephen Dedalus reflects at length on the nature and rewards of words and language:

> He drew forth a phrase from his treasure and spoke it softly to himself:
> – A day of dappled seaborne clouds.
> The phrase and the day and the scene harmonized in a chord. Words. Was it their colours? He allowed them to glow and fade, hue after hue: sunrise gold, the russet and green of apple orchards, azure of waves, the grey-fringed fleece of clouds. No, it was not their colours: it was the poise and balance of the period itself. Did he then love the rhythmic rise and fall of words better than their associations of legend and colour? Or was it that, being as weak of sight as he was shy of mind, he drew less pleasure from the reflection of the glowing sensible world through the prism of a language many-coloured and richly storied than from the contemplation of an inner world of individual emotions mirrored perfectly in a lucid supple periodic prose? (pp. 166–7)

Some of Stephen's feelings are echoed by Marcel in *A la recherche du temps perdu*, recording a particular pleasure he finds in prose in the course of describing a journey past the spires of Martinville and Vieuxvicq:

> presently their outlines and their sunlit surfaces, as though they had been a sort of rind, peeled away: something of what they had concealed from me became apparent; a thought came into my mind which had not existed for me a moment earlier, framing itself in words in my head; and the pleasure which the first sight of them had given me was so greatly enhanced that, overpowered by a sort of intoxication, I could no longer think of anything else . . . it was . . . the form of words which gave me pleasure. (I, p. 197)

Marcel's pleasure in words helps account for his conclusion that 'real life, life at last laid bare and illuminated . . . is literature'. What would normally be held to be the real, the 'sunlit surfaces' of life, are for Marcel only a kind of 'rind', a covering to be peeled away to reveal a core of vitality not in the world, nor even in thoughts about it, but in words themselves. Alongside art, reality, as for Lily Briscoe, 'melts away', or effectively 'becomes invisible': the mirror of art, for Marcel, most rewardingly reflects not upon nature but upon itself.

Stephen Dedalus's views point to a similar conclusion. In one way his musings reflect the central modernist preference discussed in Chapter 2, for an 'inner world of individual emotions' rather than the 'sensible world', the observable, objective world of realistic fiction. Yet both worlds, inner and outer, are in Stephen's view somehow separate from 'the poise and balance of the period itself . . . [the] supple periodic prose' used to record them. Words may be loved independently of their associations: for Stephen, as for Marcel, language comes close to offering more in itself than in what it signifies. In both Proust's vision and Joyce's, language edges away from the world it might represent, and from the consciousnesses that envisage it, towards an autonomous existence of its own.

This sense of language in separate, independent existence is considered later, in the next section, in relation to patterns of thought and culture developing more generally in the early twentieth century. It is worth tracing first the various ways in which it presents itself to modernist authors, as both a problem and an opportunity. These are particularly apparent in Joyce's writing after *A Portrait of the Artist as a Young Man*, firstly in *Ulysses*, which in various ways makes language a central issue. *Ulysses* is above all a parody, a form whose mockery and exaggeration generally draw attention to modes of language and styles of representation. In one way Joyce's parody also works in terms of character – his reworking of Homer casts Bloom as an unlikely modern Odysseus, journeying not through the aftermath of the Trojan War but through a single Dublin day – but the parody of *Ulysses* focuses primarily on language. Almost every chapter is written differently, and many of them appropriate and mock some specific style of literature, journalism, ordinary speech or officialdom. Constant parody, stylistic variation and exaggeration make the nature of language impossible to ignore: throughout *Ulysses* there is a central significance for Joyce's mode of representation, as well as for what is represented.

*Ulysses* in this way departs decisively from the habits of

nineteenth-century fiction, in which language most often works, as far as possible, as a transparent medium through which the world of the fiction is observed by the reader. Henry James is sometimes criticised for a language whose complexity borders on the opaque, yet in his famous metaphor of looking out through various windows in 'the house of fiction' even he assumes transparent glass for each.[5] What especially interested James was the different points of view and angles of observation each window offered for surveying the fictional scene: it did not immediately concern him that the glass might refract or colour the scene observed. For Joyce, language is never straightforwardly a window on the world, but more often as Stephen suggests a 'prism', colouring, shaping or even obscuring what is being observed – Hugh Kenner talks of Joyce's 'screens of language, through or past which it is not easy to see' (p. 41). Readers of Joyce no longer simply look through the window, but also have to examine the glass. As Joyce himself explained, 'it is the material that conveys the image . . . that interests you', however fascinating the image itself.[6]

Of course, as was suggested in Chapter 2, an interest in the material that conveys the image, a foregrounding of the language of fiction, can be seen as an enhancement of its capacity to represent the world rather than a distraction from it. Even Joyce's more eccentric uses of language may be explained as what Kenner calls 'gravitational fields' – spheres of speech and style reflecting the influence exerted by certain characters or locations. Nevertheless, though Kenner's theory helps to account for the striking, hetero-geneous styles Joyce uses, it does not really make them any less obtrusive when they appear in the novel. The newspaper headlines that figure in Chapter 7, 'Aeolus', may be explained as a conse-quence of the setting in a newspaper office, for example, but this does not diminish the unusual impact of their appearance in the text, nor the extent to which they draw attention to themselves and the language of journalism in general. Moreover, in a number of ways Kenner's idea of the 'gravitational field' provides a less thorough or satisfactory explanation for some of the later stages of *Ulysses*. Joyce's linguistic extravagance and virtuosity increase fairly steadily as the novel progresses, challenging more and more radically any attempt to account for them. At least by comparison with what follows, the early chapters of *Ulysses* seem innocent, relatively uncomplicated. Much of the novel's early stages is in the form of the 'duet for two narrators' discussed in Chapter 2, in which a supple prose slips subtly between the inner voice of Bloom (or of Stephen) and a more objective register that describes them and the Dublin world they inhabit. As the novel goes on, however, phrase and day and scene harmonise less. Joyce's language becomes a cloudier mirror of either what Stephen calls the 'inner world' or the 'glowing sensible world'. Language increasingly draws attention to itself and its own devices; inescapably so by the time Chapter 12, 'Cyclops', is reached.

In this section, Joyce's duet breaks up into two thoroughly unharmonious voices, which compete instead of co-operate in presenting the scene. Highly colloquial Dublin street-speech conflicts with a grander, inflated rhetoric throughout 'Cyclops', concluding with this description of Bloom's barely dignified exit from Barney Kiernan's pub:

> And the last we saw was the bloody car rounding the corner and old sheepsface on it gesticulating and the bloody mongrel after it with his lugs back for all he was bloody well worth to tear him limb from limb. Hundred to five! Jesus, he took the value of it out of him, I promise you.
>
> When lo, there came about them all a great brightness and they beheld the chariot wherein He stood ascend to heaven . . . And they beheld Him even Him, ben Bloom Elijah, amid clouds of angels ascend to the glory of the brightness at an angle of fortyfive degrees over Donohoe's in Little Green street like a shot off a shovel. (pp. 282–3)

Such absurdly disparate styles do arise, in one way, from the 'gravitational field' in Kiernan's pub, and the attitudes competing within it. The grandiloquence mockingly corresponds to the Citizen's heroic, romantic but phoney vision of a noble Ireland, while the other styles belong to the drab, cynical city life endured by his listeners. But the juxtaposition of styles also draws particular attention to the nature and limitations of each, making the chapter's subject not just the pub and what is seen in it, but *ways* of seeing and the effect of style in conditioning meaning. Named after the race of menacing one-eyed giants described by Homer, 'Cyclops' has as its subject narrowness of vision, and it shows how speech habits and registers contribute to this constraint. While seeming to represent the world to the mind, any single language or style actually defines, dictates and often limits what it is possible to see.

This is a limitation that *Ulysses* continues to demonstrate in the chapters that follow, and – through parody and its own repeated variations of style – also to resist. The next chapter, 'Nausicaa', goes on to mock the deadening, sentimental, namby-pamby-marmalady-drawersy style of popular magazine fiction. The following chapter, 14, 'Oxen of the Sun,' is a final, extravagantly extended 'gravitational field', deriving not from character – Bloom's voice and consciousness fade from the novel after Chapter 13 – but from place. Setting the chapter in a maternity hospital creates a kind of appropriateness – as an imitation of the nine months of foetal growth from conception to birth – for Joyce's writing in nine sections, the styles of each representing a phase in the historical development of the English language. The chapter thus moves from the archaic, alliterative style of 'Before born babe bliss had. Within womb won he worship' (p. 315) to the functional, prosaic modernity of

> Science, it cannot be too often repeated, deals with tangible phenomena. The man of science like the man in the street has to face hardheaded facts that cannot be blinked and explain them as best he can. (p. 341)

The diversity of the chapter as a whole allows – as in 'Cyclops' – languages to conflict with, criticise or clarify by contrast each other's nature and limitations. No single voice or style is left dominant overall: like the child eventually born in the hospital, language develops towards an independent life of its own, disjunct from any specific narrator, character or inner consciousness. In the next chapter, it leaves almost altogether the body of reality to which it is normally sustainingly connected, moving into the drunken hallucination and fantasy of 'Nighttown' before falling back exhausted into the monotonous clichés of Chapter 16.

Chapter 17, 'Ithaca', sobers up into what appears to be severe objectivity. In the form of what Joyce called 'mathematical catechism',[7] factual questions are often answered with long lists of apparently exact, detailed scientific data about Bloom's life and his day in Dublin. The questions and answers sound rather like a science exam, and the voices that provide them appear for the most part neutral, disembodied, independent of any character or 'gravitational field'. The very end of the chapter, however, does provide what seems to be something of a clue to its speakers' identity. When Molly hears her husband coming to bed and stirs awake to talk to him, she is described as engaging in 'catechetical interrogation . . . reiterated feminine interrogation' (pp. 605–6). Perhaps Molly is in some way a source of the questions, with Bloom – always inclined to a scientific mentality – providing the answers? Molly, however, is awake only during the last few pages of 'Ithaca'. A better clue to the chapter's nature throughout is provided by the description of the couple lying in bed as 'listener and narrator' (p. 606). Narrator and listener in 'Ithaca' are not just Bloom and Molly, but in another sense the text and its reader. Joyce described the chapter as being intended to allow 'the reader to know everything and know it in the baldest, coldest way'.[8] In one way the questions and answers of 'Ithaca' look like an opportunity for readers to get from the text 'hardheaded facts' and 'tangible phenomena', Joyce at last providing a firm reality independent of the screens and prisms of stylised language through which almost everything in the novel has hitherto been playfully refracted.

The kind of factual, precise questions asked, however, do not so much elicit absolute knowledge as parody the wish for it to exist, and the assumption that it can. Pretended scientific objectivity is often undermined, partly by Joyce's ineradicable lyricism. This lyricism continues to colour descriptions of Bloom and Stephen, for example, alone on 'the heavenborn earth', looking up from 'the penumbra of the garden' to observe 'the heaventree of stars hung with humid nightblue fruit' (pp. 573, 578). Set against this cosmic context,

Alone, what did Bloom feel?

The cold of interstellar space, thousands of degrees below freezing point or the absolute zero of Fahrenheit, Centigrade or Reaumur: the incipient intimations of proximate dawn. (p. 578)

Even at such moments, when 'Ithaca' moves from 'the heaventree of stars' to the exactness of temperature scales, seeming after all to present things in 'the baldest, coldest way', the chilliness of the language does not eradicate emotion, but actually highlights it, emphasising by contrast Bloom's lonely human warmth. Scientific objectivity is further undermined by the absurdity of some of the knowledge presented – Stephen and Bloom's views, for example, are 'equal and negative' on 'the influence of gaslight or electric light on the growth of adjoining paraheliotropic trees' (p. 545). Moreover, the text's pretence to exactness and objectivity is often exposed by obvious omissions, speculations and inaccuracies – its falsification of Bloom's spending for the day, for example; or its implausible and unverifiable list of Molly's twenty-five lovers; or its erroneous suggestion that temperatures anywhere, even in interstellar space, ever fall below absolute zero. The question 'Was the narration . . . unaltered by modifications?' is answered 'absolutely', but the evidence of 'Ithaca' suggests the impossibility of presenting an absolutely faithful, 'unmodified' version of anything. Supposedly the most precise, objective section of *Ulysses*, 'Ithaca' is actually its final demonstration of the space that inevitably exists between 'words and their associations'. Even the baldest, coldest, apparently most objective language modifies and mediates the world, refracting, colouring and re-creating it through the various screens and prisms of structure and style. Ultimately, no language can be wholly transparent. *Ulysses* constantly exposes the gap that results between word and world, language and reality, one that grows wider and more apparent as the novel goes on.

This gap widens further, and is much further explored and exploited, in Joyce's writing after *Ulysses*. This later writing first appeared as 'Work In Progress' in the Paris-based journal *transition* in the 1920s: it was eventually published in its entirety as *Finnegans Wake* in 1939. Joyce writes in its early stages, 'Here English might be seen' (p. 13) – but if it can be, it is only fragmentarily and dimly. In 'the waters of babalong' (p. 103) which express the dreams of H. C. Earwicker – the sleeping Dublin publican whose mind sustains the material of the novel – language's familiar functions largely dissolve. For example, one of the many minor stories in *Finnegans Wake* begins

> The Mookse and The Gripes.
> Gentes and laitymen, fullstoppers and semicolonials, hybreds and lubberds!
> Eins within a space and a wearywide space it wast ere wohned a Mookse. The onsesomeness wast alltolonely, archunsitslike, broady oval, and a Mookse he would a walking go. (My hood! cries Antony Romeo), so one grandsumer evening, after a great morning and his good supper of gammon and spittish, having flabelled his eyes,

pilleoled his nostrils, vacticanated his ears and palliumed his throats,
he put on his impermeable, seized his impugnable, harped on his
crown and stepped out of his immobile *De Rure Albo*. (p. 152)

'If you are abcedminded' the text comments earlier, 'what curios of
signs . . . in this allaphbed! Can you rede . . . its world?' (p. 18). If
there is a world to be read in *Finnegans Wake*, it is obviously in
unconventional ways. Rather than being meaningless, as some early
critics complained, *Finnegans Wake* causes problems because it is
actually overfraught with wayward, ever-expanding significances.
These, however, do less to communicate a story – though this
remains at least dimly visible, especially towards the end of the
above extract – than to direct attention self-referentially at Joyce's
means of expression and the curiosity of his signs. 'Eins within a
space', for example, parodies the traditional opening 'once upon a
time', emphasising Joyce's distance from narrative convention and
incidentally establishing the sort of equation of space and time
typical of thinking in the 1920s. The phrase reinforces this idea with
the use of the German for 'once', 'Eins', with its half-suggestion of
Einstein, who has also turned up as 'Winestain' a few pages earlier.

Almost every other word in the extract likewise functions
obliquely; doubly or sometimes multiply in terms of pun or hidden
suggestion. Does 'wast', for example, mean 'vast' or work as an
archaic form of the verb to be, or in both senses? Is 'wearywide' very
wide or wearisomely wide, or both? Constantly raising such
questions, always shifting its vocabulary away from single deter-
minate meanings, *Finnegans Wake* directs attention to the nature
and relationships of words, to linguistic issues such as phonetics,
etymology, or the semantics of English and sometimes of other
languages – rather than to any traditional subject of the novel.
Character, for instance, the ladies and gentlemen conventionally
central to fiction, are converted in the above extract to 'Gentes and
laitymen, fullstoppers and semicolonials', becoming features of
punctuation, adjuncts of language.

This kind of conversion, and the strategies of *Finnegans Wake* in
general, are more or less defined by one of the novel's own phrases:
'say mangraphique, may say nay por daguerre!' (p. 339). Among the
multilingual puns of this statement can be found the suggestion that
Joyce's work is primarily 'graphique', not 'por daguerre': it is
writing, writing for itself, not as daguerrotype or any other quasi-

photographic attempt to represent character or reality. In his essay 'The Revolution of Language and James Joyce', one of the editors of *transition*, Eugene Jolas, likewise remarks that 'Work in Progress' showed that

> The real metaphysical problem today is the word. The epoch when the writer photographed the life about him with the mechanics of words redolent of the daguerrotype, is happily drawing to its close. The new artist of the word has recognised the autonomy of language.[9]

Jolas's comment appeared in *Our Exagmination Round his Factification for Incamination of Work in Progress* (1929), a volume of essays defending Joyce's work against contemporary puzzlement and criticism. In another of its essays, Samuel Beckett remarked that in Joyce's latest writing 'form *is* content, content *is* form . . . His writing is not *about* something; *it is that something itself*' (p. 14). Beckett's terms help to clarify the progress or change in orientation of Joyce's writing in the 1920s. In *Ulysses*, 'form' and 'content' share attention: Bloom, Molly and Stephen remain firmly visible, even through thickening screens of language, which inevitably also draw attention to themselves. In *Finnegans Wake*, the balance shifts firmly away from 'Gentes and laitymen': screens of language thicken towards an opacity no photography or daguerrotype can wholly penetrate, and the only way to 'rede its world' is to concentrate upon the language itself. The real problem – or the real interest – of *Finnegans Wake* is not in the real but the word, a word freely fleeing its denotative function, creating an 'autonomous language', a 'new art of the word'. Representation and its medium are what *Finnegans Wake* principally represents: its language is at least as much an examination and celebration of itself as a communication of any world, inner or outer.

*Finnegans Wake* thus extends to extremes the separation of words and their associations, language and meaning, which interests Stephen in *A Portrait of the Artist as a Young Man*. Though Joyce may have felt this separation more acutely than his contemporaries, and explored it further than any of them, he was certainly not the only modernist author to puzzle over the gap between words and the world, or to negotiate in one way or another with the problems and possibilities that resulted. In *To the Lighthouse*, for example,

Woolf shows Lily Briscoe questioning in her own way words' attachment to objects or associations, and doubting language's capacity to mean or represent anything:

> Little words that broke up the thought and dismembered it said nothing. 'About life, about death; about Mrs Ramsay' – no, she thought, one could say nothing to nobody. The urgency of the moment always missed its mark. Words fluttered sideways and struck the object inches too low. Then one gave it up; then the idea sunk back again . . . For how could one express in words these emotions of the body? (p. 202)

Themes and conclusions in *To the Lighthouse* are often dramatised by the form of the text itself: in this case, something of Lily's scepticism about language reappears in the novel's own attempt to express things 'about death; about Mrs Ramsay'. Mrs Ramsay's death is framed in an odd, barely intelligible sentence, as if the ordinary shape of language could hardly contain the weight of emotion involved:

> [Mr Ramsay stumbling along a passage stretched his arms out one dark morning, but, Mrs Ramsay having died rather suddenly the night before, he stretched his arms out. They remained empty.] (pp. 146–7)

Further reservations about words and their adequacy to express or contain reality appear in *The Waves*. Throughout, Bernard uses phrase-making and storytelling as a necessary refuge from the difficulties of life, explaining, for example,

> I must make phrases and phrases and so interpose something hard between myself and the stare of housemaids, the stare of clocks, staring faces, indifferent faces, or I shall cry. (p. 25)

Bernard in this way feels compelled to seek 'among phrases and fragments something unbroken', and he believes life can be 'netted . . . with a sudden phrase . . . retrieved . . . from formlessness with words' (pp. 229, 232). Yet he is also sceptical about the process in which he finds it so necessary to engage, worrying that 'life is not susceptible perhaps to the treatment we give it' (p. 229). As Woolf also suggests in *Jacob's Room*, life may slip through the nets framed to catch it by novelists, or, if they do catch it and succeed in imposing a consoling order upon it, this is achieved at the expense of falsifying or excluding some of its raw reality. In the end Bernard seeks instead words which can themselves be more raw and immediate, or somehow able to reject conventional language altogether. He remarks that instead of

> Stories . . . phrases . . . neat designs of life . . . I begin to long for some little language such as lovers use, broken words, inarticulate words . . .

> . . words of one syllable such as children speak . . . I need a howl; a cry . . . I need no words. Nothing neat . . . I have done with phrases.
> How much better is silence . . . let me sit on and on, silent, alone. (pp. 204, 254)

Partly as a result of his particular concern with 'the emotions of the body' and 'language such as lovers use', D. H. Lawrence also experienced uneasiness with the ordinary function of words. As suggested in Chapter 2, his interest in profound emotions, love and passion – and the urge to follow these into his characters' unconscious as well as conscious minds – often severely strains ordinary language in his novels. It also leads in general to scepticism about the value of words, limited in their potential to represent what is called in *Women in Love* an 'unspeakable communication' (p. 361) – something 'beyond thought' (p. 221); beyond what can be reflected in ordinary consciousness. Birkin indicates something of this problem when he remarks of a passionate vision of Ursula that it 'could never be netted, it must fly by itself to the heart' and asks, 'What was the good of talking, anyway? It must happen beyond the sound of words' (p. 282). Ursula confirms Birkin's conclusions, remarking:

> She knew, as well as he knew, that words themselves do not convey meaning, that they are but a gesture we make, a dumb show like any other. (p. 209)

In *Lady Chatterley's Lover*, Constance Chatterley resents language in a more general way, not only for its failure to reach or represent certain of the deepest and most important feelings, but for a deadening obstruction of *all* real communication with life. Significantly, like many of Lawrence's scenes of intense emotion, her relationship with the gamekeeper Mellors unfolds in terms somewhat apart from conventional language, or at least, in this case, outwith standard English. Full of 'thees' and 'thous', his broad Derbyshire dialect helps establish a private language 'such as lovers use'; one able to generate terms for physicality and more inventive and alert to love and the body. Constance's disdain for her husband, on the other hand, focuses on 'his consciousness, his words': she despises the lifelessness and obstruction of his

> turning everything into words . . . How she hated words, always coming between her and life: they did the ravishing, if anything did: ready-made words and phrases, sucking all the life-sap out of living things . . .
>
> How ravished one could be without ever being touched. Ravished by dead words become obscene, and dead ideas become obsessions. (pp. 96–7)

The idea of words ravishing or sucking the life out of things echoes Lily Briscoe's view of language dismembering thought and saying nothing about life. Constance's feeling that words come between her and life likewise resembles Bernard's sense of phrases interposing something hard between himself and the world. Such attitudes show both Woolf and Lawrence following Joyce, finding language definitely not a transparent medium, but instead something autonomous, a screen between the individual and the world surveyed. Woolf and Lawrence, however – the latter in particular – look less positively on this autonomy of language, on words partly freed of their associations, than Stephen Dedalus does in *A Portrait of the Artist as a Young Man*, or Joyce throughout much of his work. The particular limitations indicated and parodied by Joyce in languages turned clichéd, dead or stale, Lawrence sees as inherent, ineradicable properties of *all* language. In *Psychoanalysis and the Unconscious* he remarks:

> The idea is another static entity, another unit of the mechanical-active and materio-static universe . . . Ideas are the dry, unliving, insentient plumage which intervenes between us and the circumambient universe, forming at once an insulator and an instrument for the subduing of the universe . . .
>
> 'In the beginning was the Word'. This is the presumptuous masquerading of the mind. The Word cannot be the beginning of life. It is the *end* of life . . . the mind is the dead end of life. (p. 246)

For Lawrence, language is not a prism through which reality can be refracted into new shapes and colours, but rather a kind of prison, a trapping of vital, open or profound experience into narrowing categories that the mind sets up for it – static entities; ready-made words and phrases; dead or deadening ideas. A similar view of language as a trap or prison underlies Bernard's scepticism in *The Waves* about 'netting' experience into neat designs, or about relying on 'phrases laid like Roman roads across the tumult of our lives' (p. 223). This idea of language as a grid imposed on a vital 'tumult' extends the general modernist inclination (discussed earlier) to see life and reality as fluid, continuous, perpetually creative, but falsely apprehended by the divisive, dissecting apparatus of the intellect – clocks, calendars, concepts, categories or whatever. It was suggested in Chapter 3 that modernism looked resentfully at the way in which one set of such concepts and categories had been institutionalised, shaped into the huge net spread across the world from Greenwich, formalising space and time into narrowing, defining orders. Language, for some of the modernists, was resented as in certain respects another such net, another unit of the 'mechanical . . . materio-static' forces restricting or ravishing rather than truly representing life. In this way, words and language – the very medium of their art – became for some of the modernists, as Eugene Jolas suggests, a real problem.

Significantly, Jolas suggests language to be not only a real literary problem, but 'the real metaphysical problem today'. Like the features of modernist writing discussed in the last two chapters, its new concern with language is apparent elsewhere in the life of the twentieth century, its philosophy or metaphysics included. Like the suspicion of the clock discussed in Chapter 3, modernist uneasiness with language is expressed particularly clearly in the philosophy of Henri Bergson. Like Lawrence, Bergson saw words as static and only too likely to 'impose . . . their own stability' on the true fluidity of life and consciousness. The intellect, with 'its insatiable desire to separate', seizes on language as a tool to arrest and define. As a result,

> the word with well-defined outlines overwhelms or at least covers over the delicate and fugitive impressions of our individual consciousness. (*Time and Free Will*, pp. 128, 132)

This leaves, in Bergson's view, 'no common measure between mind and language' (p. 165). Worse, it consequently encourages a kind of split in apprehension of the mind or self: because it is 'ill-suited to render the subtleties of psychological analysis' (p. 13), language helps establish 'finally two different selves' (p. 231). One is the self that can be made to belong in language: defined, solidified, made visible, but falsified. The other self runs on deeply, continuously, but almost inaccessibly, beyond the reach of words.

The suggestion that language splits the self points towards some of the later writing – Samuel Beckett's particularly – that followed from modernism. It also anticipates some later twentieth-century thinking, such as the diagnosis in Jacques Lacan's psychoanalytic criticism that language induces a continuous and permanent division of the subject. Bergson's scepticism about language was also shared by several other philosophers in his own age. William James, for example, follows Bergson in finding words isolating single, separate features from the continuity of experience, dividing it into limiting categories. This artificial quality ensures that 'language works against our perception of the truth' (I, p. 241). Like James and Bergson, Nietzsche criticises language's imposition of stasis upon fluidity, category upon continuity. He remarks that

> Through words and concepts we are still continually misled into imagining things as being simpler than they are, separate from one another, indivisible, each existing in and for itself.

Nietzsche also goes further, questioning the possibility of any valid contact between language and reality:

> mankind set up in language a separate world beside the other world, a place it took to be so firmly set that, standing upon it, it could lift the rest of the world off its hinges and make itself master of it . . . A great deal later – only now – it dawns on men that in their belief in language they have propagated a tremendous error.[10]

Nietzsche's comments suggest that his views, like those of James and Bergson, arose almost inevitably from the epistemologic shift discussed in Chapter 2. Such a shift in outlook was bound to question the nature and function of language. If authentic contacts between mind and world ceased to seem wholly possible, then language's confident provision of terms representing reality for the mind came to seem a pretence, even a delusion – an invitation to step securely on to a bridge over a gulf now considered unbridgeable. Language's innocence seemed to have been lost. Talking about this, Michel Foucault suggests that

> in its original form, when it was given to men by God himself,

language was an absolutely certain and transparent sign for things. (p. 36)

Since, however,

the profound kinship of language with the world was . . . dissolved . . . things and words were to be separated from one another. (p. 43)

This sort of separation was further reflected and formalised in the linguistics of the period: in particular by Ferdinand de Saussure's influential *Cours de linguistique générale*, first published in 1916. Saussure suggests that words and concepts, signifiers and signifieds – rather than being connected absolutely, innocently or transparently – relate to one another only arbitrarily, as a result of habit and convention. Contemporary science also undermined secure contact between language and reality. Describing the astonishing session of the Royal Society at which confirmation of Einstein's theories was announced in 1919, *The Times* reported the President of the Society – after stating that the meeting had just listened to 'one of the most momentous, if not the most momentous, pronouncements of human thought' – as admitting that 'no-one had yet succeeded in stating in clear language what the theory of Einstein really was'.[11] A relativistic reality eluded description other than in the language of mathematics: the most 'momentous' thoughts of humanity, as well as the profoundest of its passions, were now generally conceived as taking place beyond the certain reach of words.

Many thinkers, then, in the early twentieth century, contributed to a sense of language detached on the one hand from a reality it could no longer pretend wholly to master, and on the other from a mind whose fluid movements tended to be misrepresented by its static, defining aspects. As Nietzsche suggests, language came to seem a separate domain of its own, with no common measure securely existing between either words and mind or words and the world. The 'autonomy of language' was thus not simply an invention of James Joyce and modernist authors, but a 'real metaphysical problem' of much more far-reaching concern at the time – and also since. Modernism's investigations of how representation operates, of how art shapes itself in language, participate in an uneasy fascination with how reality can be signified, the world given form in words, which runs throughout the twentieth century, a recurrent stress in its thoughts. Miriam Henderson sums up doubts wider than her own, wider even than those of modernist fiction in general, when she remarks in *Pilgrimage*:

> *All* that has been said and known in the world is in *language*, in words ... then no one *knows* anything for certain. Everything depends upon the way a thing is put, and that is a question of some particular civilisation ... language is the only way of expressing anything and it dims everything ... words ... get more and more wrong. (II, p. 99)

In addition to contemporary philosophy, several other factors in the early twentieth century contributed to the kind of stresses on language that modernist fiction reflects. Psychoanalysis was obviously one. Freud encouraged the kind of deeper attention to individual consciousness that appears in modernism: he also , like D. H. Lawrence, showed how such attention encounters limits in the powers of language. In *The Interpretation of Dreams* (1899), Freud asks:

> what representation can 'if' 'because' 'as though' 'although' 'either-or'
> and all the other conjunctions without which we cannot understand a phrase or sentence, receive in the dream? (p. 290)

Freud answers by suggesting that the dream can only 'reproduce logical connections in the form of simultaneous' (p. 292), leaving language – if it exists in the dream at all – fractured, unstructured, without ordinary sense. At one point at least, following a character towards unconsciouness and dream, modernist fiction moves towards such a language. At the end of 'Ithaca', as Bloom's thoughts revolve darkly towards sleep, the 'baldest, coldest' scientific language dissolves and collapses completely:

> Going to bed there was a square round Sinbad the Sailor's roc's auk's egg in the night of the bed of all the auks of the rocs of Darkinbad the Brightdayler.
>
> Where?
> .     (p.607)

Drifting towards unconsciousness, Bloom's language first expands into apparent nonsense, then shrinks to a final, silent point. Each movement indicates a different terminus of modernism's urge to 'look within' and 'examine the mind'. In one direction, this urge leads to a full stop on the edge of unconsciousness, the blankness and silence which follows the final period – '.' – to Bloom's thoughts in *Ulysses*. This is also close to the position Bernard reaches in *The Waves* when he decides how much better it is to sit on, silent and alone, rather than engage in howls, cries or even the broken language of love. It is the logic Lawrence admits when he talks in *Women in Love* of an

> unspeakable communication . . . the reality of that which can never be known, vital, sensual reality that can never be transmuted into mind content, but remains outside, living body of darkness and silence. (p. 361)

Language, in this view, can reach only so far into the mind: the rest is silence.

Or – the other terminus – what rests outside the realm of consciousness or ordinary sense may still be approximated by a language that seeks, as best it can, verbal equivalents for the unconscious and unspeakable. This is the direction Joyce briefly establishes in his very last attention to Bloom, in the passage above, in *Ulysses*, and which he follows much further in *Finnegans Wake*. 'All the auks of the rocs of Darkinbad the Brightdayler' show Joyce's language moving from the bright day of *Ulysses* and the streams of consciousness that run through it towards the great night language, the stream of unconsciousness, which he considered *Finnegans Wake* and its burden of dreams. If, as Proust suggests, dreams leave language 'void of content' (II, p. 1014), or in Freud's view, devoid of ordinary logic or conjunction, then a promising approximation to the language of dream may be offered by the style of *Finnegans Wake*. Its self-referential, puzzling 'curios of signs', denying ordinary meaning, ensure as Beckett suggests that 'form *is* content, content *is* form'. Considered in this way, however nonsensical it seems – in fact, *because* it seems nonsensical, or at least beyond ordinary sense – *Finnegans Wake* can be seen as the ultimate, logical extension of modernism's urge to examine the mind.

The two movements, however – towards silence or the floods of 'babalong' in *Finnegans Wake* – mutually expose what comes close to a contradiction in this modernist urge. If pursued far enough and deeply enough, one way or the other, the determination to look within may simply lead beyond what can be realised in the linguistic medium of fiction, at the very least requiring the complete reforging of language that appears in *Finnegans Wake*. The new modernist wish to 'examine the mind' not only revealed that at times 'little words . . . broke up the thought and dismembered it', but also that in certain areas they might be able to say nothing at all. In an age made by Freud's work more than ever aware of the nature and depth of the mind, ordinary words and language seemed more than ever limited and particular in what they could achieve. Almost inevitably, given its interests, modernist fiction grew self-conscious and in some ways sceptical about its own medium, its use of language. If they moved deeply into the workings of the mind in their fiction, modernist authors were likely to experience a version of the feelings of Samuel Beckett's Unnamable, paradoxically concluding 'in the silence you don't know, you must go on, I can't go on, I'll go on' (p. 382). Silence tells readers nothing: the novel must go on in language, yet knowing that language cannot go on very far in recording the 'living body of darkness' within the self.

An 'unspeakable experience' of a different sort, the First World War, had its own effects in placing stresses on language and in opening up gaps between reality and representation. In one way, these were the direct result of ruin and desolation on a scale so far beyond anything known before that they eluded assimilation in familiar words or literary forms. Some of Ernest Hemingway's fiction dramatises the impossibility of rendering authentic war experience within conventions wholly inadequate to contain such monstrous events. In his short story 'Soldier's Home' (1926), for example, Hemingway shows a hero who is forced to fabricate and lie in order to interest his audience, or even to seem to be telling the truth. In *The Great War and Modern Memory*, Paul Fussell examines at length how the familiar forms of expression that presented themselves for description of the war failed to match the reality, or were used inappropriately and misleadingly, even by participants in the action who had every intention of remaining as truthful to it as possible.

The lasting effects of the war on language, however, were the work not of participants overwhelmed by the indescribable, but of governments and propagandists who quite deliberately over-whelmed the actual in words, screening terrible truths from the public, turning carnage into patriotic glory. Talking about the start of the war, Richard Aldington remarks in *Death of a Hero*:

> The long, unendurable nightmare had begun. And the reign of Cant, Delusion and Delirium . . .
>
> If the War had been an honest affair for any participant, it would not have needed the preposterous bolstering up of Cant . . .
>
> One human brain cannot hold, one memory retain, one pen portray the limitless Cant, Delusion, and Delirium let loose on the world during those four years . . . this sort of criminal rant was called Pisgah-Heights of Patriotism. (pp. 221–3)

Like his fellow German war-novelist Erich Maria Remarque, in his ironically entitled *All Quiet on the Western Front* (*Im Westen nichts Neues*, 1929), Aldington shows at several points in *Death of a Hero* the gap between actual experience and official report:

> Four or five times they passed corpses being carried down the trenches as they went up. There was, of course, nothing to report on the Western front. (p. 279)

Aldington's example is relatively innocuous compared to some of the actual delusions practised by Press and propaganda during the war. Describing the first day's action in the battle of the Somme, for example, *The Times* reported:

> Sir Douglas Haig telegraphed last night that the general situation was favourable . . .
>
> The great offensive in the West has made a good beginning and promises exceedingly well . . .
>
> The day goes well for England and France . . . as far as can be ascertained our casualties have not been heavy.[12]

This was the report. In reality the first morning of the Somme, 1 July 1916, saw the heaviest casualties ever sustained by the British army, devastating in the space of a few hours the 60,000 British soldiers involved in the first assault: 420,000 were killed or wounded before the battle eventually ended, months later.

Such gaps between reality and report multiplied throughout the war to an extent that induced a permanent scepticism about the agencies responsible for them. As Paul Fussell suggests,

> there is a sense in which public euphemism as the special rhetorical sound of life in the latter third of the twentieth century can be said to originate in the years 1914–18. It was perhaps the first time in history

that official policy produced events so shocking, bizarre, and stomach-turning that the events had to be tidied up for presentation to a highly literate mass population . . .

A lifelong suspicion of the press was one lasting result of the ordinary man's experience of the war. It might even be said that the current devaluation of letterpress and even of language itself dates from the Great War. (pp. 178, 316)

As Fussell indicates, the latter part of the twentieth century has done nothing to diminish scepticism about Press and official report. For example, 1973 found the Press secretary to the President of the United States, Richard Nixon, announcing with apparent equanimity that earlier statements to the media were 'inoperative' – a public euphemism about a public lie.[13] Throughout the twentieth century the multiplying lies of governments and official institutions – as well as advertisers – have steadily added to language's potential for distortion rather than representation; to its capacity for rhetorical manipulation almost independently of meaning or truth. This capacity has sometimes been directly examined and exploited in literature – by Ernest Hemingway, for example, likely to be more conscious than other modernist writers of the war's effects on language since he was a journalist himself. Early short stories such as 'The Killers' (1928) or 'Hills Like White Elephants' (1928) show the possibilities of using language, almost independently of the usual meaning of words, as a means of manipulating or enforcing power. Much the same dissembling and manipulation appear in the early work of Harold Pinter, an admirer of Hemingway, as well as of Joyce and Beckett, who continues in the later twentieth century to dramatise the potential and peculiarities of what he calls a language 'where under what is said, another thing is being said'.[14] For Hemingway and Pinter at least, the distortion and corruption of the twentieth-century's language by its agencies of power is a source of fascination and literary opportunity, rather than only regret.

For most of the modernists in the early part of the century, however, the principal effect of the war was not in opening up new layers, capacities or opportunities in language. Rather, the war's unspeakable experience and the cant that reigned around it simply diminished confidence in language's reliability, and in its communicative function in general, while also exercising a particularly corrosive effect on the significance of certain words. Writing before the war's effects were felt, in *The Good Soldier* (1915), Ford Madox Ford's narrator still talks of the way 'good soldiers' found their profession 'full of the big words, courage, loyalty, honour, constancy' (p. 31). By contrast, in *A Farewell to Arms* (1929), written after the war and from Hemingway's own experience of the Italian campaign, the narrator remarks that 'abstract words such as glory, honour, courage or hallow were obscene'. He adds that

> I was always embarrassed by the words sacred, glorious, and sacrifice and the expression in vain . . . I had seen nothing sacred, and the things that were glorious had no glory and the sacrifices were like the stockyards at Chicago if nothing was done with the meat except to bury it. There were many words that you could not stand to hear. (p. 202)

Living after 'the cataclysm . . . among the ruins', Constance Chatterley likewise regrets a kind of devaluation in the currency of certain words:

> 'Home!' . . . it was a word that had had its day. It was somehow cancelled. All the great words, it seemed to Connie, were cancelled for her generation: love, joy, happiness, home, mother, father, husband, all these great, dynamic words were half dead now, and dying from day to day. (p. 64)

For good soldiers and civilians alike, the disillusion of the war and the ruins that followed it disallowed great words, big words, or abstract words. Yet of course these 'cancelled' words did not simply disappear. They continued in everyday usage, but hollowed out, emptied of meaning, a rhetoric disjunct from reality. Like other contemporary influences, the war in this way helped detach signifiers from signifieds. It played its part in ensuring – in Foucault's terms – that 'the profound kinship of language with the world was dissolved' and that 'things and words were . . . separated from one another'. For the hollow men and women of the 1920s, only a hollow language was left – another kind of 'autonomous language', bereft of common measure with mind or world.

Gaps between word and world were also widened by the experience of exile, an experience shared in one way or another, as critics have often noticed, by very many modernist authors. Joseph Conrad was a Pole who travelled the world before settling in Britain; Ford

Madox Hueffer – who changed his name to Ford during the First World War – was of German extraction; Henry James was originally American before becoming a country gentleman in Sussex and eventually seeking British citizenship. Though D. H. Lawrence was native-born in Nottinghamshire, much of his life was spent abroad, eventually in Italy and Mexico, fleeing Britain in ways some of his characters contemplate in *Women in Love*. Born in Nova Scotia, Wyndham Lewis spent several of his formative years, early in the century, wandering on the Continent. Dorothy Richardson grew up in London, but left by the age of 17 to work, like her heroine Miriam Henderson, as an English-language teacher in a school in Germany.

Miriam's experience of this polyglot school community with its babble of conflicting languages – French, German, strange versions of English – provides one basis for her conclusion, quoted earlier, that 'language is the only way of expressing anything and it dims everything'. Another basis for this conclusion, however, was available to Richardson, or to any woman writer, even without leaving London. Unusually among modernist authors, Virginia Woolf was British both by origin and domicile: her Bloomsbury literary circle, and the London setting for *Mrs Dalloway*, seem to place her at the heart of metropolitan culture. Yet Woolf points to a particular form of exile for women writers when she talks (in the passage from *A Room of One's Own* quoted in Chapter 2) about feeling 'outside . . . alien and critical' even when walking through Whitehall in central London. This sense of exile, of exclusion from a male-dominated culture and society, Woolf also sees as having particular consequences for the language of women's writing. She remarks in *A Room of One's Own* that, for a woman novelist,

> it is useless to go to the great men writers for help . . . the first thing she would find, setting pen to paper, was that there was no common sentence ready for her use . . . a man's sentence . . . was unsuited for a woman's use. (p. 76).

Dorothy Richardson likewise asked for a 'feminine prose' to escape the stricture of a male language unsuited to her purposes. Miriam Henderson discusses some of these restrictions, and the disparities between the language of men and women:

> In speech with a man a woman is at a disadvantage – because they speak different languages. She may understand his. Hers he will

never speak nor understand . . . she must therefore, stammeringly, speak his. (II, p. 210)

Yet no woman, Miriam adds, will ever reveal 'her mental measure . . . even the fringe of her consciousness' by speaking the language of men (II, p. 210). Since culture is constructed in what Miriam sees as effectively a foreign language, she finds 'there was nothing to turn to. Books were poisoned. Art. All the achievements of men were poisoned at the root' (II, p. 222).

Miriam's comments – like those of Richardson herself, or Virginia Woolf – highlight a specific, aggravated lack of 'common measure' between women's consciousness and the conventional language and forms available to express it. This lack contributed to a certain state of exile, metaphorically at least, for women at the time, though in a way a fruitful one. Uneasiness with ordinary language and consequent readiness to reject conventional forms of representation almost forced women writers, in the early twentieth century, into the position suggested in Chapter 2 that they occupied – at the centre of modernist innovation and stylistic experiment. Being partly outside a culture, alien and critical, is not always a comfortable position, but it can encourage productive re-examination and reconstruction of that culture's conventional forms and styles.

Exile in reality – geographic rather than only metaphoric – affected modernist authors and their work in a variety of ways. Some of Conrad and James's personal experience as foreigners, for example, may be reflected in the frequent interest of their novels in a 'first-person singular' – one who is often a lonely stranger, gradually puzzling out the demands of the complex new environment confronting him. For Conrad himself, who spoke French as well as Polish before he learned English, part of this puzzle was with language, a difficulty often examined in his fiction. The speech of many of the minor narrators who add to Marlow's story in *Lord Jim*, for example, and of several other characters, shows strong traces of syntax or vocabulary retained from languages more familiar to them than English. Thus when he provides Marlow with the account of how he helped rescue the *Patna*, the French Lieutenant describes as follows his first encounter with the ship's frightened passengers:

'*Impossible de comprendre – vous concevez* . . . They crowded upon

us. There was a circle round that dead man (*autour de ce mort*) . . .
One had to attend to the most pressing. These people were beginning
to agitate themselves – *Parbleu!*' (p. 108)

The wise German merchant, Stein, draws his conclusions about
Jim, and about life in general, in a manner similarly bilingual:

> Because you not always can keep your eyes shut there comes the real
> trouble – the heart pain – the world pain . . . You not strong enough
> are, or not clever enough. Ja! (p. 163)

When recording the language of the Captain who takes Jim to
Patusan – whose 'flowing English seemed to be derived from a
dictionary compiled by a lunatic' (p. 182), and who talks of
'laughable hyaenas' and the 'weapons of a crocodile' – Conrad's
tortuous speech forms move towards the absurd.

Throughout *Lord Jim*, however, alternation between languages
has the serious purpose of emphasising the absurdity of what one
character calls the attempt to 'see a thing as it is' (p. 130). Conrad's
careful particularisation of points of view, for each of the multiple
narrators of *Lord Jim*, highlights the way any account of reality is
ineradicably coloured by the nature and outlook of individual
observers. The novel also shows how the singularity of any
individual outlook is itself conditioned by the particular qualities of
the language in which it is framed. *Lord Jim* shows that nothing can
be seen absolutely 'as it is': nothing can be seen independently of
ways of seeing it which are inevitably specific to individuals,
cultures and ultimately languages. Throughout, *Lord Jim* demonstrates the kind of conclusion Miriam Henderson reaches when she
remarks that 'everything depends upon the way a thing is put, and
that is a question of some particular civilisation'. Juxtaposition of
different languages emphasises the particularity, the arbitrariness of
each: in the end Conrad's shifting screens of language create a sense
of exile not so much from individual nations or civilisations, but
from reality itself. Like Jim himself, the world 'as it is' remains at
most only barely visible through the shifting mists of words used to
represent it. No language can make more than an incomplete
contact with a world that exists, *Lord Jim* suggests, across 'a broad
gulf that neither eye nor voice could span' (p. 256). Many of the
novel's crucial moments – Jim's crisis of conscience in Marlow's
hotel in Chapter 15, or his concluding desire to sacrifice himself to
Doramin – take place in a silence that almost mocks the powers of

the word. While Jim soundlessly agonises in Marlow's room, Marlow writes endless, purposeless letters. When Jim makes his final, suicidal decision to present himself to Doramin's fury, his journal records, 'I must now at once . . .'. – followed by nothing except a blot in the shape of the head of an arrow (p. 256). As Marlow reflects, language can never achieve a finality, a fullness, a complete consummation of the desires of its speakers or a true encapsulation of their world:

> the last word is not said . . . Are not our lives too short for that full utterance which through all our stammerings is of course our only and abiding intention? I have given up expecting those last words, whose ring, if they could only be pronounced, would shake both heaven and earth . . . The heaven and the earth must not be shaken. (pp. 171–2)

Linguistic concern and experiment in the fiction of later modernists may have been partly owed, like Conrad's, to a background of exile and an experience of conflicting languages. James Joyce was probably the most thoroughgoing of all modernist exiles: following his hero Stephen's strategy of leaving Ireland to 'forge . . . the uncreated conscience' of his race, he worked as an English teacher in Trieste before moving on to Zurich in 1915 and finally settling in Paris after the war. Lengthy foreign domicile, and perhaps especially work, like Dorothy Richardson's, as a teacher of English, placed Joyce in a permanent context of linguistic contrasts and conflicts after he left Ireland. Yet in some ways this sort of experience actually began much earlier, as an inevitable part of Joyce's Irishness. This is suggested in *A Portrait of the Artist as a Young Man* when Stephen Dedalus encounters an English priest and reflects that

> The language in which we are speaking is his before it is mine. How different are the words *home*, *Christ*, *ale*, *master*, on his lips and on mine! I cannot speak or write these words without unrest of spirit. His language, so familiar and so foreign, will always be for me an acquired speech. I have not made or accepted its words. My voice holds them at bay. My soul frets in the shadow of his language. (p. 189)

Stephen's 'fretting' against standard English, and its existence for him as an 'acquired speech', help account for his self-conscious fascination for words, and his sense of their objective existence partly independent of their 'associations'. For Joyce himself, languages later encountered in France, Switzerland and Italy – foreign yet eventually familiar – simply added to a critical, objective distance from English and its accepted forms which already existed before he left Ireland. Conflicting shadows of many languages played across Joyce's whole life – an obvious encouragement to the verbal inventiveness and concentration on words and speech that appear in *Ulysses*, and to the eventual creation in *Finnegans Wake* of a polyglot, autonomous language in which English can sometimes only barely be seen.

The last line of *Ulysses* – not Molly's 'yes', but Joyce's note of where the novel was written, in 'Trieste-Zurich-Paris' – thus provides a key to the nature of his writing as a whole, and indeed to the development of other contemporary novelists, or even of modernism in general. Fretting against foreign languages, confrontation with alien yet apparently self-consistent systems of words, confirms a sense of arbitrariness in the relation of signifier and signified, adding to a need for the nature of language and representation to become a subject of enquiry. Awareness of foreign cultures and their alternative systems for envisaging the world may also have heightened, for the authors mentioned above, critical awareness of the specific conventions of the language and culture in which they worked, adding to a readiness to reshape or abandon these conventions in favour of new techniques. In this way, not only women writers, but all modernist exiles may have found the experience of being 'outside . . . alien and critical' a provocative, shaping influence in the evolution of their art. It is not simply an interesting coincidence that many modernists were exiles. The experience of exile significantly added to readiness to reconstruct the novel form – to engage in the stylistic, structural innovation that became the defining characteristic of modernism.

Some of the narrative and linguistic theory of Mikhail Bakhtin further clarifies why this was so. As discussed in Chapter 2, Bakhtin defines the language of the novel as essentially 'a *system* of languages that mutually and ideologically interanimate each other' (p. 47). In this polyphonic or (in Bakhtin's terminology) 'polyglossic' system, simultaneous allegiances to more than one language – or form of language – fret, compete and interfuse. Such tension and fretting between languages Bakhtin shows to be fundamental to the origins as well as to the continuing existence of the novel form. Historically, the novel genre first appeared and developed at a time when the autonomy of national languages was being challenged – when

> the period of national languages, coexisting but closed and deaf to each other, comes to an end. Languages throw light on each other: one language can, after all, see itself only in the light of another language . . . In this actively polyglot world, completely new relationships are established between language and its object (that is, the real world) . . . the novel emerged and matured precisely when intense activization of external and internal polyglossia was at the peak of its activity; this is its native element . . .

> Thus did the interanimation of languages occur in the very epoch that saw the creation of the European novel. Laughter and polyglossia had paved the way for the novelistic discourse of modern times. (pp. 12, 82)

If, as Bakhtin indicates, 'interanimation of languages' is fundamental to the creation and development of the novel, *re*-creation and *re*development of the genre – the business of modernism – may also be most likely to occur at historical points where 'intense peaks' of polyglossia recur. The opening years of the twentieth century constitute such a point, a point where intimate contacts between foreign and native elements of speech and culture were once again a central, everyday experience of many people, and many authors. New relations were once again – for the complex of historical and cultural reasons examined above – established between language and its object. The new 'autonomy of language', bereft of the absolute certainty that Foucault sees as characterising its earlier relations with reality, created at the time a linguistic shift as profound as the epistemological shift earlier discussed. A 'new artist of the word', in Eugene Jolas's description, reshaped the novel around new perceptions of the nature of language, as well as new outlooks on the world in general.

The peculiar position of language in the early twentieth century, and the general stress on means of representation, can therefore be seen not only as an anxiety for the literature of the time, but as among the conditions and challenges that actually brought modernism into being. Lack of 'common measure' between mind and word, word and world, may be disturbing: it is also potentially liberating, and in any case a context that demands new creativity.

Not for all modernist novelists, but certainly for the greatest of them, James Joyce, it offered almost a cause for celebration. It provided, at any rate, the opportunity for wit, humour and play which drew upon and re-created for the modernist period some of what Bakhtin defines as the novel's deepest powers. Laughter, celebration, mockery and parody Bakhtin sees as fundamental conditions of the novel's origins, with many continuing echoes throughout the subsequent history of the genre. Bakhtin traces the novel's polyglossic nature, its competing 'system of languages', back to the bawdy, irreverent, radical, liberating energies of popular carnival in the Middle Ages. In these celebrations, 'parodic and travestying forms . . . kept alive the memory of . . . linguistic struggle' (p. 67), and through mockery and satire resisted the narrowing, deadening effects of official, institutionalised culture and language. Surviving echoes or reanimations of these conditions of origin Bakhtin defines as a continuing 'carnivalesque' aspect of the novel. In these terms *Ulysses* is a thoroughly carnivalised text. It parodies and mocks the styles of institutions and officialdom; of science; of journalism and of advertising – as well as of literary language and everyday speech. It is thoroughly heterogeneous and inventive in its own use of words; constantly shifting and reorienting its language around the various speech patterns of its characters; avoiding any single, narrowing, definitive register of its own. It is eventually enormously, sometimes grotesquely, affirmative of the body, life and sex. In *Ulysses* at least, 'linguistic struggle' and the fretting of language figure not as a difficulty but as excitement; not as painful necessities for the novel to deal with, but as sources of virtue and vitality for the text to exploit – above all, as a context for the display of Joyce's own extraordinary virtuosity with words.

Not every reader or critic finds this virtuosity happily – or even at all accessibly – extended in *Finnegans Wake*. Yet the inaccessibility of ordinary meaning is a necessary condition – or again, in a way a virtue – of a text which goes much further even than *Ulysses* in exploiting and celebrating aspects of language other than the semantic. Julia Kristeva suggests of 'resistance against modernist literature' in general that it may result from 'an obsession of meaning' (p. 142) which treats too narrowly the range of language's joys and powers: her warning is particularly relevant to *Finnegans Wake*. Locating Joyce firmly in Bakhtin's category of the carnivalesque, Kristeva suggests that readers should understand that the aim of [his] practice, which reaches us as a language, is . . . not only to impose a music, a rhythm – that is, a polyphony – but also to wipe out sense through nonsense and laughter. This is a difficult operation that obliges the reader not so much to combine significations as to shatter his own judging consciousness. (p. 142)

Kristeva's approval of 'nonsense and laughter' wiping out sense offers a way to 'rede' the world Joyce created, independently of too much anxiety about its intelligibility. Obsession with meaning, as she points out, obscures the capacity of words to approximate to the condition of music as well as to convey ordinary sense; to create a rhythm and polyphony able to contact powers deeper than those of intellect and meaning. Proust, in *A la recherche du temps perdu*, thinks of music as 'the means of communication between souls' which 'might have been – if the invention of language, the formation of words, the analysis of ideas had not intervened' (III, p. 260). Joyce, on the other hand, fascinated by sounds and their qualities throughout his fiction, considers the possibilities offered by music always available – sometimes even more fully available – in language. In *A Portrait of the Artist as a Young Man*, for example, Stephen finds 'the soft beauty of the . . . word' possessed of 'a touch fainter and more persuading than the touch of music' (p. 244). Chapter 11 of *Ulysses*, 'Sirens', opens with two pages of fragmentary, syncopated, onomatopoeic phrases, barely communicative of sense but resonant with the random sounds of the city – a kind of urban word-jazz, typical of innovations in style modernism makes in response to the new experiences and rhythms of twentieth-century city life; and of the verbal music which variously sounds at many stages of *Ulysses*.

Such verbal music is audible throughout *Finnegans Wake*. While Lily Briscoe complains in *To the Lighthouse* of 'little words that broke up the thought and dismembered it', the language of *Finnegans Wake* partly gives up thought, and the compromised, doubtful relations of word and world, re-membering instead other powers of language – rhythmic, musical, close to Bernard's demand in *The Waves* for the spontaneous 'howl and cry'; remote from the corruption of meaning in public language wrought by the rhetoric of the First World War; far from the intellect's narrowing 'analysis of ideas' which made language, not only for Lily Briscoe but also for so many writers and thinkers in the early twentieth century, not a reliable means of representation but a kind of prison for imagination and emotion. Far more than any other text in the history of fiction, *Finnegans Wake* achieves the condition of 'words-in-freedom' which one of F. T. Marinetti's Futurist Manifestos, in 1913, claimed as the likely way ahead for literature. As Samuel Beckett warned in 1929, Joyce's work 'is not to be read – or rather it is not only to be read. It is to be looked at and listened to.' [15]

It is another question whether the joys of such a free, polyphonic, multi-layered language are best appreciated at the lengths to which Joyce extends them in *Finnegans Wake*, or whether they may not ideally be the province of poetry rather than fiction. At any rate, however fully or finally the methods of *Finnegans Wake* can be justified, they can be seen as full, final, logical extensions of developments taking place throughout the modernist period, and in many ways central to it. The interest in an autonomous language, in 'the rhythmic rise and fall of words' themselves, begins on Stephen's 'day of dappled seaborne clouds', or with Marcel's journey past Martinville. It grows further in the work of the later modernist writers discussed above, Joyce particularly, and is consummated by him in *Finnegans Wake*. Since in some ways it is difficult to see how its experimentation could be taken much further, and since the novel was finally published in the conveniently epochal year of 1939, *Finnegans Wake* is often held to mark a kind of final terminus for modernism itself.

## MODERNISM AND POSTMODERNISM

Finnegans, however, never end but always begin again, and *Finnegans Wake* marks in twentieth-century writing a point of transition, even new beginning, as much as conclusion. Joyce's novel is in one way a final extension of modernist self-consciousness about art, representation and language: it is also, as such, an antecedent for a self-referential, self-conscious writing – what Fredric Jameson defines as a 'language-centred postmodernism' – which has followed. [16] Several other critics have seen Joyce's 'autonomy of language' and 'new art of the word' helping to instigate a phase of writing that extends – though into distinctly new areas – some of the initiatives of modernism. Christopher Butler, for example, takes *After the Wake* (1980) as the title for his

'Essays on the Contemporary Avant-Garde'. Ihab Hassan talks of *Finnegans Wake* as 'a "monstrous prophecy of our postmodernity" . . . both augur and theory of a certain kind of literature' (pp.xiii-xiv).

Joyce's development towards *Finnegans Wake* also helps confirm the distinctions Brian McHale establishes in his study *Postmodernist Fiction* (1987) between modernism and postmodernism. McHale sees modernism as dominated by epistemological questions, and postmodernism by ontologic ones. The epistemological shift and other general changes in world outlook at the end of the nineteenth century led, in modernism, to questioning and experiment which reflect uncertainty about how reality can be known or assimilated by mind or text. Postmodernism radically extends such uncertainty, often assuming reality – if it exists at all – to be quite unknowable, or inaccessible through a language grown detached from it. Postmodernism investigates instead what worlds can be projected or constructed by language and text themselves. Stephen Dedalus's pondering of how or whether relations can be sustained between word and world shows *A Portrait of the Artist as a Young Man* sharing in the generally epistemological phase of modernism. In *Finnegans Wake*, the breach between word and world is no longer a matter of doubt but of assumption. Contact with a recognisable world is overwhelmed, in McHale's view, by 'the competing reality of language' (p. 234) which establishes *Finnegans Wake* as an ontologically separate, autonomous world.

If this kind of development made *Finnegans Wake*, as Ihab Hassan suggests, an augur and a prophecy, what did it prophesy, and what literature did it inaugurate? Fulfilment of its 'prophecy' is most immediately apparent in the fiction of Samuel Beckett. Aware of Joyce's work throughout its progress, Beckett was naturally one of the first to respond to its 'autonomy of language'. In the central part of his own work, the trilogy *Molloy, Malone Dies, The Unnamable* (1950–2), the Unnamable remarks, 'it all boils down to a question of words . . . all words, there's nothing else' (pp. 308, 381). Each of the trilogy's aging narrators compensates for his failing life by endlessly spinning distracting stories, evasive artifices in words. Yet each constantly demonstrates and comments upon the inadequacies of the linguistic medium he employs. Language and the nature of narrative imagination thus become central subjects in the trilogy. Contact with a recognisable, extra-textual reality is further overwhelmed by the eventual exposure of each narrator as only an imaginative figment or device of a subsequent one, a means whereby he seeks to distract himself from the 'black void' around him (p. 278). Progressive revelation of all these figures as mere narrative devices and verbal constructs creates in Beckett's trilogy a kind of autonomy of fiction or imagination, extending the autonomy of language created by its continuously self-questioning discourse. Beckett's novels reveal themselves as fictions about the creation of fiction, demonstrating and discussing both the potential and the limitation of language and narrative as consolations for the black emptiness of life.

Flann O'Brien's *At Swim-Two-Birds* (1939) also follows fairly closely, though more cheerfully, in the wake of Joyce. It is another fantasy, like *Finnegans Wake*, about a Dublin publican, though one whose sleep is troubled by more than dreams. O'Brien's publican is also an author, one who tries to control his characters firmly by locking them up at night to limit their incessant drinking. Unfortunately, they escape while he sleeps, taking over his narrative themselves and filling it with bizarre tortures for their creator. Like Beckett's trilogy, *At Swim-Two-Birds* is thus a story about telling a story about storytelling, with much reflection about the nature of storytelling, the novel's own methods not least, also included. Each work extends in this way the self-reflexive autonomy, the ontologic separateness, of *Finnegans Wake*. Each is also a postmodernist paradigm, a prophecy of the self-reflexive foregrounding of language and fiction-making that has become one of the central, distinguishing characteristics of postmodernism. There are now almost too many authors to list who have expanded the self-consciousness of modernist art, writing stories about storytelling, or intruding into the fiction to comment on their own practice and proceedings or to discuss other problems in relating language, fiction and reality. Lawrence Durrell, Doris Lessing, John Fowles, Christine Brooke-Rose, Rayner Heppenstall, John Berger, B. S. Johnson, Alasdair Gray and Julian Barnes figure, among many others, in this postmodernist idiom which has continued to expand and experiment with the conventions of fiction down to the present day. The French experimental novelist Alain Robbe-Grillet remarked in the 1960s that, 'after Joyce' and other modernists,

it seems that we are more and more moving towards an age of fiction
in which the problems of writing will be lucidly envisaged by the
novelist, and in which his concern with critical matters, far from
sterilising his creative faculties, will on the contrary supply him with
motive power . . .

Invention and imagination may finally become the subject of the
book. (pp. 46–7, 63)

The self-conscious interest in the imagination and its apparatus
established by modernism has become more and more frequently a
central subject within recent fiction: for some time now it has been
clear that Robbe-Grillet's postmodernist age has arrived.

As it differs at least in emphasis from its modernist predecessor,
further discussion of this age lies outwith the scope of this study. Its
consequential relation to modernism, however, is worth stressing
for at least two reasons. Firstly, it can help to clarify the term
'postmodernism', which seems to grow vaguer as it is more and
more fashionably and frequently employed. What McHale calls the
'element of logical and historical *consequence*' with which
'postmodernism follows *from* modernism' (p. 5) helps place recent
writing within a clear critical and historical perspective. Secondly,
looking at this recent writing in terms of its antecedents shows that
– despite the changing historical stresses, discussed in the next
chapter, which moved the novel substantially away from
modernism, even during the early 1930s – modernist initiatives
distinctly survived and were extended in one phase of the fiction
that followed. Despite general changes in interest at the time, these
modernist initiatives were in some instances carried forward into
later writing by authors whose work actually began in the 1930s,
such as Beckett, Flann O'Brien, Lawrence Durrell, Malcolm Lowry
or Jean Rhys.

Postmodernism is in any case only the most direct illustration of
ways modernism has affected later writing. Adding greatly to what
Ezra Pound once called 'the international store of literary technique',[17] modernism's innovative styles have continued to influence
later authors much more generally. Without necessarily engaging in
the radical, self-questioning artifice of postmodernism, writers since
the 1930s have often simply borrowed or adopted the kind of
techniques – for entering individual consciousness, or reshaping the
chronology of the novel, or generally re-examining the resources of

fiction – which modernism spectacularly established in the early decades of the century. Modernism's influence on writing, as the century ends, continues to be felt as the major new initiative to have appeared during it.

# — 5 —

# *VALUE*

## THE END OF MODERNISM

> In 1930 it was impossible – if you were young, sensitive,
> imaginative – not to be interested in politics; not to find
> public causes of much more pressing interest than
> philosophy. In 1930 young men . . . were forced to be aware
> of what was happening in Russia; in Germany; in Italy; in
> Spain. They could not go on discussing aesthetic emotions
> and personal relations . . . they had to read the politicians.
> They read Marx. They became communists; they became
> anti-fascists. (Virginia Woolf, 'The Leaning Tower', 1940)[1]

Not all the 'young men' Woolf refers to immediately conformed to
the pattern she outlines. At least one member of 'the group which
began to write about 1925' (p. 170) whom she considers in 'The
Leaning Tower,' Christopher Isherwood, went on discussing 'aesthetic emotions and personal relations' in his early fiction, and in
ways very similar to those of the modernists. Isherwood later
acknowledged that he had 'learned a few lessons from these masters
and put them into practice':[2] various 'echoes', as he calls them, of
the work of James Joyce and Virgina Woolf appear in his first two
novels, *All the Conspirators* (1928) and *The Memorial* (1932). In
each, interior monologue often predominates over conversation or
action, much as it does in Woolf's fiction. In *All the Conspirators*,
there are also sections of randomly associating thoughts closer to
the stream-of-consciousness method of Joyce, and the novel's
concern with art and writing – sometimes apparently autobiographical – resembles Joyce's interests in *A Portrait of the Artist as
a Young Man* (1916), or Woolf's use of the artist Lily Briscoe in *To
the Lighthouse* (1927). *The Memorial* shows affinities between
Isherwood's style and modernism extending into the areas of

structure and temporality. The novel's sections are headed '1928', '1920', '1925' and '1929': conventional chronology is further renounced, in favour of 'time in the mind', by the intense memories and recollections that break into the characters' interior monologues. Repeated flashbacks and deferred explanations show Isherwood apparently acting on Ford Madox Ford's suggestion that 'to get . . . a man in fiction you could not begin at his beginning . . . you must . . . work backwards and forwards over his past'. Isherwood later explained that in *The Memorial* he tried 'to start in the middle and go backwards, then forwards again . . . time is circular, which sounds Einstein-ish and brilliantly modern'.[3]

Such 'brilliantly modern' techniques make *The Memorial* an outstanding novel, deserving fuller critical attention than it has usually received. A significant aspect of Isherwood's modernist technique, however, is how quickly it disappears from his fiction later in the 1930s. His next novel, *Mr Norris Changes Trains* (1935), set in Berlin, has very little of the structural complexity or inward registration of thought that mark *The Memorial* and *All the Conspirators*. Instead, it is largely straightforward in chronology, and objective in recording visual detail and observation of characters' behaviour and the state of their city. *Goodbye to Berlin* (1939) is similar. Preference for direct, uncomplicated contact with observed reality is emphasised by Isherwood's narrator describing himself as 'a camera with its shutter open, quite passive, recording, not thinking' (p. 11). In a way, of course, a genuinely 'passive recording' is unrealisable: just as a camera has to be pointed somewhere, any recording in language is 'pointed' by its point of view and style. Nevertheless, Isherwood's idea of the narrator as a camera shows how far he had moved away from modernism by the end of the 1930s. Discussing Joyce's work in 1929, Eugene Jolas suggested that 'the epoch when the writer photographed the life about him with the mechanics of words . . . is happily drawing to its close'. Writing ten years later, Isherwood apparently wanted to open up this epoch once again. Though *All the Conspirators* and *The Memorial* so clearly 'echo' modernist determination to 'illumine the mind within rather than the world without', in the thirties Isherwood's priorities reversed – 'the world without', rather than inward attention to mind and consciousness, becoming the principal focus of his attention.

Isherwood's career is exemplary in this way, indicating the shape and the strength of modernist influence at the end of the 1920s, but also how quickly this seemed to fade in the decade that followed. Modernist fiction continued to appear during it – Woolf's *The Waves* in 1931; Joyce's *Finnegans Wake* in 1939; the early novels of some of the writers mentioned at the end of Chapter 4 – but in general the 1930s are considered to be a period of decline or redirection of modernism's innovative energies. Many of the generation of novelists Woolf points to, emerging in the late 1920s, followed the same pattern of development as Isherwood, or more or less began from the conclusion – in favour of realist rather than modernist methods – that he eventually reached. Both George Orwell and Graham Greene, for example, sometimes echo the modernists. Orwell's third chapter in *A Clergyman's Daughter* (1935) resembles the 'Nighttown' section (Chapter 15) of *Ulysses*, and the interior monologues and occasional stream of consciousness of Greene's *England Made Me* (1935) also suggest a debt to Joyce. Such echoes, however, are occasional and fragmentary in work which is on the whole much more conventional in style. Orwell, in particular, deliberately looks back to model his strategies on the work of writers modernism rejected, such as H. G. Wells.

In 'The Leaning Tower', Woolf indicates several factors – some obvious, some more complex – that help account for this general movement away from modernist methods in the 1930s. As the passage already quoted suggests, novelists were inevitably subject to the intensifying pressure of the decade's politics and 'public causes'. By the mid-1930s British writers – and to some extent the public in general – were preoccupied by the rise of Hitler in Germany, by the continuing menace of Mussolini in Italy, and perhaps above all by the Spanish Civil War. In addition, as Woolf rather complacently concedes, though there was 'neither war nor revolution in England itself', there was nevertheless 'the influence of change . . . the threat of war' (II, p. 170). In fact, the economic depression that followed the collapse of the Wall Street stock market late in 1929 – as well as facilitating Hitler's rise to power in Germany – thoroughly dominated British affairs throughout the 1930s. Even by 1931, the pound had been devalued, the Labour Party ousted by a National Government created to deal with the emergency, and unemployment had reached a scale that provoked hunger marches and riots.

Such crises, domestic as well as international, were likely to have discouraged novelists in the 1930s – as Woolf suggests – from continuing to write about the kind of 'aesthetic emotions', profound relations or subjective states that had occupied the attention of the modernists. 'Young men' writing in 1930 might have been drawn back to realist style, to straightforward representation of 'the world without', simply by the urgency of what was happening in that world, in reality itself. A major factor in Christopher Isherwood's change of tactics between *The Memorial* and *Mr Norris Changes Trains*, for example, might have been the need to represent to the British public, as clearly and immediately as possible, the threat of Adolf Hitler that Isherwood had discovered for himself on visits to Berlin in the early 1930s. A lucid, documentary style, with the supposed objectivity of a camera, 'recording, not thinking', might have seemed the best possible vehicle for communicating the threatening political problems of the time.

Background and education also particularly disposed members of Isherwood's generation to attend to these problems. Woolf points out in 'The Leaning Tower' that for her own generation, the modernist generation,

> when the crash came in 1914 all those . . . who were to be the representative writers of their time, had their past, their education, safe behind them, safe within them. They had known security; they had the memory of a peaceful boyhood, the knowledge of a settled civilisation. (pp. 169–70)

Rather than having 'their education . . . safe within them' by 1914, the generation after the modernists, the 1930s generation, experienced a schooling that was significantly shaped by the First World War. As Woolf points out, the majority of the new writers emerging in the 1930s were educated at public schools. In these traditional bastions of English social structure, they encountered with particular immediacy the kind of establishment values that were implicated in the conduct of the war and therefore considered profoundly corrupt by many members of the younger generation at the time. This common educational background probably contributed to the readiness of 1930s' writers to 'become communists or anti-fascists'; to adopt anti-establishment political commitments that further heightened their attentiveness to the 'public causes' of their day.

Though sharpened by the circumstances of their education,

attentiveness to contemporary events was in any case almost inevitable for 1930s' novelists. Unlike the modernists, they lacked an experience that could have distracted them from the immediate life of their times. Modernist writers, after all, were confronted challengingly enough by public causes and events: these could hardly have existed more disturbingly than they did in the course of the First World War. The difference, however, as Woolf indicates, is that the modernists were able to look back to a stable pre-war past; to engage with memories of 'a peaceful boyhood, the knowledge of a settled civilisation'. As suggested in Chapter 3, knowledge of security lost in the past created for the modernists particular incentives to reshape time and history in their fiction; to re-establish connections with a vanished epoch. In *A la recherche du temps perdu*, for example, or in *To the Lighthouse*, Proust and Woolf indicate the recovery of the past through art and memory as one of few consolations available to a generation living on in a desolate post-war world. Such consolation was difficult enough for the modernists to establish: it was still less accessible to the generation which succeeded them.

This is reflected in the dates Isherwood chooses for the four sections of *The Memorial* – 1928, 1920, 1925, 1929. However much the younger generation of writers wished to follow the modernists in reshaping time and history in their fiction – in working 'backwards and forwards over the past' – there were difficulties for them in extending this process back into the years before the war. For Christopher Isherwood, born in 1904, and his contemporaries, these years and the 'knowledge of a settled civilisation' they might have offered existed not as an adult memory but at most as a recollection of early childhood. Perhaps as a result, his generation was readier than the modernists to deal with contemporary history not through imaginative strategies that transformed or sought to escape its processes, but instead through direct, political commitment to transforming reality and historical process themselves. Lacking an ideal or settled civilisation in memory, younger writers in the 1930s were more disposed to commit themselves to the creation of one in actuality; to espouse the political ideologies – communism or socialism – likeliest to assist in this process; and to direct their fiction at the immediate 'public causes' and political problems of their world.

## THE EVASIONS OF MODERNISM

The disposition to deal directly with political issues led not only to the shift away from modernist styles and structures exemplified by Isherwood's writing, but at times to hostile criticism of modernism, often on the grounds of its supposed evasiveness and self-indulgence. Looking back on the modernist inclination of his early novels, Isherwood commented ruefully on the 'excessive reverence for Mrs Woolf' that had marked this stage of his writing. Other contemporary novelists were more vehement in their rejection of modernism. In his essay 'Inside the Whale' (1940), for example, George Orwell suggests of the modernists that

> what is noticeable about all these writers is that what 'purpose' they have is very much up in the air. There is no attention to the urgent problems of the moment, above all no politics in the narrower sense . . . when one looks back at the twenties . . . in 'cultured' circles art-for-art's sake extended practically to a worship of the meaningless. Literature was supposed to consist solely in the manipulation of words.[4]

Factors that turned novelists against the styles dominating the previous decade also affected 1930s' critics, some of whom denounced modernism in terms similar to Orwell's, or stronger. Commitment to communism and anti-fascism encouraged particular interest in what was happening in Russia at the time: some British critics were therefore quickly aware of Karl Radek's famous denunciation of modernism at the Soviet Writers Congress of 1934, and inclined to extend some of its implications in their own work.[5] Philip Henderson, for example, incorporates a reference to Radek's attack on Joyce into the highly critical view of modernism he outlines in *The Novel Today: Studies in Contemporary Attitudes* (1936). Henderson considers that

> it is the duty of writers, as those who express the creative needs of the race, not only to hope for the establishment of a reasonable society, but actively to assist, as writers, towards bringing such a society into being. (p. 52)

He therefore regrets that 'many modern writers dare not look too closely at social reality' (p. 14) but choose instead to remain 'enmeshed in the chaos of subjectivism' (p. 81). Reacting to 'a sense of the collapse of their world', modernist writers, in Henderson's view,

> retired further and further into private worlds detached from social reality, their characters attempting to lead lives either entirely on an intense emotional, passional plane as with Lawrence, or on a plane of aesthetic abstraction and contemplative withdrawal from all significant activity whatsoever, as in the case of Joyce and Virginia Woolf. (p. 103)

Henderson's criticism of modernism's 'detachment from social reality' was echoed by other commentators at the time, such as Alick West, in *Crisis and Criticism* (1937), or Ralph Fox, who complained in *The Novel and the People* (1937) of the 'false outlook on life . . . in Proust and Joyce' and of their apparent reluctance to see 'the individual as a whole, as a social individual' (p. 105).

Adverse criticism of modernist writers was not new to the 1930s: many of the first reactions to their work, to Joyce's *Ulysses* in particular, expressed a more complete – sometimes shocked – rejection than anything that came later. The 1930s' criticism, however, remains particularly significant for two reasons. Firstly, its preference for 'social reality' – rather than anything 'enmeshed in the subjective' and apparently detached from it – helps define the particular climate of opinion in which modernism slipped away from the more central position it had occupied in the literary imagination of the previous decade. Secondly, the views expressed by Henderson and others in the 1930s indicate a direction followed by some later criticisms and expanded into a more thoroughgoing, substantial rejection of modernism. Thus in 'The Ideology of Modernism' (1955) the Hungarian Marxist Georg Lukács develops more fully and articulately the same sort of thinking as Henderson follows in the passages quoted above. For Lukács, as for Henderson, modernism is limited by its characters' existence in 'private worlds, detached from social reality'. Lukács considers that 'attenuation of reality underlies Joyce's stream of consciousness': this 'rejection of narrative objectivity, the surrender to subjectivity' contributes to 'reduction of reality to a nightmare' – to a vision of 'ghostly un-reality, of a nightmare world'. In this modernist world, both social relationships and their historical context seem to Lukács to disappear:

in the work of leading modernist writers . . . Man . . . is by nature
solitary, asocial, unable to enter into relationships with other human
beings . . .
Man, thus conceived, is an ahistorical being.

By directing attention away from social reality, and through what
Lukács calls 'the denial of history, of development, and thus, of
perspective', modernist writing establishes an 'assumption that the
objective world is inherently inexplicable' and therefore beyond
improvement or change. For Lukács,

the ideology of most modernist writers asserts the unalterability of
outward reality . . . human activity is, *a priori*, rendered impotent
and robbed of meaning.[6]

Lukács's criticisms are worth quoting at length, as they provide
what is probably still the most substantial negative view of
modernism, one necessary to consider in any assessment of this
phase of writing. Moreover, Lukács's views are usefully typical of a
wider range of negative reactions. Though not all criticism of
modernism is based specifically on its supposed lack of political or
social relevance, most hostile views do take something of the same
form as those of Lukács. Hugh Walpole, for example, offered in the
1930s a negative perspective different from many other commentators at the time, complaining of what he calls the 'modern'
phase of recent fiction that 'there *is* a moral world, and . . . the
novelists of [this] generation are losing a great deal by disregarding
it' (p. 29). Though emphasising different priorities, Walpole's
reasoning remains comparable to that of Lukács. For each,
modernism ignores conventional fiction's capacity to contribute
wisdom or ideas to the organisation of ordinary life and the social
sphere. This 'attenuation of reality' leaves modernism out of touch
with the world and bereft of a central dimension in its experience –
political, in Lukács's view; moral in Walpole's. A reply to Lukács's
criticisms, therefore, can help to provide something of an answer to
other commentators, and to criticism of modernism in general,
contributing to an evaluation of this phase of writing as a whole.

It might at first be supposed that such a reply could be easily and
clearly based on the fiction of D. H. Lawrence, shown throughout
the present study to be thoroughly concerned with the new
conditions and pressures in what he calls 'the modern industrial and
financial world'. 'The Industrial Magnate' chapter of *Women in*

*Love* probably gives as full an account as any twentieth-century novel of the restructuring of industry around Taylorist imperatives, and of the reifying consequences of this process both for a particular workforce and ultimately for the whole of modern industrialised society. In more general terms, *The Rainbow* and *Women in Love* offer a very wide-ranging history of social change in Britain between the Industrial Revolution and the time of the First World War. An actual social historian could hardly offer anything more thorough or compelling, at least in tracing the effects of these changes within the modern psyche.

And yet, even in the course of presenting what seems such thorough social awareness, Lawrence's fiction nevertheless reveals something of the evasive assumption of 'the unalterability of outward reality' that Lukács complains of. In *Lady Chatterley's Lover*, for example, Lawrence records that

> when Connie saw the great lorries full of steel-workers from Sheffield, weird, distorted smallish beings like men, off for an excursion to Matlock, her bowels fainted and she thought: Ah God, what has man done to man? What have the leaders of men been doing to their fellow-men? They have reduced them to less than humanness; and now there can be no fellowship any more! It is just a nightmare. (p. 159)

Lawrence raises a genuine question about social organisation: 'What have the leaders of men been doing to their fellow-men?' He even offers a genuine answer – 'They have reduced them to less than humanness' – confirmed by many pages at this point in the novel presenting 'apartness and hopelessness [in] . . . this terrifying new and gruesome England' (pp. 159, 163). But although conditions of modern industrial reality are established, and questions raised about them, Lawrence's presentation of a 'new and gruesome England' does not extend to a point where it could suggest means of progress or even the possibility of change. Instead, just as this point seems to be reached, the whole issue of industrialism's dehumanising effect on modern life is consigned to the domain of 'nightmare'. Since no answers or alternatives can be further pursued rationally in this domain, the clear vision of terrible and gruesome processes in *Lady Chatterley's Lover* remains one which accepts them as inevitable. Connie's reflections in the passage that follows extend this view of a terrible yet unalterable modern existence. She considers industrial development in the past, and surveys the dreary, wasted landscape that is its result in the present, but adds, 'God alone knows where the future lies' (p. 161). Any possibility of purposeful movement towards a better future is further negated when, thinking of the colliers – reduced like the steel-workers to a less than human existence – Connie comments, 'Supposing the dead in them ever rose up! But no, it was too terrible to think of' (p. 166).

There are other indications in Lawrence's fiction that he finds – like Connie – that however nightmarish contemporary reality may be, any attempt to alter its inhuman structuring may be worse still, too difficult or too terrible to contemplate. It is only at the end of *The Rainbow* that he suggests the possibility of 'a new architecture' for society as a whole, with 'the old, brittle corruption of houses and factories swept away' (p. 496). Yet even here, the forces that might sweep the world clean, changing 'the face of the world's corruption' (pp. 495–6), are, as suggested in Chapter 3, vague and visionary, mystical rather than practical – a 'new germination' (p. 496), rather than a new set of economic or social structures. Such an ending remains largely consistent with the rest of Lawrence's fiction. Throughout his work, alternatives to the rigours of 'the modern industrial and financial world' are generally presented in emotional rather than rational terms – most often shown arising from the redeeming power of individual relationships and the dark energies of sexuality contained within them. *The Rainbow* differs from Lawrence's other fiction only in being more than usually optimistic – or just mystic – in envisaging this redeeming potential extended over a whole society, rather than just two elect members of it, such as Birkin and Ursula in *Women in Love*.

Such faith in relationships and their redeeming psychic energies is consoling but also limiting. Part of Lawrence's complaint about modern industrialism, repeated in Connie's reflections quoted above, is that its Taylorist rationalisation of labour left workers effectively more like machines than human beings. Lawrence's own rejection of the rational, however, simply concedes, as an inevitable adjunct of the nightmare modern world, one of the faculties that most urgently needed to be contested and repossessed. The kind of economic reasoning draining 'humanness' out of modern life might reasonably have been resisted: analysed and challenged on its own terms. Instead, by relying on the dark, mystic and intuitional, Lawrence leaves little solid ground for purposeful change in society, but at best only for the construction of personal refuges more or less outside it – for the creation of 'private worlds, detached from social reality', in fact. Views of modern reality as nightmare, and the projection principally of visionary or emotional solutions to its problems, are in the end, as Lukács suggests, a kind of evasiveness, even of escapism. Lawrence's own flight from an irredeemable, industrialised Britain is anticipated by his fiction some time before his actual departure with his wife Frieda in the 1920s.

Lawrence's ultimate evasion of issues of political or historical change is particularly disappointing – given the extent of social awareness his fiction also shows – but not unusual. As Lukács suggests, such evasiveness or 'denial of history' is discernible more generally in modernist fiction. Joyce's *Ulysses*, for example, seems equally committed to the view that the course of history is something to be ignored or escaped rather than confronted or altered – a view overtly stated in one of the novel's most quoted lines: 'History, Stephen said, is a nightmare from which I am trying to awake' (p. 28). This, of course, is not necessarily Joyce's own opinion. Stephen is closer to expressing Joyce's views in *A Portrait of the Artist as a Young Man* than he is in *Ulysses*, which on the whole presents Leopold Bloom in a much more favourable light. Yet Bloom, in his own way, denies history almost as firmly as Stephen, remarking in Chapter 12, 'Cyclops', that

> it's no use . . . Force, hatred, history, all that. That's not life for men and women, insult and hatred. And everybody knows that it's the very opposite of that that is really life . . .
> – Love, says Bloom. I mean the opposite of hatred. (p. 273)

Bloom's alternative to the pangs of history sounds rather like D. H. Lawrence's, love providing a way out of the depredations of force and hatred; the integrity of individual relationships compensating for wider social disintegration. This kind of possibility is in a way further endorsed by the novel's conclusion – Molly's sleepy recollections of love and passion assembled, as suggested in Chapter 3, into an affirmation of mankind that transcends particular time, place or history and soothes her back into unconsciousness again. It is a conclusion in one way emblematic of the wider tactics of modernism in transforming or escaping history through vision; in making it dream-like or impalpable. Such tactics confirm the appropriateness of Fredric Jameson's suggestion that modernist narrative possesses a 'political unconscious'. Contemporary society and history are assigned a 'nightmare' character often enough by modernist novelists to suggest that the unconscious – the domain of dreams and nightmares, beyond rational control – is the only place they wish to envisage for politics. Such thinking curiously inverts other new habits of mind of the modernist age. In particular, Freud's doctrines suggest that dream and nightmare are worth bringing to light and analysing to see what they contribute to understanding of the real psychic condition of the patient. Modernist fiction, on the other hand, consigns the real conditions of history to the realm of nightmare apparently in order to avoid analysing them, or at any rate to avoid taking such analysis far enough to suggest more than a release of sexual or emotional energies as an antidote to force and hatred in the modern industrial and financial world.

When history and contemporary politics are not suppressed into nightmare in this way, they are often escaped or transcended through myth or art. A sense of timeless and transcendental order in myth particularly appealed to the modernists, especially to the poets, and most notably to T. S. Eliot in *The Wasteland* (1922). In discussing fiction, however – specifically *Ulysses* – Eliot talks of myth and Joyce's pattern of references to Homer also offering the contemporary novel

> a way of controlling, of ordering, of giving a shape and a significance to the immense panorama of futility and anarchy which is contemporary history.[7]

In Woolf's *To the Lighthouse*, Lily Briscoe similarly refers to an artist's brush as 'the one dependable thing in a world of strife, ruin, chaos' (p. 170). Woolf and Eliot seek a transcendence of strife, ruin, futility and anarchy by means of myth or art: neither, however, much considers how the problems of contemporary life might be addressed in fact. Instead, as Lukács suggests, historical reality is held to be nightmarish but unalterable. Priority is given to establishing shape or significance only in art: for this to be achieved, art has to remain aloof from the supposedly anarchic historical reality it surveys. Art therefore seems to become, for the modernists, as suggested in Chapter 4, a self-contained alternative to reality, rather than a means through which life itself can be more clearly envisaged, regulated or understood. In this way, the modernists can indeed be seen to have renounced some of art's traditional responsibility as – in Hugh Walpole's terms – a moral agent in the world, or – in those of Lukács – a political one.

## THE VALUE OF MODERNISM

How should modernist fiction be assessed in the light of such views, and what value assigned to it in the history of literature in the twentieth century? How far can Lukács's criticisms be answered? From one point of view, of course, they might not entirely need to be. Despite the substance and seriousness of his charges, confirmed in the discussion above, they might be considered to point only to a negative aspect of a literature that has usually been seen to offer far more in the way of admirable features, and has generally been very positively assessed. Modernism has not only – as the last chapter concluded by suggesting – continued as a major influence on subsequent generations of writers, more or less recovering from its loss of esteem in the 1930s, it has for the most part steadily gained in critical interest and estimation in recent decades. Lukács's remains a relatively rare dissenting voice, raised against a phase of writing analysed in many shelves of mostly favourable criticism, and firmly installed within the teaching of most universities.

This kind of esteem, however, raises as many difficulties in evaluation as it solves – in particular the problem that modernism has often been seen as an intellectual, élitist form of art, more certain of critical and academic success than genuine popularity. Interior monologues, unusual chronologies, self-conscious concerns with language and with art contribute to a complexity that makes modernist fiction rarely as easy to read as its nineteenth-century predecessors, whose authors are generally much more ready to follow straightforward plots and to make the world presented easily and directly comprehensible. Until the work of Henry James, critical success and popularity in the novel form were largely synonymous. Since, they have grown apart, the highest praise often reserved by critics or academics for novels that sold relatively few copies at the time of their first publication, and in some cases also thereafter. To the charges raised by Lukács, in other words, there might be added the suggestion that modernist fiction lost touch with the everyday world not only by ceasing to write about it, but by ceasing to write about anything in ways easily accessible to the majority of its inhabitants. Opponents of modernism have often extended this charge, suggesting that, at a time when culture was becoming more and more the possession of the masses – through the general spread of literacy and new media such as the cinema – modernist writers quite deliberately chose to create a difficult, challenging art, which only an intellectual élite could fully appreciate or understand. This attempt to retain culture as the possession of an élite can be seen as consistent with the anti-democratic politics which many modernists – T. S. Eliot, Wyndham Lewis, D. H. Lawrence, for example – embraced in one way or another.

Such accusations of élitism or lack of responsibility to ordinary readers are further considered below, after first outlining one answer to the charge of irresponsibility to contemporary society and history. This can be established by looking further at some of the fiction which followed modernism in the 1930s. Not all novelists at the time, not even those most firmly committed politically, turned against modernist styles. For example, in one of the most accomplished of novels published in the 1930s, *A Scots Quair* (1932–4), Lewis Grassic Gibbon uses a range of interior monologues not only to communicate the thoughts and feelings of a few principal characters, but to gain access to the consciousnesses of many members of a working, rural community. The kind of Free Indirect Discourse characteristic of D. H. Lawrence's fiction – very flexibly employed – allows Gibbon to alternate the novel's attention freely between many individuals, and at times to develop a kind of choric voice for the community as a whole. The novel's structure is equally sophisticated. Rather in the manner of Ford Madox Ford's *Parade's End*, chapters are circular, beginning at a moment later than the events they go back to describe, ending with the story advanced again to the time from which the chapter began. This pattern allows immediate events to be held alongside wider vision of their significance; actuality to be juxtaposed with the ideal. Rather than denying history or politics, such patterning remains completely engaged with contemporary conflicts and injustices, while also showing the possibility of a more worthwhile future beyond them, and sometimes the kind of organisation which could allow movement towards it. In these ways, both the structure and the communism of insight and utterance in *A Scots Quair* establish an exact formal reflex for the generally left-wing ideology of the 1930s.

Like Lewis Grassic Gibbon, Malcolm Lowry remains in touch with contemporary history and politics while also adopting modernist methods. Lowry's *Under the Volcano* (1947), begun in the late 1930s, resembles *Ulysses* fairly closely in construction and technique. Its chapters occupy hours in a single day, and its narrative is principally focused within the minds of three characters, transcribed in a complex mixture of stream of consciousness, Free Indirect Discourse and interior monologue. This transcription is further complicated by the nearly permanent drunkenness of Lowry's central figure, the Consul Geoffrey Firmin. His thoughts at times tumble almost indecipherably among distorted fragments of conversation, perception and hallucination: the result is a 'whirling cerebral chaos' (p. 309) sometimes resembling the 'Nighttown' section of *Ulysses* (Chapter 15) more than any other. Yet even such a highly private, nightmare world is neither wholly 'detached from social reality' nor a 'denial of history'. Instead, much of what impinges upon characters' internal consciousness – newsreels of the civil war in Spain, the growth of fascism in Mexico – troublingly reflects the origin and nature of political conflicts darkening the late 1930s. Firmin's drunkenness is itself related to contemporary history both consequentially and metaphorically, as a response to, and a reminder of, its unendurable quality. In Lowry's own view,

> The drunkenness of the Consul is used on one plane to symbolise the universal drunkenness of mankind during the war, or during the period immediately preceding it . . . his fate should be seen also in its universal relationship to the ultimate fate of mankind.[8]

Though at a moment of particular intoxication the Consul talks of history and 'its worthless stupid course' (p. 311) as being unalterable, this is an idea not accepted but often contested throughout *Under the Volcano* – in particular, in this drunken scene, by the Consul's half-brother Hugh, committed to the Republican cause in Spain. In general, as Lowry suggests, confinement within the Consul's consciousness is not a refuge from the course of history, but a highlighting of its threats, focused unusually immediately through the experience of a character whose pain and stupidity is emblematic of the wider uneasiness of his time.

Both Malcolm Lowry and Lewis Grassic Gibbon thus suggest that modernist techniques are neither invariably nor necessarily ahistoric or apolitical. This, of course, is not much of a defence against Lukács's charge that such techniques *were* employed evasively and irresponsibly by modernist authors themselves. Yet there is also evidence that the modernists' own use of these techniques was less negative and limiting than Lukács claims. Modernism, as suggested earlier, continues to provide a major influence on writing in the twentieth century: its effect on reading has in some ways been equally decisive. This is not, or not only, a matter of the difficulty and complexity with which modernist texts confront their readers, denying them the relative straightforwardness of plot and exposition characteristic of the Victorian novel and much fiction written since the 1920s. Modernist novels *are* genuinely difficult and challenging, but this can also – if not for Georg Lukács, at least for another thinker of the left, Roland Barthes – be seen to establish for readers a freedom and responsibility that more conventional fiction denies them. Barthes clarifies the source of this modernist potential in distinguishing what he calls 'readerly' (*'lisible'*) and 'writerly' (*'scriptible'*) texts. 'Readerly' texts are closer to the conventions of nineteenth-century fiction, presenting a ready-made world, one that can be comprehended with the minimum of effort by a reader who finds the fiction straightforwardly constructed and the nature and motives of characters clearly, objectively explained. Modernist fiction, on the other hand, challenges its readers to reconsider the nature of fiction and its relation to reality, and to reconstruct for themselves fictional worlds complexly envisaged through the consciousness of characters, often transcribed in diverse styles and contained in unusual structures. In such ways, modernist fiction comes closer to the 'writerly' text. In Barthes's view, this writerly text is one in which readers are almost forced to become writers themselves – or at least to enter into an active collaboration with the author, who obliges them to construe meanings and develop the text's significances for themselves. Barthes draws an analogy between the challenges of this type of text and those created by the kind of musical composition that succeeded the work of Schoenberg:

> we know that today post-serial music has radically altered the role of the 'interpreter', who is called on to be in some sort the co-author of

the score, completing it rather than giving it 'expression'. The Text is very much a score of this new kind: it asks of the reader a practical collaboration.

This kind of collaboration, Barthes suggests, leaves the reader 'no longer a consumer, but the producer of the text'.[9]

Like several of the differences separating modernist fiction from its predecessors, Barthes's distinction may be essentially one of degree, rather than entirely qualitative. Every novel, nineteenth-century, modernist or other, requires to some extent the practical, imaginative collaboration of its readers. Yet what modernism demands of readers in this way certainly is greater, quantitatively, and more challenging than almost anything in nineteenth-century fiction. As well as contributing to a more active involvement or 'collaboration' in the novel, these demands also establish a more decisive, responsible attitude towards the novel's values. The realism of nineteenth-century literature can seduce readers into accepting uncritically – as similar or even identical to reality – fictional worlds that are actually thoroughly conditioned by the politics and values of their authors. Since readers of a writerly or modernist text are more involved in producing its meanings and values for themselves, they are more likely to avoid simply accepting those of the author.

At certain levels they may also be more disposed, by such texts, to look beyond 'social reality' in its current shape. Even when it happens to offer explicit proposals about how society might be reorganised, nineteenth-century fiction's realism retains a degree of implicit commitment to the world as it exists; to reality as it is conventionally structured and represented. Moreover, nineteenth-century writing most often offers a reassuring sense of completeness, in the portrayal of the fictional world itself, which may be a disincentive to look at the possibilities or need for change in 'social reality' beyond the novel. The difference in modernism's tactics – in some novels at least – can be illustrated by returning to the contrast of Lawrence's *The Rainbow* and *Women in Love* that concluded Chapter 3. Consecutive construction and a firm conclusion, even one on the level of vision and Lawrentian mysticism, leave *The Rainbow* closer to nineteenth-century conventions than is *Women in Love*. The latter is denied a consoling sense of order or completeness by its fragmentary structure and an apparent scepticism about the very possibility of satisfactory endings. Birkin's refusal, on the last page, to acknowledge the stability or wholeness of his relationship with Ursula leaves *Women in Love* without a secure, final sense of order in the society and relationships portrayed. Readers close the novel in uncertainty, returning from fiction to life with a raw sense of incompleteness and – possibly – a particular readiness to question what denies order and coherence to modern society in general.

To some extent such questioning is invited throughout *Women in Love*, as well as at its end. The need to reconstruct meaning and coherence from a fragmentary fiction may leave readers, at every stage, more disposed to question forces that leave modern life incoherent and fragmented in fact. Though in *Lady Chatterley's Lover* and elsewhere Lawrence stops short of providing satisfactory answers of his own to such questions – and even hesitates to pursue them very far in directions his fiction logically suggests he might – this does not prevent readers from doing so for themselves. In fact, it might encourage them to investigate areas that the author leaves open or incompletely resolved. This openness may be morally as much as politically enabling. Though Hugh Walpole complains of the absence of a moral dimension from modernist fiction, it may be that the most moral sort of text is one that leaves readers free to determine morality for themselves. Modernism is closer to doing so than is nineteenth-century fiction, often ready to draw general conclusions on behalf of its readers and to point out regularly what they might be thinking about individual characters and actions.

Other worthwhile consequences follow from the writerly aspect of modernist fiction. Involving readers in producing rather than passively consuming texts can help to alert them to devices – and motives – through which meaning is produced and reality made consumable in other media as well as in literature. In a century more than ever dominated by its media, and by the power of advertising and other forms of manipulation that these disseminate, this is more than ever a necessary concern. As suggested in the last chapter, it is a concern variously highlighted by modernist fiction's uneasiness with language and means of representation, and particularly emphasised by Joyce in *Ulysses*. Joyce's constant alternations of style require readers to recognise how completely any view of the world is conditioned by the language in which it is framed; how 'outward reality', far from being unalterable, is inescapably altered and particularised by styles, forms and words chosen to frame it. By demonstrating so thoroughly language's capacity to warp and shape the world, Joyce's narrative frees readers to recognise how easily it can be used as a tool of commercial, political or other forms of manipulation. This kind of manipulation is sometimes specifically illustrated in the novel's occasional concern with journalism and advertising: Bloom himself is after all an advertising man of a kind.

Like other difficult, challenging aspects of modernist style, the self-reflexive concern with language in Joyce's work may therefore be seen as neither wilful élitism nor an arid intellectual exercise, however much it may be a source of difficulty for readers accustomed to the relative straightforwardness and stylistic homogeneity of nineteenth-century fiction. Moreover, as suggested in Chapter 4, some of the problems inherent in language are not only recognised but partly redressed in Joyce's writing and in modernist fiction generally. Stylistic diversity and linguistic inventiveness help to make modernism a carnivalised literature, one that resists language's servitude to existing social ordering and systems of power, keeping it open instead as a domain of contention, play and change.

Roland Barthes's views provide one starting point for an answer to Georg Lukács and other critics of modernism: Fredric Jameson offers material for another. Jameson's ideas have already been discussed in Chapters 2 and 3 – in particular, his view that modernism offers

> Utopian compensation for increasing dehumanization on the level of daily life . . .

> A Utopian compensation for everything reification brings with it . . .
> for everything lost in the process of the development of capitalism.
> (pp. 42, 236)

This kind of thinking reappears in Jameson's comments on Lukács, underlying an attempt to modify his arguments. In particular relation to visual art, for example, Jameson suggests:

> Lukács is not wrong to associate the emergence of . . . modernism with the reification which is its precondition; but he oversimplifies and deproblematizes a complicated and interesting situation by ignoring the Utopian vocation . . . the mission to return at least a

symbolic experience of libidinal gratification to a world drained of it, a world of extension, gray and merely quantifiable. (p. 63)

Thinking of modernism in general, Jameson adds:

> In short, it is evidently wrong to imagine, as Lukács sometimes seems to do, that modernism is some mere ideological distraction, a way of systematically displacing the reader's attention from history and society to pure form, metaphysics, and experiences of the individual monad; it is all those things, but . . . the modernist project is more adequately understood as the intent . . . to 'manage' historical and social, deeply political impulses, that is to say, to defuse them, to prepare substitute gratifications for them. (p. 266)

Jameson's argument in *The Political Unconscious* does generally justify his claim that modernism is a more complex and interesting phenomenon than Lukács seems to allow. However, this does not necessarily help to demonstrate that it is any more responsible to its age and its history than Lukács suggests. In fact, what claims to be an alternative or modified form of Lukács's view is at times differentiated from it only precariously. Jameson's idea of symbolic or 'substitute gratification' does not seem very different from the 'ideological distraction' and 'displacement of attention' which, in his assessment, is all that Lukács considers modernism to offer.

Acknowledging Lukács as 'right', even in the course of proposing modifications to his ideas, Jameson helps confirm a core of validity for his criticisms, ones that cannot be wholly denied or dismissed. Yet it is worth taking Jameson's idea of 'substitute gratification' further – perhaps slightly further, even, than he takes it himself. Much of the present study has followed his kind of thinking, showing modernist fiction's formal innovations opening up dimensions – spatial, temporal or linguistic – in which individual existence can still be considered integral and whole despite the reifying, fragmenting processes of the modern industrialised world of late capitalism. As Jameson suggests, these innovations can indeed be seen as ways of defusing, in imagination, this world's real tensions; of providing gratifying or 'Utopian' consolations that might in the end function principally as distractions from actual history and society, much as Lukács considers. It is also possible, however, that at the symbolic or imaginative level Jameson discusses, modernist fiction can offer more. It keeps open at least in imagination alternative possibilities, substitute visions, which function not only as distractions from contemporary social reality, but potentially as critiques of it. For example, as indicated in Chapter 3, time in the modernist age had not been lost – as Proust's title suggests – so much as stolen. By the early twentieth century a Taylorised industry had established more and more rigorous methods of converting time into money; placing modern life more and more exclusively in the hands of the 'commercial clock'. Modernist fiction resists this appropriation of the dimension of time not only by its explicit hostility to the clock, but by means of unconventional, non-chronological narratives that ensure readers engage with alternative ways of conceiving experience. The writerly task of reconstructing a fictional world and its temporality out of the unconventional material of a modernist text enables readers to recognise *any* ordering of temporality as a construct, an artifice and not an absolute. The clock can therefore be placed as only one of several possible means of shaping the dimension of time – rather than the agent of a primary, universal order that many interests, commercial or otherwise, sought to make it by the end of the nineteenth century. Much the same sort of alternative vision or critique of the way modern reality had come to be habitually – but often dehumanisingly – conceived and organised is made available by other aspects of modernist innovation, in ways discussed earlier in relation to language and to the internalisation of narrative perspective. Modernism may not have done much directly, of course, in any of these ways, to reshape the modern world or alter its politics. Yet in this respect it is not really more limited than the art of any other period. In general, as Jameson suggests, 'it is clear that the work of art cannot itself be asked to change the world or to transform itself into political praxis' (p. 234). More reasonably, it can be asked to shape and facilitate imagination of how the world might be ordered differently, a demand which, in some ways, modernism fulfils.

Jameson's explanation of how narrative creates its 'substitute gratifications' also opens up another possibility, if not necessarily for a defence of modernist strategies themselves, at least for a reading that defines for them a lasting significance and interest. Jameson suggests that

> the production of aesthetic or narrative form is to be seen as an
> ideological act in its own right, with the function of inventing

imaginary or formal 'solutions' to unresolvable social contradictions. (p. 79)

Whether in the sublime form of myths, or the ridiculous one of jokes, or in many variously respectable manifestations between, all narratives work at one level, as Jameson suggests, as an imaginative resolution of problems or 'contradictions' in contemporary actuality. Seen in this way, however much or little modernist authors reflected social reality deliberately, it inevitably remained an influential presence in their work, their narrative forms conditioned or 'produced' by the challenges of their age. So even if modernism's unusual, innovative narratives do seem a 'denial of history', they can still be seen as a denial of history which – like any other choice of narrative forms – is itself historically conditioned. Moreover, the nature of the denial may have much to reveal about the nature of what is denied, about the pressures of history within the contemporary imagination. As Jameson suggests, there is in any reading of narrative the possibility of 'construing purely formal patterns as a symbolic enactment of the social within the formal and the aesthetic' (p. 78). Analysis of narrative forms developed by the modernists, therefore, need not be distracted from the forces of contemporary history, politics or social reality. On the contrary, in tracing the ways narrative comes to terms with these forces, something of the nature and operation of these forces themselves can be illumined.

This potential can be summed up through a metaphor about the aims of art, artists and criticism which Joseph Conrad includes in his Preface to *The Nigger of the 'Narcissus'* (1897):

Sometimes, stretched at ease in the shade of a roadside tree, we watch the motions of a labourer in a distant field, and after a time, begin to wonder languidly as to what the fellow may be at. We watch the movements of his body, the waving of his arms, we see him bend down, stand up, hesitate, begin again. It may add to the charm of an idle hour to be told the purpose of his exertions. If we know he is trying to lift a stone, to dig a ditch, to uproot a stump, we look with a more real interest at his efforts; we are disposed to condone the jar of his agitation upon the restfulness of the landscape . . . we understood his object.

And so it is with the workman of art . . . We talk a little about the aim – the aim of art which, like life itself, is inspiring, difficult – obscured by mists. (pp. 13–14)

Conrad's languid picture seems at first to offer the kind of perspective, aloof from the hard world of labour, for which Lukács resented modernist writers. But in fact, for Conrad, the labourer is equated with the writer – 'the workman of art' – while it is the critic or reader who is the indolent observer. His metaphor suggests two principal ways in which such 'observation', the business of reading or criticism, may be conducted. Firstly, work in the field of modernism can simply be admired for itself. Criticism can concentrate on the modernist novel's energy in breaking from the past; its exertions in creating new shapes and forms; the flexibility of its style; the ingenuity of its construction, and so on. The shelves of admiring criticism of modernism are mostly devoted, legitimately enough, to this sort of analysis.

Secondly, however, it can add to more than just 'the charm of an idle hour' to assess the work of modernist writers in terms not only of the nature but 'the purpose of [their] exertions'. Modernism now belongs to 'a distant field': distant enough, as the preface suggested, for its movements to be related to the historical terrain on which it stood; the objects and realities that resisted, challenged and shaped its labours. Wallace Stevens suggests that modern poetry can be described as 'the poem of the mind, in the act of finding/What will suffice'. Modernist fiction can be considered in similar terms. Writing which so thoroughly reoriented the conventions of the novel can still be admired and enjoyed as an outstanding act of the literary mind in the twentieth century. The 'real interest in [its] efforts', however, relates to the question of why such efforts in reshaping time, space, language and art seemed to the modernists to be all that would suffice. Looking for answers to this question, making the aims and needs of modernist art less misty and obscure, has been a main object of the present study. There is still much to admire in the power and promise of modernism's imagination, but also much to learn from the way this imagination relates to the pressures of the 'modern industrial and financial world' in the twentieth century's first three decades. In its closing years, such pressures have certainly not diminished: looking back on the distant field of modernism offers some ways of understanding them; of seeing how they can be imagined.

# NOTES

## CHAPTER 1

1. The *Oxford English Dictionary* records Jonathan Swift, for example, remarking on 'abominable curtailings and quaint modernisms' in 1737; and another commentator talking of 'imperfections and modernisms' in 1897.

   For a recent discussion of the complex question of how – and with what degree of approval – terms such as 'modern', 'modernism' and 'modernity' are employed, see Jürgen Habermas, *The Philosophical Discourse of Modernity* (Cambridge: Polity, 1987), especially Chapter 1.

   R. A. Scott-James borrows the term 'modernism' from Thomas Hardy and from contemporary theology, where it was used to refer to the liberalising movements that attempted to update traditional beliefs and religious doctrines in the early years of the century.

2. Virginia Woolf, 'Mr. Bennett and Mrs. Brown' (1924), rpt. in *Collected Essays* (London: Hogarth Press, 1966), vol. I, p. 326; and 'Modern Fiction' (1919), rpt. in *Collected Essays*, vol. II, pp. 106–7.

3. Quoted in Virginia Woolf, *A Writer's Diary: Being Extracts from the Diary of Virginia Woolf*, ed. Leonard Woolf (1953; rpt. London: Triad, 1985), p. 97.

4. Quoted in Michael Levenson, *A Genealogy of Modernism* (Cambridge: Cambridge University Press, 1984), p. 217.

5. Robert P. Morgan, 'Secret Languages: The Roots of Musical Modernism' in Monique Chefdor, Ricardo Quinones and Albert Wachtel (eds.), *Modernism: Challenges and Perspectives* (Chicago: University of Illinois Press, 1986), p. 41.

6. Virginia Woolf, letter of 6 May 1922, rpt. in *The Letters of Virginia Woolf*, ed. Nigel Nicholson and Joanne Trautmann (London: Chatto, 1975–80), vol. II, p. 525; see also *A Writer's Diary*, p. 138.

7. Virginia Woolf, *A Writer's Diary* (see n. 3), pp. 55–6; Woolf, letter of 25 June 1921, *Letters*, (see n. 6), vol. II, p. 476. In this letter Woolf

does however add of Lawrence that 'he is honest, and therefore he is 100 times better than most of us'.

8. Friedrich Nietzsche, 'The Wanderer and his Shadow' (1880), rpt. in *Human, all too Human: A Book for Free Spirits*, trans. R. J. Hollingdale (Cambridge: Cambridge University Press, 1986), p. 378.

9. F. T. Marinetti, 'Destruction of Syntax – Imagination without Strings – Words-in-Freedom' (1913), rpt. in Umbro Apollonio (ed.), *Futurist Manifestos* (London: Thames and Hudson, 1973), p. 96.

10. *ibid.*, p. 97; 'The Founding and Manifesto of Futurism' (1909), p. 22.

11. Carola Giedion-Welcker, 'On *Ulysses* by James Joyce', *Neue Schweizer Rundschau* (1928), rpt. in Robert H. Deming (ed.), *James Joyce: The Critical Heritage* (London: Routledge and Kegan Paul, 1970), vol. II, p. 443.

## CHAPTER 2

1. Marcel Proust, *Remembrance of Things Past* (1913–27), trans. C. K. Scott-Moncrieff and Terence Kilmartin (Harmondsworth: Penguin, 1983), vol. III, pp. 585, 931, 950. Virginia Woolf, 'Phases of Fiction' (1929), rpt. in *Collected Essays* (London: Hogarth Press, 1966), vol. II, p. 81.

2. C. H. Rickword, 'A Note on Fiction', *The Calendar of Modern Letters*, October 1926; rpt. in Peter Faulkner (ed.), *A Modernist Reader: Modernism in England 1910–1930* (London: Batsford, 1986), p. 160.

3. Henry James, Prefaces to *The Spoils of Poynton*, *The Tragic Muse*, *The Princess Casamassima*, *The Portrait of a Lady*; rpt. in R. P. Blackmur (ed.) *The Art of the Novel: Critical Prefaces*, (London: Charles Scribner's Sons, 1934), pp. 120, 85, 70, 51.

4. *ibid.*, Prefaces to *The Princess Casamassima* and *The Portrait of a Lady*, pp. 65, 46.

5. J. Hillis Miller, 'The Interpretation of *Lord Jim*', in Morton W. Bloomfield (ed.), *The Interpretation of Narrative: Theory and Practice* (Cambridge, MA: Harvard University Press, 1970), p. 220.

6. Henry James, 'The New Novel' (1914), rpt. in *Notes on Novelists: with some other Notes* (London: Dent, 1914), p. 276.

7. Ford Madox Ford, *The Good Soldier* (1915; rpt. Harmondsworth: Penguin, 1977), p. 167.
   Conrad's views are recorded in his 'Author's Note' in *Lord Jim*.

8. Henry James, 'The Younger Generation' (1914), rpt. in Leon Edel and Gordon N. Ray (eds.), *Henry James and H. G. Wells* (London: Rupert Hart-Davis, 1958), p. 200.

9. D. H. Lawrence, letter of 5 June 1914, *The Collected Letters of D. H.*

*Lawrence*, ed. Harry T. Moore (London: Heinemann, 1962), vol. I, p. 282.

10. In *The Dialogic Imagination*, ed. Michael Holquist, trans. Caryl Emerson and Michael Holquist (Austin, TX: University of Texas Press, 1981), Bakhtin remarks that, in general, 'The novel can be defined as a diversity of social speech types (sometimes even diversity of languages) and a diversity of individual voices, artistically organized', p. 262. For his particular idea of 'hybridisation', see pp. 358–62.

11. Dorothy Richardson, Foreword to *Pilgrimage* (1915–67; rpt. London: Virago, 1979), vol. I, pp. 10, 11.

12. J. D. Beresford, Introduction to Dorothy Richardson, *Pointed Roofs: Pilgrimage* (London: Duckworth, 1915), p. vi.

13. May Sinclair, 'The Novels of Dorothy Richardson', *The Egoist*, April 1918, p. 58.

14. My translation of '. . . sa nouveauté, sa hardiesse, et les possibilités qu'elle offrait pour exprimer avec force et rapidité les pensées les plus intimes, les plus spontanées, celles qui paraissent se former à l'insu de la conscience et qui semblent antérieur au discours organisé . . . une forme qui permettait d'atteindre si profondement dans le Moi le jaillissement de la pensée et de la saisir si près de sa conception.' Valery Larbaud, 'Preface' to Edouard Dujardin, *Les lauriers sont coupés* (1888; rpt. Paris: Albert Messein, 1925), p. 6.

   Joyce picked up a copy of Dujardin's novel on a station bookstall in Paris in 1903. Joyce was ready to acknowledge a certain borrowing from it: see Richard Ellmann, *James Joyce* (Oxford: Oxford University Press, 1982), pp. 126, 519–20. Debate about the nature and extent of his debt continues among critics: see, for example, Anthony Burgess, 'French Pioneer in the Music of Language', review of Edouard Dujardin, *The Bays are Sere*, trans. Anthony Suter, *The Independent*, 1 March 1991, p. 23.

15. Henry James, 'The Future of the Novel' (1899), rpt. in Edel and Ray, *op. cit.* (see n. 8), p. 57.

16. D. H. Lawrence, letter of 22 April 1914, *Collected Letters* (see n. 9), vol. I, p. 273; and *England, My England* (1924; rpt. Harmondsworth: Penguin, 1960), p. 20.

17. 'H.C.H', review of *The Trap*, *The Calendar of Modern Letters*, June 1925, pp. 328–9.

18. James Joyce, letter of 3 January 1920, in *Selected Letters of James Joyce*, ed. Richard Ellmann (London: Faber and Faber, 1975), p. 246.

19. Quoted in Frank Budgen, *James Joyce and the Making of Ulysses* (London: Grayson & Grayson, 1934), pp. 15, 17.

20. Virginia Woolf, 'Modern Fiction', *Collected Essays*, (see n. 1), vol. II, p. 107.

21. Virginia Woolf, *A Writer's Diary: Being Extracts from the Diary of Virginia Woolf*, ed. Leonard Woolf (1953; rpt. London: Triad, 1985), p. 102; J. Hillis Miller, 'The Rhythm of Creativity in *To the Lighthouse*', in Robert Kiely (ed.), *Modernism Reconsidered* (London: Harvard University Press, 1983), pp. 171, 173. Hillis Miller's use of the phrase *style indirect libre* (p. 173) confirms that he has Free Indirect Discourse in mind.

22. Ford Madox Ford, *The Critical Attitude* (London: Duckworth, 1911), p. 97; D. H. Lawrence, 'John Galsworthy' (1928), rpt. in Anthony Beal (ed.), *Selected Literary Criticism* (London: Heinemann, 1955); Henry James, 'The Younger Generation', rpt. in Edel and Ray, *op. cit.* (see n. 8), pp. 187, 195.

23. H. G. Wells, letter to Henry James, 8 July 1915, rpt. in Edel and Ray, *op. cit.* (see n. 8), p. 264; H. G. Wells, *Kipps* (1905; rpt. London: Fontana, 1973), p. 241; H. G. Wells, 'The Contemporary Novel' in Edel and Ray, pp. 148, 141.

24. See Philip Henderson, *The Novel Today: Studies in Contemporary Attitudes* (London: John Lane, 1936), p. 27; J. B. Priestley, *Literature and Western Man* (London: Heinemann, 1960), pp. 425–6; Angus Wilson, 'Arnold Bennett's Novels', *London Magazine*, October 1954, p. 60.

25. A selection of Freud's papers was published in 1909; *Three Contributions to a Theory of Sex* in 1910; and *The Interpretation of Dreams* in 1913. Havelock Ellis's six-volume *Studies in the Psychology of Sex* (1897–1910) refers frequently to Freud.

26. D. H. Lawrence, *St Mawr* in *St Mawr and The Virgin and the Gypsy* (1925, 1930; rpt. Harmondsworth: Penguin, 1988), p. 55. Throughout his story, Lawrence uses the horse St Mawr partly to represent 'terrible mystery' and physical or natural forces beyond what can be understood intellectually.

27. D. H. Lawrence, letter of 16 September 1916, *Collected Letters* (see n. 9), vol. I, p. 475; D. H. Lawrence, *Fantasia of the Unconscious and Psychoanalysis and the Unconscious* (1923; rpt. London: Heinemann, 1961), pp. 11, 208, 246.

28. The opinion is expressed by Tommy Dukes in D. H. Lawrence, *Lady Chatterley's Lover* (1928; rpt. Harmondsworth: Penguin, 1982), p. 39. Lawrence himself puts forward similar views in, for example, *Fantasia of the Unconscious* (see n. 27), p. 170ff., or in his letter of 8 December 1915, in which he states, 'I am convinced . . . that there is another seat of consciousness than the brain and the nerve system: there is a blood-consciousness which exists in us independently of ordinary mental consciousness', *Collected Letters* (see n. 9), vol. I, p. 373.

29. Virginia Woolf, 'Character in Fiction', *The Essays of Virginia Woolf*, ed. Andrew McNeillie (London: Hogarth Press, 1988), vol. III, p. 504.
30. 'The Contemporary Novel', in Edel and Ray, *op. cit.* (see n. 8), p. 147.
31. Friedrich Nietzsche, *Human, all too Human: A Book for Free Spirits* (1878), trans. R. J. Hollingdale (Cambridge: Cambridge University Press, 1986), p. 13; *The Gay Science* (1882), trans. Walter Kaufmann (New York: Vintage Books, 1974), p. 219.
32. Nietzsche quotes this view, approvingly, from Kant in *Human, all too Human* (see n. 31), p. 22; *The Will to Power* (1901), trans. Walter Kaufmann and R. J. Hollingdale (London: Weidenfeld and Nicolson, 1968), p. 265.
33. Quoted in Stanford Schwartz, *The Matrix of Modernism* (Princeton, NJ: Princeton University Press, 1985), p. 14.
34. Friedrich Nietzsche, *Beyond Good and Evil* (1886), trans. R. J. Hollingdale (Harmondsworth: Penguin, 1990), p. 44.
35. Virginia Woolf, 'The Narrow Bridge of Art' (1927), *Collected Essays* (see n. 1), vol. II, p. 219.
36. T. S. Eliot, 'Rhapsody on a Windy Night' (1914), *Collected Poems: 1909-1962* (London: Faber and Faber, 1974), p. 27. I am grateful to Faber and Faber for permission to quote from T. S. Eliot's *Collected Poems*.
37. D. H. Lawrence, letter of 5 June 1914, *Collected Letters* (see n. 9), vol. I, p. 282.
38. Andrew Marvell, 'The Garden' (1681), *Collected Poems*, ed. Elizabeth Story Donno (Harmondsworth: Penguin, 1972), p. 101.

## CHAPTER 3

1. Virginia Woolf, *A Writer's Diary: Being Extracts from the Diary of Virginia Woolf*, ed. Leonard Woolf (1953; rpt. London: Triad, 1985), p. 138.
2. These plans are reproduced in, for example, Richard Ellmann, *Ulysses on the Liffey* (London: Faber and Faber, 1974), p. 188ff.
3. Henri Bergson, *Mind Energy: Lectures and Essays* (1919), trans. H. Wildon Carr (London: Macmillan, 1920), p. 94.
4. D. H. Lawrence, letter of 5 June 1914, *The Collected Letters of D. H. Lawrence*, ed. Harry T. Moore (London: Heinemann, 1962), vol. I, p. 282.
5. Quoted in Joseph Blotner, *Faulkner: A Biography* (New York: Random House, 1984), p. 563.
6. See Wyndham Lewis, *Time and Western Man* (London: Chatto and Windus, 1927), pp. 13–18, for Lewis's account of how Einstein might

have derived his ideas from Bergson. Lewis suggests that 'In any reasonable, and not romantic, account of the matter, we must suppose the mathematical physicist not entirely unaffected by neighbouring metaphysical thought.'

7. Alexander Moszkowski, *Einstein the Searcher: His Work Explained from Dialogues with Einstein*, trans. Henry L. Brose (London: Methuen, 1921), pp. 114, 117; My translation of 'il n'y a qu'un temps psychologique, différent du temps du physicien', a remark attributed to Einstein in François Heidsieck, *Henri Bergson et la notion de l'éspace* (Paris: Le Cercle du Livre, 1957), p. 164.

8. Friedrich Nietzsche, *The Birth of Tragedy*, in *The Birth of Tragedy and The Genealogy of Morals* (1871; 1887), trans. Francis Golffing (New York: Doubleday, 1956), p. lll; *The Gay Science* (1882), trans. Walter Kaufmann (New York: Vintage Books, 1974), pp. 172, 173; *Human, all too Human: A Book for Free Spirits* (1878), trans. R. J. Hollingdale (Cambridge: Cambridge University Press, 1986), p. 20.

9. Sigmund Freud, *The Interpretation of Dreams* (1899), trans. A. A. Brill (London: George Allen and Co., 1913), p. 15. Freud quotes 'toute impression, même la plus insignifiante, laisse une trace inaltérable, indéfiniment susceptible de reparaître au jour' from J. Delboeuf, *Le Sommeil et les rêves* (Paris, 1885). In the passage quoted below, he refers to Fr. Scholz, *Schlaf und Traum* (Leipzig, 1887), and J. Volkelt, *Die Traumphantasie* (Stuttgart, 1875).

10. See Lewis's short story, 'You Broke My Dream', which mentions 'R. Dunne, Esq.', in Wyndham Lewis, *The Wild Body* (London: Chatto and Windus, 1927), p. 295.

11. Wyndham Lewis, *Paleface* (London: Chatto and Windus, 1929), p. 255; *Time and Western Man* (London: Chatto and Windus, 1927), p. 129.

12. Wyndham Lewis, *The Art of Being Ruled* (London: Chatto and Windus, 1926), p. 389.

13. Fredric Jameson, *Fables of Aggression: Wyndham Lewis, the Modernist as Fascist* (London: University of California Press, 1979), pp. 124, 123.

14. Quoted in Shiv K. Kumar, *Bergson and the Stream of Consciousness Novel* (London: Blackie, 1962), pp. 36–7.

15. John Stevenson's *British Society 1914–45* (London: Allen Lane, 1984) records, 'A report on bad time-keeping in the ship-building, munitions and transport industries at the end of April 1915 blamed lost time on the ease with which highly paid workers could purchase beer and spirits' (p. 71). Even by the end of 1914, earlier closing times had been introduced by about half the local authorities in England.

16. Edward Said, 'Yeats and Decolonization', *Literature in the Modern*

*World: Critical Essays and Documents*, ed. Dennis Walder (Oxford: Oxford University Press and the Open University Press, 1990), p. 36.

17. Quoted in Stephen Kern, *The Culture of Time and Space 1880–1918* (Cambridge, MA: Harvard University Press, 1983), p. 18.

18. In Marcel Proust, *Remembrance of Things Past* (1913–27), trans. C. K. Scott-Moncrieff and Terence Kilmartin, (1981; rpt. Harmondsworth: Penguin, 1983), vol. II, p. 1029, Marcel records his lover Albertine's absolute wonder at finding that she is able to visit by car, in a single afternoon, several villages each of which was previously separated by a day's journey.

19. As well as apparently misunderstanding Bergson's philosophy, Moszkowski gives the wrong date for Max Planck's Nobel Prize.

20. Anton Giulio Bragaglia, 'Futurist Photodynamism' (1911), rpt. in Umbro Apollonio (ed.), *Futurist Manifestos* (London: Thames and Hudson, 1973), p. 39. See also pp. 14–15 and pp. 39–40 for an account of the work of Muybridge and Marey. *Futurist Manifestos* also reproduces 'Dynamism of a Dog on a Leash' and 'Little Girl Running on a Balcony', Figures 30 and 31.

21. The quotation is from the opening page (15) of the first United States edition of *Tarr* (New York: Alfred Knopf, 1918). Neither the serialisation of the novel in *The Egoist*, nor the one-volume British edition of 1918, nor Lewis's revised edition of 1927 contains the strange form of punctuation '.='. But there is evidence that the edition published in the United States was closest to Lewis's original manuscript and reproduces the form of punctuation he chose for it.

22. Hugh Kenner, *The Stoic Comedians: Flaubert, Joyce and Beckett* (London: University of California Press, 1962), p. 59.

23. The phrase was coined by Herbert Spencer, but accepted by Darwin himself.

24. Virginia Woolf, 'The Leaning Tower' (1940), rpt. in *Collected Essays* (London: Hogarth Press, 1966), vol. II, pp. 166–7.

25. Henry James, letter of 5 August 1914, quoted in Paul Fussell, *The Great War and Modern Memory* (London: Oxford University Press, 1979), p. 8; letter of 18 June 1915, quoted in Compton Mackenzie, *Gallipoli Memories* (London: Cassell, 1929), pp. 141–2; Wyndham Lewis quoted in Michael Levenson, *A Genealogy of Modernism* (Cambridge: Cambridge University Press, 1984), p. 9.

26. Virginia Woolf, 'The Leaning Tower' (see n. 24), pp. 167, 170.

27. H. M. Tomlinson, 'All Our Yesterdays', rpt. in George Bruce, (ed.), *Short Stories of the First World War* (London: Sidgwick and Jackson, 1971), p. 48.

28. Bakhtin, of course, refers to an earlier period of history than the one beginning around 1840 which Lawrence describes. Lawrence stresses,

however, that the quality of life the Brangwens enjoyed at this time had lasted more or less unchanged for centuries. And Bakhtin suggests (pp. 217–18) that the 'ancient matrices' he discusses occasionally survive or leave 'traces' in the literature of later periods.

29. Quoted in Harry T. Moore, *The Priest of Love: A Life of D. H. Lawrence* (London: Heinemann, 1974), p. 73; D. H. Lawrence, letter of 5 June 1914, *Collected Letters* (see n. 4), vol. I, p. 282.

30. D. H. Lawrence, letter of 5 June 1914 (see n. 29).

31. D. H. Lawrence, letter of 19 December 1916, in Aldous Huxley, (ed.), *The Letters of D. H. Lawrence* (London: Heinemann, 1932), p. 386.

32. The Kaiser's remark 'I never wanted this' is quoted in Alan Palmer, *The Kaiser: Warlord of the Second Reich* (London: Weidenfeld and Nicolson, 1978), p. 188. The remark grew famous in Britain after the war was over.

33. D. H. Lawrence, letter of 27 July 1917, *Collected Letters* (see n. 4), vol. I, p. 519.

34. Italo Calvino, *If on a Winter's Night a Traveller*, trans. William Weaver (London: Picador, 1982), p. 13.

35. T. S. Eliot, 'Ulysses, Order, and Myth' (1923), rpt. in Frank Kermode (ed.), *Selected Prose of T. S. Eliot* (London: Faber and Faber, 1975), p. 177.

## CHAPTER 4

1. Henry James, 'The Younger Generation' (1914), rpt. in Leon Edel and Gordon N. Ray (eds.), *Henry James and H. G. Wells* (London: Rupert Hart-Davis, 1958), p. 215; Henry James, 'The Art of Fiction' (1884), rpt. in Leon Edel (ed.), *The House of Fiction: Essays on the Novel by Henry James* (London: Rupert Hart-Davis, 1957), pp. 23–4.

2. Virginia Woolf, *A Writer's Diary: Being Extracts from the Diary of Virginia Woolf*, ed. Leonard Woolf (1953; rpt. London: Triad, 1985), p. 178.

3. Stephen Spender, *The Struggle of the Modern* (London: Hamish Hamilton, 1963), p. x.

4. Quoted in Jean Radford, 'Introduction to May Sinclair', *Mary Olivier: A Life* (1919; rpt. London: Virago, 1980), p. [vii]; Wyndham Lewis, letter of March 1916, in W. K. Rose (ed.), *The Letters of Wyndham Lewis* (London: Methuen, 1963), p. 76.

5. Henry James, Preface to *The Portrait of a Lady*, rpt. in *The Art of the Novel: Critical Prefaces* ed. R. P. Blackmur (London: Charles Scribner's Sons, 1934), p. 46ff.

6. Quoted in Frank Budgen, *James Joyce and the Making of Ulysses* (London: Grayson & Grayson, 1934), p. 180.

7. *ibid.*, p. 263.

8. *ibid.*, p. 263.

9. Eugene Jolas, 'The Revolution of Language and James Joyce', in Samuel Beckett *et al.*, *Our Exagmination Round his Factification for Incamination of Work in Progress* (1929; rpt. London: Faber and Faber, 1972), p. 79.

10. Friedrich Nietzsche, 'The Wanderer and his Shadow' (1880), rpt. in *Human, all too Human: A Book for Free Spirits*, trans. R. J. Hollingdale (Cambridge: Cambridge University Press, 1986), p. 306; *Human, all too Human*, p. 16.

11. 'Revolution in Science: New Theory of the Universe: Newtonian Ideas Overthrown', *The Times*, 7 November 1919, p. 12.

12. 'Forward in the West', 'The Battle of the Somme', 'The Day Goes Well', *The Times*, 3 July 1916, pp. 8, 9, 10.

13. 'This is the operative statement . . . The others are inoperative.' Ronald L. Ziegler, addressing a White House Press conference in April 1973, quoted in Bob Woodward and Carl Bernstein, *All the President's Men* (London: Quartet, 1974), p. 292.

14. Harold Pinter, 'Writing for the Theatre': speech to the National Student Drama Festival, 1962, included as 'Introduction to Harold Pinter', *Plays: One* (London: Methuen, 1976), p. 14.

15. F. T. Marinetti, 'Destruction of Syntax – Imagination without Strings – Words-in-Freedom' (1913), rpt. in Umbro Apollonio (ed.), *Futurist Manifestos* (London: Thames and Hudson, 1973), p. 95; Samuel Beckett, 'Dante. . . Bruno. Vico. . Joyce', in Samuel Beckett *et al.*, *Our Exagmination Round his Factification for Incamination of Work in Progress* (1929; rpt. London: Faber and Faber, 1972), p. 14.

16. Fredric Jameson, *Fables of Aggression: Wyndham Lewis, the Modernist as Fascist* (London: University of California Press, 1979), p. 123.

17. Ezra Pound, 'Paris Letter', *The Dial*, June 1922, p. 625.

## CHAPTER 5

1. Virginia Woolf, *Collected Essays* (London: Hogarth Press, 1966), vol. II, p. 172.

2. Christopher Isherwood, Foreword (1957) to *All the Conspirators* (1928; rpt. London: Methuen, 1984), p. 7.

3. Ford Madox Ford, *Joseph Conrad: A Personal Remembrance*

(London: Duckworth, 1924), pp. 129–30; Christopher Isherwood, *Lions and Shadows* (1938; rpt. London: Methuen, 1982), p. 182.

4. Christopher Isherwood, Foreword to *All the Conspirators* (see n. 2), p. 8; George Orwell, 'Inside the Whale' (1940), rpt. in Sonia Orwell and Ian Angus (eds.), *The Collected Essays, Journalism and Letters of George Orwell* (1968; rpt. Harmondsworth: Penguin, 1970), vol. I, p. 557.

5. See Karl Radek, 'James Joyce or Socialist Realism', a report delivered at the Congress of Soviet Writers, August 1934, rpt. in Robert H. Deming, *James Joyce: The Critical Heritage* (London: Routledge and Kegan Paul, 1970), vol. II, pp. 624–6.

6. Georg Lukács, 'The Ideology of Modernism' (1955), rpt. in David Lodge, *20th Century Literary Criticism: A Reader* (London: Longman, 1972), pp. 480, 479, 484, 480, 476–7, 486, 480, 487.

7. T. S. Eliot, 'Ulysses, Order, and Myth' (1923), rpt. in Frank Kermode, (ed.), *Selected Prose of T. S. Eliot* (London: Faber and Faber, 1975), p. 177.

8. Malcolm Lowry, letter of 2 January 1946, rpt. in Harvey Breit and Marjorie Bonner Lowry (eds.), *Selected Letters of Malcolm Lowry* (1967; rpt. Harmondsworth: Penguin, 1985), p. 66.

9. Roland Barthes, *Image Music Text*, trans. Stephen Heath (London: Fontana, 1982), p. 163; Roland Barthes, *S/Z*, trans. Richard Miller (New York: Hill and Wang, 1974), p. 4.

# SELECT BIBLIOGRAPHY

## FICTION

Alain-Fournier, *Le Grand Meaulnes*, 1913, trans. Frank Davidson, Harmondsworth: Penguin, 1974.

Aldington, Richard, *Death of a Hero*, 1929 (rpt. London: Hogarth Press, 1984).

Beckett, Samuel, *The Beckett Trilogy: Molloy, Malone Dies, The Unnamable*, 1950–2 (rpt. London: Picador, 1983).

Bruce, George (ed.), *Short Stories of the First World War*, London: Sidgwick and Jackson, 1971.

Conrad, Joseph, *Chance*, 1913 (rpt. Harmondsworth: Penguin, 1984).

—— *Heart of Darkness*, 1902 (rpt. Harmondsworth: Penguin, 1973).

—— *Lord Jim*, 1900 (rpt. Harmondsworth: Penguin, 1968).

—— *Nostromo*, 1904 (rpt. Harmondsworth: Penguin, 1969).

—— *The Nigger of the 'Narcissus': Typhoon and Other Stories*, 1897, 1903 (rpt. Harmondsworth: Penguin, 1968).

—— *The Secret Agent*, 1907 (rpt. Harmondsworth: Penguin, 1967).

—— *Under Western Eyes*, 1911 (rpt. Harmondsworth: Penguin, 1975).

—— *Victory*, 1915 (rpt. Harmondsworth: Penguin, 1976).

Dickens, Charles, *David Copperfield*, 1849–50 (rpt. Harmondsworth: Penguin, 1977).

Dujardin, Edouard, *Les lauriers sont coupés*, 1888 (rpt. Paris: Albert Messein, 1925).

Faulkner, William, *The Sound and the Fury*, 1929 (rpt. Harmondsworth: Penguin, 1971).

Fitzgerald, F. Scott. *The Great Gatsby*, 1926 (rpt. Harmondsworth: Penguin, 1968).

Ford, Ford Madox, *Parade's End*, 1924–8 (rpt. Harmondsworth: Penguin, 1982).

—— *The Good Soldier*, 1915 (rpt. Harmondsworth: Penguin, 1977).

Forster, E. M., *A Passage to India*, 1924 (rpt. Harmondsworth: Penguin, 1967).

—— *Howards End*, 1910 (rpt. Harmondsworth: Penguin, 1969).

Gibbon, Lewis Grassic (James Leslie Mitchell), *A Scots Quair*, 1932–4 (rpt. London: Pan, 1982).

Hemingway, Ernest, *The Essential Hemingway*, London: Panther, 1977.

Huxley, Aldous, *Point Counter Point*, 1928; (rpt. Harmondsworth: Penguin, 1975).

Isherwood, Christopher, *All the Conspirators*, 1928 (rpt. London: Methuen, 1984).

—— *Goodbye to Berlin*, 1939 (rpt. London: Panther, 1977.

—— *Mr Norris Changes Trains*, 1935 (rpt. London: Panther, 1977).

—— *The Memorial*, 1932 (rpt. London: Panther, 1978).

James, Henry, *The Ambassadors*, 1903 (rpt. Harmondsworth: Penguin, 1973).

—— *The Portrait of a Lady*, 1881 (rpt. Harmondsworth: Penguin, 1973).

—— *What Maisie Knew*, 1897 (rpt. Harmondsworth: Penguin, 1977.

Joyce, Mames, *A Portrait of the Artist as a Young Man*, 1916 (rpt. Harmondsworth, Penguin, 1973).

—— *Dubliners*, 1914 (rpt. Harmondsworth: Penguin, 1971).

—— *Finnegans Wake*, 1939 (rpt. London: Faber and Faber, 1971).

—— *Stephen Hero*, 1944 (rpt. London: Panther, 1977).

—— *Ulysses*, 1922 (rpt. Harmondsworth: Penguin, 1986).

Lawrence, D. H., *England My England*, 1924 (rpt. Harmondsworth: Penguin, 1960).

—— *Kangaroo*, 1923 (rpt. Harmondsworth: Penguin, 1976).

—— *Lady Chatterley's Lover*, 1928 (rpt. Harmondsworth: Penguin, 1982).

—— *St Mawr and the Virgin and the Gypsy* 1925, 1930 (rpt. Harmondsworth: Penguin, 1988).

—— *Sons and Lovers*, 1913 (rpt. Harmondsworth: Penguin, 1968).

—— *The Rainbow*, 1915 (rpt. Harmondsworth: Penguin, 1971).

—— *Three Novellas: The Fox, The Ladybird, The Captain's Doll*, 1923 (rpt. Harmondsworth: Penguin, 1971).

—— *Women in Love*, 1921 (rpt. Harmondsworth: Penguin, 1971).

Lewis, Wyndham, *Tarr*, London: The Egoist Press, 1918.

—— *The Wild Body*, London: Chatto and Windus, 1927.

Lowry, Malcolm, *Under the Volcano*, 1947 (rpt. Harmondsworth: Penguin, 1983).

Mackenzie, Compton, *Sinister Street*, 1913–14 (rpt. Harmondsworth: Penguin, 1983).

O'Brien, Flann, *At Swim-Two-Birds*, 1939 (rpt. Harmondworth: Penguin 1975).

Orwell, George, *Coming up for Air*, 1939 (rpt. Harmondsworth: Penguin, 1962).

Proust, Marcel, *Remembrance of Things Past*, 1913–27, trans. C. K. Scott-Moncrieff and Terence Kilmartin, 3 vols., Harmondsworth: Penguin, 1983.

Remarque, Erich Maria, *All Quiet on the Western Front*, 1929, trans. A. W. Wheen, London: Mayflower, 1968.

Richardson, Dorothy, *Pilgrimage*, 1915–67 (rpt. in 4 vols., London: Virago, 1979).

Sinclair, May, *Life and Death of Harriett Frean*, 1922 (rpt. London: Virago, 1980).

—— *Mary Olivier: A Life*, 1919 (rpt. London: Virago, 1980).

Stein, Gertrude, *Three Lives*, 1909 (rpt. Harmondsworth: Penguin, 1984).

Woolf, Virginia, *Between the Acts*, 1941 (rpt. London: Panther, 1978).

—— *Jacob's Room*, 1922 (rpt. London: Panther, 1976).

—— *Mrs Dalloway*, 1925 (rpt. Harmondsworth: Penguin, 1976).

—— *Orlando*, 1928 (rpt. Harmondsworth: Penguin, 1975).

—— *To the Lighthouse*, 1927 (rpt. Harmondsworth: Penguin, 1973).

—— *The Waves*, 1931 (rpt. Harmondsworth: Penguin, 1973).

## BACKGROUND AND CRITICAL

Apollonio, Umbro (ed.), *Futurist Manifestos*, London: Thames and Hudson, 1973.

Bakhtin, Mikhail, *The Dialogic Imagination: Four Essays*, ed. Michael Holquist, trans. Michael Holquist and Caryl Emerson, Austin, TX: University of Texas Press, 1981.

Barthes, Roland, *Image Music Text*, trans. Stephen Heath, London: Fontana, 1982.

—— *S/Z*, trans. Richard Miller, New York: Hill and Wang, 1974.

Beckett, Samuel, *et al.*, *Our Exagmination Round his Factification for Incamination of Work in Progress*, 1929 (rpt. London: Faber and Faber, 1972).

Bergson, Henri, *Creative Evolution*, 1907, trans. Arthur Mitchell, London: Macmillan, 1911.

—— *Durée et simultanéité: à propos de la théorie d'Einstein*, Paris: Librairie Felix Alcan, 1922.

—— *Mind Energy: Lectures and Essays*, 1919, trans. H. Wildon Carr, London: Macmillan, 1920.

—— *Time and Free Will: An Essay on the Immediate Data of Consciousness*, 1889, trans. F. L. Pogson. London: George Allen and Unwin, 1971.

Bloomfield, Morton W. (ed.), *The Interpretation of Narrative: Theory and Practice*, Cambridge, MA: Harvard University Press, 1970.

Bradbury, Malcolm, and James McFarlane (eds.), *Modernism: 1890–1930*, Harmondsworth: Pelican, 1976.

Budgen, Frank, *James Joyce and the Making of Ulysses*, London: Grayson & Grayson, 1934.

Bullett, Gerald, *Modern English Fiction: A Personal View*, London: Herbert Jenkins, 1926.

Butler, Christopher, *After the Wake: Essays on the Contemporary Avant Garde*, Oxford: Oxford University Press, 1980.

Carruthers, John, *Scheherazade: or the Future of the English Novel*, London: Kegan Paul, Trench, Trubner and Co., 1928.

Chefdor, Monique, Ricardo Quinones and Albert Wachtel (eds.), *Modernism: Challenges and Perspectives*, Chicago, IL: University of Illinois Press, 1986.

Cohn, Dorrit, *Transparent Minds: Narrative Modes for Presenting Consciousness in Fiction*, Princeton, NJ: Princeton University Press, 1978.

Daiches, David, *The Novel and the Modern World*, Cambridge: Cambridge University Press, 1960.

Deming, Robert H. (ed.), *James Joyce: The Critical Heritage*, 2 vols., London: Routledge and Kegan Paul, 1970.

Drew, Elizabeth, *The Modern English Novel: Some Aspects of Contemporary Fiction*, London: Jonathan Cape, 1926.

Dunne, J. W., *An Experiment with Time*, London: A. and C. Black, 1927.

Edel, Leon, and Gordon N. Ray (eds.), *Henry James and H. G. Wells*, London: Rupert Hart-Davis, 1958.

Eliot, T. S., *Selected Prose of T. S. Eliot*, ed. Frank Kermode, London: Faber and Faber, 1975.

Ellmann, Richard, *James Joyce*, Oxford: Oxford University Press, 1982.

Faulkner, Peter, *Modernism*, London: Methuen, 1977.

—— (ed.), *A Modernist Reader: Modernism in England 1910–1930*, London: Batsford, 1986.

Ford, Ford Madox, *Joseph Conrad: A Personal Remembrance*, London: Duckworth, 1924.

—— (as Ford Madox Hueffer) *The Critical Attitude*, London: Duckworth, 1911.

Forster, E. M., *Aspects of the Novel*, 1927 (rpt. Harmondsworth: Penguin, 1971).

Foucault, Michel, *The Order of Things: An Archaeology of the Human Sciences*, 1966, London: Tavistock, 1970.

Fox, Ralph, *The Novel and the People*, London: Lawrence and Wishart, 1937.

Freud, Sigmund, *The Interpretation of Dreams*, 1899, trans. A. A. Brill,

London: George Allen and Co., 1913.

Friedman, Alan, *The Turn of the Novel*, New York: Oxford University Press, 1966.

Fussell, Paul, *The Great War and Modern Memory*, London: Oxford University Press, 1979.

Genette, Gérard, *Narrative Discourse*, 1972, trans. Jane E. Lewin, Oxford: Blackwell, 1986.

Gilbert, Sandra M., and Susan Gubar, *No Man's Land: The Place of the Woman Writer in the Twentieth Century*, 3 vols., London: Yale University Press, 1988–

—— (eds.), *The Female Imagination and the Modernist Aesthetic*, London: Gordon and Breach, 1986.

Habermas, Jürgen, *The Philosophical Discourse of Modernity*, Cambridge: Polity, 1987.

Hassan, Ihab, *The Postmodern Turn: Essays in Postmodern Theory and Culture*, Lincoln, OH: Ohio State University Press, 1987.

Heidsieck, François, *Henri Bergson et la notion de l'éspace*, Paris: Le Cercle du Livre, 1957.

Henderson, Philip, *The Novel Today: Studies in Contemporary Attitudes*, London: John Lane, 1936.

Isherwood, Christopher, *Lions and Shadows: An Education in the Twenties*, 1938 (rpt. London: Methuen, 1982).

James, Henry, *Notes on Novelists: with some other Notes*, London: Dent, 1914.

—— *The Art of Fiction and Other Essays*, New York: Oxford University Press, 1948.

—— *The Art of the Novel: Critical Prefaces*, ed. R. P. Blackmur, London: Charles Scribner's Sons, 1934.

—— *The House of Fiction: Essays on the Novel by Henry James*, ed. Leon Edel, London: Rupert Hart-Davis, 1957.

James, William, *The Principles of Psychology*, 2 vols., London: Macmillan, 1890.

Jameson, Fredric, *The Political Unconscious: Narrative as a Socially Symbolic Act*, London: Methuen, 1981.

Joyce, James, *Selected Letters of James Joyce*, ed. Richard Ellmann, London: Faber and Faber, 1975.

Keating, Peter, *The Haunted Study: A Social History of the English Novel 1875–1914*, London: Secker & Warburg, 1989.

Kenner, Hugh, *Joyce's Voices*, London: Faber and Faber, 1978.

Kern, Stephen, *The Culture of Time and Space 1880–1918*, Cambridge, MA: Harvard University Press, 1983.

Kiely, Robert (ed.), *Modernism Reconsidered*, London: Harvard University Press, 1983.

Kristeva, Julia, *Desire in Language: A Semiotic Approach to Literature and Art*, 1977, ed. Leon S. Roudiez, trans. Thomas Gora, Alice Jardine and Leon S. Roudiez, Oxford: Blackwell, 1981.

Kumar, Shiv K., *Bergson and the Stream of Consciousness Novel*, London: Blackie, 1962.

Lacan, Jacques, *The Four Fundamental Concepts of Psycho-Analysis*, 1973, ed. Jacques-Alain Miller, trans. Alan Sheridan, Harmondsworth: Penguin, 1977.

Lawrence, D. H., *Collected Letters*, ed. Harry T. Moore, 2 vols., London: Heinemann, 1962.

—— *Fantasia of the Unconscious and Psychoanalysis and the Unconscious*, 1923 (rpt. London: Heinemann, 1961).

—— *Selected Literary Criticism*, ed. Anthony Beal, London: Heinemann, 1955.

Levenson, Michael H., *A Genealogy of Modernism: A Study of English Literary Doctrine 1908-1922*, Cambridge: Cambridge University Press, 1984.

Lewis, Wyndham, *Men without Art*, 1934 (rpt. New York: Russell and Russell, 1964).

—— *Paleface*, London: Chatto and Windus, 1929.

—— *The Art of Being Ruled*, London: Chatto and Windus, 1926.

—— *Time and Western Man*, London: Chatto and Windus, 1927.

Lodge, David, *After Bakhtin: Essays on Fiction and Criticism*, London: Routledge, 1990.

—— (ed.), *20th Century Literary Criticism: A Reader*, London: Longman, 1972.

Lubbock, Percy, *The Craft of Fiction*, London: Jonathan Cape, 1921.

Marx, Karl, *Capital: A Critique of Political Economy*, 1867-94, trans. Ben Fowkes, 3 vols., Harmondsworth: Penguin, 1979.

McHale, Brian, *Postmodernist Fiction*, London: Methuen, 1987.

Milton, Colin, *Lawrence and Nietzsche: A Study in Influence*, Aberdeen: Aberdeen University Press, 1987.

Moszkowski, Alexander, *Einstein the Searcher: His Work Explained from Dialogues with Einstein*, trans. Henry L. Brose., London: Methuen, 1921.

Nietzsche, Friedrich, *Beyond Good and Evil: Prelude to a Philosophy of the Future*, 1886, trans. R. J. Hollingdale, Harmondsworth: Penguin 1990.

—— *Human, all too Human: A Book for Free Spirits*, 1878, trans R. J. Hollingdale, Cambridge: Cambridge University Press, 1986.

—— *The Birth Of Tragedy and The Genealogy of Morals*, 1871, 1887, trans. Francis Golffing, New York: Doubleday, 1956.

Nietzsche, Friedrich, *The Gay Science*, 1882, trans. Walter Kaufmann, New York: Vintage Books, 1974.

—— *The Will to Power*, 1901, trans. Walter Kaufmann and R. J Hollingdale, London: Weidenfeld and Nicolson, 1968.

—— *Thus Spoke Zarathustra: A Book for Everyone and No One*, 1892, trans. R. J. Hollingdale, Harmondsworth: Penguin, 1971.

Orr, John, *The Making of the Twentieth-Century Novel: Lawrence, Joyce, Faulkner and Beyond*, London: Macmillan, 1987.

Orwell, George, *The Collected Essays, Journalism and Letters of George Orwell*, ed. Sonia Orwell and Ian Angus, 4 vols., 1968 (rpt. Harmondsworth: Penguin, 1970).

Priestley, J. B., *Literature and Western Man*, London: Heinemann, 1960.

Quennell, Peter, *A Letter to Mrs. Virginia Woolf*, London: Hogarth Press, 1932.

Read, Herbert, *Art Now: An Introduction to the Theory of Modern Painting and Sculpture*, London: Faber and Faber, 1933.

Richards, Jeffrey, and John M. MacKenzie, *The Railway Station: A Social History*, Oxford: Oxford University Press, 1988.

Robbe-Grillet, Alain, *Snapshots and Towards a New Novel*, 1963, trans. Barbara Wright, London: Calder and Boyars, 1965.

Robson, W. W., *Modern English Literature*, Oxford: Oxford University Press, 1970.

Russell, Bertrand, *The ABC of Relativity*, London: Kegan Paul, Trench, Trubner and Co., 1926.

Schwartz, Stanford, *The Matrix of Modernism*, Princeton, NJ: Princeton University Press, 1985.

Scott, Bonnie Kime (ed.), *The Gender of Modernism: A Critical Anthology*, Bloomington, IN: Indiana University Press, 1990.

Scott-James, R. A., *Modernism and Romance*, London: John Lane, 1908.

Smyth, Edmund (ed.), *Postmodernism and Contemporary Fiction*, London: Batsford, 1991.

Spender, Stephen, *The Struggle of the Modern*, London: Hamish Hamilton, 1963.

Spengler, Oswald, *The Decline of the West*, 1918–22, trans. Charles Francis Atkinson, London: G. Allen and Unwin, 1934.

Stevenson, John, *British Society 1914–45*, London: Allen Lane, 1984.

Taylor, Frederick W., *The Principles of Scientific Management*, New York and London: Harper and Brothers, 1911.

Trilling, Lionel, *The Liberal Imagination*, London: Secker & Warburg, 1951.

Walder, Dennis (ed.), *Literature in the Modern World: Critical Essays and Documents*, Oxford: Oxford University Press and Open University Press, 1990.

Walpole, Hugh, *A Letter to a Modern Novelist*, London: Hogarth Press, 1932.

West, Alick, *Crisis and Criticism*, London: Lawrence and Wishart, 1937.

Woolf, Virginia, *A Room of One's Own*, 1929 (rpt. Harmondsworth: Penguin, 1975).

—— *A Writer's Diary: Being Extracts from the Diary of Virginia Woolf*, ed. Leonard Woolf, 1953 (rpt. London: Triad, 1985).

—— *Collected Essays*, 4 vols., London: Hogarth Press, 1966.

—— *The Letters of Virginia Woolf*, 6 vols., ed. Nigel Nicholson and Joanne Trautmann, London: Chatto, 1975–80.

Zegger, Hrisey Dimitrakis, *May Sinclair*, Boston, MA: Twayne, 1976.

# INDEX

Aldington, Richard, 138, 140, 142, 184
  *Death of a Hero* (1929), 10, 62,
    106, 138, 142, 184
Alexander, Samuel, 107, 126
Austen, Jane, 34
Ayer, A. J., 111

Bakhtin, Mikhail, ix, 11, 34, 48, 89, 144,
    191–4
Balla, Giacomo, 129–30, 231, n.20
  'Dynamism of a Dog on a
    Leash'(1912), 129
  'Little Girl Running on a
    Balcony'(1912), 129
Barnes, Julian, 197
Barthes, Roland, 106, 216–17, 219
Beckett, Samuel, 174, 179, 182,
    183, 185, 195, 196–7, 198
  *Molloy, Malone Dies, The Unnam-*
    *able* (1950–2), 196–7
  Beckett, Samuel, *et al.*, *Our Exagmi-*
    *nation Round his Factificationfor*
    *Incamination of Work inProgress*
    (1929), 174
Bennett, Arnold, 3, 4, 58, 59, 60, 157
  *Clayhanger* series (1910–18), 157
Beresford, J. D., 36
Berger, John, 197
Bergson, Henri, 10, 11, 69,
    102–13*passim*, 124, 126, 127–9,
    130, 131, 135, 136, 178–9
  *Creative Evolution* (1907), 128
  *Durée et Simultanéité* (1922), 108
  *Time and Free Will* (1889), 103–5, 178
*Bildungsroman*, the, 29, 87, 92, 100, 141,
    157–8
Bragaglia, Anton, 129
Brooke-Rose, Christine, 197
Budgen, Frank, 118
Bullett, Gerald, 17–18, 157

*Modern English Fiction* (1926), 27
Butler, Christopher, 195–6
  *After the Wake* (1980), 195–6

Calvino, Italo, 151
carnivalesque, the 193–4, 219
  *See also* Bakhtin, Mikhail
Carruthers, John, 10, 18, 62, 64, 68, 81,
    157
Chaplin, Charlie, 111, 112
  *Modern Times* (1936), 123
'chronophotography', 123, 128–31, 136,
    214
city, the, 78, 113, 120, 146, 194
Cohn, Dorrit, 47
Conrad, Joseph, xi, 2, 18, 22–5, 27,
    28, 37, 60, 69, 85–6, 93–7, 98,
    120–2123, 186, 188, 222–3
  *Chance* (1913), 24, 75
  *Heart of Darkness* (1902), 24, 75,
    7697, 120
  *Lord Jim* (1900), 22–6, 60, 85,
    93–4, 95, 96, 97, 120, 123, 188–90
  *Nostromo* (1904), 76, 85, 96, 123
  *The Nigger of the 'Narcissus'*
    (1897), 222–3
  *The Secret Agent* (1907), 85–6,
    96–7, 98, 110, 119–122
  *Typhoon* (1903), 120
  *Under Western Eyes* (1911), 85
Cubism, 6, 52

Daiches, David, 28
Darwin, Charles, 68, 140
Defence of the Realm Act, the, 116
Derrida, Jacques, 106
Dickens, Charles, 34, 48, 90–1
  *David Copperfield* (1849–50), ix,
    26, 29, 90–1, 92
  *Great Expectations* (1860–1), 26

*Pickwick Papers* (1837), 5
Drew, Elizabeth, 2, 37, 62, 63–4, 68,
  157
  *The Modern English Novel: Some
    Aspects of Contemporary Fiction*
    (1926), 1, 40
Dujardin, Edouard, 39, 227 n.14
Dunne, J. W., 110–11
  *An Experiment with Time* (1927),
    110–11
Durrell, Lawrence, 197, 198

*Egoist, The*, 164
Einstein, Albert, 10, 70–1, 103, 107–8,
  109, 111, 112, 118, 123, 125, 173,
  180, 202
  General Theory of Relativity (1916),
    125
Eleatic paradoxes, the, 126–7
Eliot, T. S., 76, 151–2, 163, 214
  'Rhapsody on a Windy Night', 75,
    135–6
  'The Hollow Men', 75
  *The Wasteland*, 6, 116, 212
élitism, 213–4, 219
Ellis, Havelock, 62
Ellman, Richard, 47, 48
Empire, British 122
epistemologic shift, the, 11, 26–7, 70,
  109, 179, 192, 196
exile, 186–93

Faulkner, Peter, 28
  *Modernism* (1977), 28
Faulkner, William, 8, 106
  *The Sound and the Fury* (1929), 86,
    136
'feminine prose', 41–2, 49, 187–8
First World War, the, 9, 14, 27, 35, 62,
  64, 68, 74, 80–1, 116, 125, 127,
  136–53, 161–3, 183–6, 194, 204,
  205, 209
Fitzgerald, F. Scott, 86
  *The Beautiful and Damned* (1922),
    106
  *The Great Gatsby* (1926), 86
Ford, Ford Madox, xi, 18, 25–8, 37,
  40, 59, 69, 94–6, 98–9, 138, 186–7,
  202
  *Henry James* (1915), 25
  *Joseph Conrad: A Personal Remem-
    brance* (1924), 94–5
  *Parade's End* (1924–8), 27–8, 35–6,

  37, 62, 98–9, 139, 142, 214
  *The Good Soldier* (1915), 25–7, 63,
    95–6, 97–8, 186
Forster, E. M., 86–7
  *Aspect of the Novel* (1927), 63, 86–7,
    110
  *Howards End* (1910), 79
Foucault, Michel, 11–12, 13, 14, 15,
  179–80, 186, 192
Fowles, John, 197
Fox, Ralph, 207
  *The Novel and the People* (1937),
    207
Free Indirect Discourse/Style, 31–6,
  37, 40, 44, 45, 46, 47, 51, 53, 98,
  214, 215
Freud, Sigmund, 62–7, 68, 109–10,
  137, 181–3, 212
  *The Interpretation of Dreams*
    (1899), 110, 181
  *See also* psychology and psychoa-
    nalysis
Friedman, Alan, ix, 8, 9, 12, 15
  *The Turn of the Novel* (1966), ix
Fry, Roger, 7, 61
Fussell, Paul, 142, 183, 184–5
  *The Great War and Modern
    Memory* (1979), 142, 183
Futurism, 8, 9, 14, 15, 129–30, 131
  Futurist Manifestos, 9–10, 14, 126,
    195

Galworthy, John, 3, 58, 59, 60, 149
Genette, Gérard, ix, 21, 27, 32, 47, 88,
  91–2, 97, 101–2
  *Narrative Discourse* (1972), 88, 91–2
Gibbon, Lewis Grassic, 214–5
  *A Scots Quair* (1932–4), 214–5, 216
Gide, André, 6
Gilbert, Sandra M. and Susan Gubar,
  43
  *The Female Imagination and the
    Modernist Aesthetic* (1986), 43
Gray, Alasdair, 197
Greene, Graham, 203
  *England Made Me* (1935), 203
Greenwich Mean Time, 116–22, 125,
  134–5, 178

Habermas, Jürgens, 225 n.1
Haeckel, Ernst, 66
Haig, Sir Douglas, 184
Hardy, Thomas, 2, 4, 5, 9, 225 n.1
Hassan, Ihab, 196

Heisenberg, Werner, 70
  The Uncertainty Principle, 70
Hemingway, Ernest, 8, 183, 185, 186
  *A Farewell to Arms* (1929), 186
  'Hills Like White Elephants' (1928),
    185
  'Soldiers's Home' (1926), 183
  'The Killers' (1928), 185
Henderson, Philip, 60, 206–7
  *The Novel Today: Studies in Con-
    temporary Attitudes* (1936), 206–7
Heppenstall, Rayner, 197
Hillis Miller, J., 24, 26, 55, 56, 69
Hitler, Adolf, 203, 204
Homer, 167, 169, 212
  *The Odyssey*, 101
Huxley, Aldous, 40, 152
  *Point Counter Point*, 152, 156

Imagism, 6, 8
Impressionism, 24
Industrial Revolution, the, 78, 145,
  150, 151, 209
industrial and mechanisation, 9,
  14–15, 72–8, 81, 83, 113–18, 123,
  145, 147–8, 208–11, 220, 223
  *See also* reification
intellect and intuition, 65, 104–5, 122,
  135, 178–9
interior monologue, 2, 55–6, 98, 102,
  213, 214, 215
Isherwood, Christopher, 201–3, 204,
  205–6
  *All the Conspirators* (1928), 201, 202
  *Goodbye to Berlin* (1939), 202
  *Mr Norris Changes Trains* (1935),
    202, 204
  *The Memorial* (1932), 201–2, 204,
    205

James, Henry, xi, 2, 18–22, 24, 25, 27,
  28, 36, 37, 39, 40, 46, 59, 69, 77,
  93, 141–2, 156–7, 163, 168, 187,
  188, 213
  *The Ambassadors* (1903), 19–22, 24
    35
  *The Golden Bowl* (1907), 19
  *The Portrait of a Lady* (1881), 19
  'The Younger Generation' (1914), 59
  *What Maisie Knew* (1897), 19
James, William, 11, 39, 43, 69, 105, 179
  *The Principles of Psychology* (1890),
    39
Jameson, Fredric, x, 15, 22, 24, 25, 78,

112, 113, 123, 195, 211–2, 219–22
  *The Political Unconscious: Narrative
    as a Socially Symbolic Act*
    (1981), 76–7, 220
Johnson, B. S., 197
Jolas, Eugene, 174, 178, 192, 202
  'The Revolution of Language and
    James Joyce' (1929), 174
Joyce, James, xi, 2, 3, 4, 5, 7, 8, 11,
  18, 28, 39, 44, 45–53, 54, 58, 59,
  60, 63–4, 99, 100–2, 103, 107, 110,
  118, 119, 124, 158, 164, 166–74,
  177, 180, 182, 185, 190–1, 193–5,
  196, 197, 201, 202, 203, 206, 207,
  211, 218–9
  *A Portrait of the Artist as a Young
    Man* (1916), 44, 45, 46, 47, 84,
    156, 158–9, 164, 166–7, 177, 190,
    194, 196, 201, 211
  *Dubliners* (1914), 45
  *Finnegans Wake* (1939), 49, 63, 64,
    107, 136, 172–4, 182–3, 191, 193–
    6, 197, 203
  *Stephen Hero* (1944), 45–6, 71, 158
  *Ulysses*, ix, 2, 46–53, 54, 56, 63–4, 87,
    100–2, 103, 105, 110, 113, 115, 119,
    124, 128, 132–3, 134, 139, 151, 152,
    153, 167–72, 181–2, 191, 193, 194,
    203, 207, 211, 212, 215, 218–9
  'Work in Progress', 63, 172, 174

Kafka, Franz, 6
Keating, Peter, 157
Kenner, Hugh, 21, 47–8, 52, 53, 132,
  168
Kern, Stephen, x, 118, 124–4, 140
  *The Culture of Time and Space
    1880–1918* (1983), x, 119
Kristeva, Julia, 193–4
  *Künstlerroman*, 157–8, 164

Lacan, Jacques, 179
language of modernist fiction, the, 30-
  1, 46–8, 165–97, 218–9, 221, 223
  *See also* Free Indirect Discourse/
    Style; stream of consciousness;
    interior monologue
Larbaud, Valery, 39, 45, 48, 49, 54
Lawrence, D. H., xi, 2, 3, 7, 8, 12–13,
  18, 28–36, 37, 40, 41, 59, 62–3,
  64–6, 68, 70–4, 76–7, 105–6, 112,
  119, 121, 123, 137–8, 155, 157,
  165, 176–8, 181, 182, 187, 207,
  208–11, 214, 217–8

*Fantasia of the Unconscious and Psychoanalysis and the Unconscious* (1923), 12–13, 63, 66, 70–1, 177–8
*Lady Chatterley's Lover* (1928), 30, 74, 106, 115, 138, 142, 176–7, 186, 209–10, 218
*Sons and Lovers* (1913), 29, 31, 64, 72–3, 155–6, 157–8
'The Fox' (1923), 79, 122
*The Rainbow* (1915), 29, 30–4, 40, 73, 143–51, 153, 209, 210, 217–8
'The Sisters', 143
*Women in Love* (1921), 29, 30–4, 40, 65, 68, 73–4, 77, 83–4, 87, 92, 104, 110, 114–17, 123, 136, 137, 143, 148–51, 152, 155, 165, 176, 182, 187, 208–9, 210, 217–8
Leavis, F. R., 6
Lessing, Doris, 197
Levenson, Michael, 136
Lewis, Wyndham, x, xi, 13, 40, 60, 67–8, 102–3, 106, 107, 108, 111–13, 118, 124, 126, 131–2, 136, 141, 142, 157, 187, 214
*Blast*, 68
*Men without Art* (1934), 8
*Tarr* (1918), 131–2, 156, 164–5
*The Art of Being Ruled* (1926), 157
*Time and Western Man* (1927), 5, 8 13, 102–3, 108–9, 111–13, 126, 131, 157, 164
Loos, Anita, 111
Lowry, Malcolm, 198, 215–6
*Under the Volcano* (1947), 215–6
Lubbock, Percy, 157
*The Craft of Fiction* (1921), 157
Lukács, Georg, 207–23 *passim*
'The Ideology of Modernism' (1955), 207
Lumière brothers, 129

McHale, Brian, 196, 198
*Postmodernist Fiction* (1987), 196
Mackenzie, Compton, 158
*Sinister Street* (1913–14), 158, 159
Mach, Ernest, 125
*The Science of Mechanics* (1883), 125
Mann, Thomas, 6
Marey, E. J., 128, 129–30, 231, n.20
Marinetti, F. T., 9–10, 14, 126
*See also* Futurism

Márquez, Gabriel Garcia, 96
Marvell, Andrew, 81
'The Garden' (1681), 81
Marx, Karl, 75–6, 201
Maugham, Somerset, 157
*Of Human Bondage* (1915), 157
Maxwell, James Clerk, 127
Moszkowski, Alexander, 108, 127–8
*Einstein the Searcher* (1921), 108
Muir, Edwin, 157
Mussolini, Benito, 203
Muybridge, Eadweard, 128, 231, n.20
myth, 101, 212, 222

*New Age, The*, 67
Newton, Isaac, 108, 125
Nietzsche, Friedrich, 9, 11, 14, 67–70, 109, 126, 179, 180
*Beyond Good and Evil* (1886), 67
nineteenth-century fiction, 3, 4, 21, 24–5, 26–7, 29, 33, 35, 51, 53, 60, 68, 87, 92, 140–1, 143, 149, 151, 152, 163, 168, 213, 216–19
*See also Bildungsroman*, the; Dickens, Charles
Nixon, Richard, 185

O'Brien, Flann, 197, 198
*At Swim-Two-Birds* (1939), 197
Orwell, George, 138, 141
*A Clergyman's Daughter* (1935), 203
*Coming up for Air* (1939), 138–9
'Inside the Whale' (1940), 206
*Oxford English Dictionary, The*, 3

philosophy and its influence, 11–14, 67, 111–13
*See also* Bergson, Henri; James, William; Nietzsche, Friedrich.
Picasso, Pablo, 6
'Les Demoiselles d'Avignon' (1906–7), 6
Pinero, Arthur Wing, 118, 119
*The Magistrate* (1885), 118
Pinter, Harold, 185
Planck, Max, 127–8
Post-Impressionist exhibition (1910), the, 7, 61
Pound, Ezra, 6, 198
*The Cantos*, 6
Priestley, J. B., 60, 137
Prime Meridian Conference (1884), the, 118, 122, 125
Proust, Marcel, x, 6, 7, 8, 22, 36, 42,

63, 87–93, 94, 96, 97, 99, 100,
103, 106, 130, 133, 139–40, 142,
155, 160, 164, 182, 207, 220
*A la recherche du tempts perdu*
*(Remembrance of Things Past*
(1913–27), 14, 17, 58, 63, 71–2,
83, 87–92, 101–2, 103, 104–5,
106–7, 110, 117–19, 122, 124,
126–7, 130–1, 139–40, 155, 156,
158, 160, 164, 165–7, 194, 205
psychology and psychoanalysis, 1, 2, 8,
22, 24, 26, 27, 29–30, 43, 61–2,
64, 181
*See also* Freud, Sigmund

Quatum Theory, 127–8, 133–4, 136
Quennell, Peter, 138
*A Letter to Mrs Virginia Woolf*
(1932), 138

Radek, Karl, 206
Radford, Jean, 64
Read, Herbert, 5, 6, 11
*Art Now* (1933), 5
reification, 75–7, 81, 83–4, 85, 115,
123, 135, 209, 219–20
Relativity, *see* Einstein, Albert
religion, 1, 44, 68–71, 140, 158–60
Remarque, Erich Maria, 184
*All Quiet on the Western Front*
(1929), 184
Rhys, Jean, 198
Richards, Jeffrey and Mackenzie, John
M., 117
Richardson, Dorothy, x, 3, 5, 7, 18,
28, 36–43, 44–5, 49, 54, 62, 112,
133, 187–8, 190
*Pilgrimage* (1915–67), 36–43, 44–5,
56, 68, 77, 133, 156, 181, 187–8
Rickword, C. H., 18
Robbe-Grillet, Alain, 197–8
Robson, W. W., 28
Romanticism, 78–9
Russell, Bertrand, 107, 126
*The ABC of Relativity* (1926), 108,
109

Said, Edward, 122
Saussure, Ferdinand de, 180
*Cours de linquistique générale* (1916)
Schoenberg, Arnold, 6, 216
Scott-James, R. A., x, 1–5, 11, 14
*Modernism and Romance* (1908), x, 1
Shakespeare, William, 113, 133

*The Sonnets*, 113
*As You Like It*, 113
Sinclair, May, xi, 3, 18, 28, 38, 43–4,
54, 62, 64, 164
*Life and Death of Harriet Frean*
(1922), 64
*Mary Olivier* (1919), 10, 43–4, 64,
72, 156, 159, 164
Soviet Writers Congress (1934), the,
206
Spanish Civil War, the, 203, 215
Spender, Stephen, 163
Spencer, Theodore, 46
Spengler, Oswald, 141
*The Decline of the West* (1918–22),
141
Stein, Gertrude, 8, 43, 103, 111
steam of consciousness, 2, 5, 30, 38–
43, 48–53, 54, 64, 81, 97, 100,
102, 105, 111, 124, 132–3, 136,
152, 164, 182, 201, 203, 207, 215
suffragette movement, 40, 43
symbolism, 31, 65, 147

Taylor, Frederick W., 114–15, 151,
209, 210, 220
*The Principles of Scientific Manage-*
*ment* (1911), 114, 122
Thomson, Silvanus R., 127
*Calculus Made Easy* (1900), 127
time and chronology in the novel, 4, 7,
10–11, 15, 81, 83–152 *passim*, 202,
205, 221, 223
*Times, The*, 125, 180, 184
Tomlinson, H. M., 142
*All our Yesterdays* (1930), 142
*transition*, 172
Trilling, Lionel, 12, 13, 67

Vargas Llosa, Mario, 96
Vorticism, 8
Victorian fiction, *see* nineteenth-
century fiction

Walpole, Hugh, 17, 18, 59–60, 95, 208,
213, 218
*A Letter to a Modern Novelist*
(1932), 60
Wells, H. G., 3, 58, 59, 60, 68, 141,
203
*Kipps* (1905), 60
*The History of Mr Polly* (1910), 141
West, Alick, 207

*Crisis and Criticism* (1937), 207
Wharton, Edith, 157
Whitehead, A. N., 107, 11, 126
Wilde, Oscar, 159
Wilhelm II, Kaiser, 150
Wilson, Angus, 60
women's writing and modernism, 40–44, 187–8, 191
  *See also* Richardson, Dorothy; Sinclair, May; Woolf, Virginia
Woolf, Virginia, xi, 2, 3, 4, 7–8, 9, 17, 18, 28, 42, 53–8, 60, 61, 65, 67, 71, 83, 84–5, 87, 96, 99–100, 105, 119, 124, 133–5, 138, 141, 142, 157, 165, 175–6, 177, 187–8, 201, 203, 204–5, 206, 207, 212
  *A Room of One's Own* (1929), 42 187
*A Writer's Diary* (1953), 7, 87, 99, 133
  *Jacob's Room* (1922), 137, 175

'Modern Fiction' (1919), 3, 4, 7, 58–9, 60, 62, 87, 133, 135
'Mr. Bennett and Mrs. Brown' (1924), 3, 7, 58, 60, 61, 66–7, 138
*Mrs Dalloway* (1925), 53–4, 55, 64, 66, 87, 99, 100, 119, 134–5, 136, 137, 187
*Orlando* (1928), 83, 84–5, 99, 135
'Phases of Fiction' (1929), 17
'The Leaning Tower' (1940), 201, 203, 204
*The Waves* (1931), 54–5, 84, 100 133, 135, 156, 159, 175–6, 178, 182, 194, 203
*To the Lighthouse* (1927), 55–8, 79–81, 99–100, 104, 106, 133–4, 139, 142–3, 150, 152, 159–63, 165, 174–5, 194, 201, 205, 212

Zeno of Elia, 126, 127